Reading Prophetic Poetry

Reading Prophetic Poetry

Parallelism, Voice, and Design

Barbara Bakke Kaiser

PICKWICK Publications • Eugene, Oregon

READING PROPHETIC POETRY
Parallelism, Voice, and Design

Copyright © 2019 Barbara Bakke Kaiser. All rights reserved. Except for brief quotations in critical publications or reviews, no part of this book may be reproduced in any manner without prior written permission from the publisher. Write: Permissions, Wipf and Stock Publishers, 199 W. 8th Ave., Suite 3, Eugene, OR 97401.

Pickwick Publications
An Imprint of Wipf and Stock Publishers
199 W. 8th Ave., Suite 3
Eugene, OR 97401

www.wipfandstock.com

PAPERBACK ISBN: 978-1-5326-6291-1
HARDCOVER ISBN: 978-1-5326-6292-8
EBOOK ISBN: 978-1-5326-6293-5

Cataloguing-in-Publication data:

Names: Kaiser, Barbara Bakke, author.

Title: Reading prophetic poetry : parallelism, voice, and design / Barbara Bakke Kaiser.

Description: Eugene, OR: Pickwick Publications, 2019. | Includes bibliographical references.

Identifiers: ISBN 978-1-5326-6291-1 (paperback). | ISBN 978-1-5326-6292-8 (hardcover). | ISBN 978-1-5326-6293-5 (ebook).

Subjects: LCSH: Hebrew poetry—Biblical. | Bible—Prophets—Language, style.

Classification: PJ4781 K35 2019 (print) | PJ4781 (ebook)

Most scriptural quotations are the author's own translations from *Biblia Hebraica Stuttgartensia* or *Biblia Hebraica Quinta*. A few scriptural quotations are from New Revised Standard Version Bible, copyright © 1989 National Council of the Churches of Christ in the United States of America. Used by permission. All rights reserved worldwide.

Manufactured in the U.S.A.   09/30/19

To Tom, Katherine, and David—with love

Contents

Preface and Acknowledgments | ix

1. Introduction: Rhythm and Immensity | 1

Part I: Parallelism

2. Parallelism: Vertical Reading and the Cosmic Slide | 17
3. The Day of the Lord/Locust: Moving Up and Down the Cosmic Slide in Joel 2 | 69

Part II: Voice

4. Hearing Voices in Prophetic Poetry | 107
5. Reader's Theater for the Traumatized: An Interpretation of Jeremiah 4 | 149

Part III: Design

6. Seeing Shapes in Prophetic Poetry | 195
7. Divine Mayhem and Prophetic Rebuke: The "Fearful Symmetry" of Isaiah 24 | 223

Bibliography | 249

Preface and Acknowledgments

I WRITE THIS BOOK as I retire from a thirty-nine-year teaching career. It is in some sense a valediction, a clearing and organization of files of translations, interpretations, lectures, presentations, and ideas that I have been contemplating since graduate school and testing in classrooms and workshops. There are many to acknowledge for their support along the way, but here I can recognize only a few of them.

My fascination with the biblical prophets developed at The University of Chicago with a course on translation and interpretation of the book of Amos, under the exacting leadership of the late Professor Gösta Ahlström, from whom I learned critical study of the Hebrew Bible. Beneath his imposing façade I discovered a good-humored and generous guide, who agreed to advise my literary dissertation on Lamentations, though his own major interest was history and archaeology of ancient Israel. I remember him with admiration and thanks.

I gratefully acknowledge years of support from Wittenberg University, Springfield, Ohio, where I have taught courses in Bible throughout my career. I wrote most parts of this book during several sabbatical leaves awarded by the University. The library staff granted me a distraction-free office, which I affectionately called my "monastic cell," ideal for reading, rereading, and contemplating the intricacies of prophetic poetry. I am also grateful for thoughtful and creative students, who sometimes caught—and sometimes endured—the intensity of my attachment to ancient Hebrew poetry. At Wittenberg I have enjoyed the friendship, wisdom, and support of dedicated colleagues, for whom I am most thankful, especially Jennifer Oldstone-Moore, Rochelle Millen, Paul Nelson, Warren Copeland, and Dave Barry.

During two three-month sabbatical periods the Theology faculty at the University of Otago, Dunedin, New Zealand, received me with generous hospitality. Under the leadership of Murray Rae and Paul Trebilco, the department granted me office space, access to the library, computing and copying privileges, participation in seminars and lectures, hospitable conversation at departmental lunches, and the chance to try out my ideas on biblical poetry at a seminar and a public lecture. Chapter 2 on parallelism and chapter 7 on Isaiah 24 had their beginnings in presentations at the University of Otago. I also gratefully acknowledge the wisdom and friendship of Hebrew professors James Harding and Judith McKinlay, both literary enthusiasts and creative interpreters interested in the ongoing life of texts. Thanks too to Linda Cowan, friend and Presbyterian Church leader in Christchurch, who agreed to serve as my "ideal reader" of drafts of the chapters. And I should not forget to acknowledge the companionable and encouraging chatter of the tui outside the window of my fifth floor office in the Arts Building.

Although I must admit to working mostly as a solitary figure bent over my Hebrew Bible, I certainly acknowledge the help of a whole community of scholars, most of whom I name in the footnotes and bibliography of the book. *Reading Prophetic Poetry* is primarily a work of practical criticism for non-specialists, which applies to specific poems many ideas that have been developed by others, notably insights on trauma studies, grammatical parallelism, polyphony and dialogic relationship among voices, and performance criticism. I gratefully acknowledge and build on those ideas as I seek to make ancient Hebrew poetry accessible to any attentive reader.

Finally, I thank my family, who had little direct role in the content of the book, but without whose support I would not have written it. In grateful acknowledgment of their inspiration, I thank my husband Tom for his curiosity and sense of adventure, my daughter Katherine for the power and beauty of voice, and my son David for his depth and prophetic passion for the environment.

1

Introduction

Rhythm and Immensity

On Aramoana Beach

What makes prophetic poetry so powerful and endurable? Certainly its privileged status as part of the Jewish and Christian canons contributes to its durability, but that does not wholly account for its power. I might want to answer that it is the *messages* of the prophets about righteousness and justice, aspiration and hope that speak with such force. But many have spoken or written on these topics, and their words like parabolic seeds have failed to take root in the heart or have been choked out by the weeds of everyday commerce.

I find another suggestion on winter walks along Aramoana Beach, a two-kilometer expanse of sand on the Otago harbor north of Dunedin, New Zealand. On one side is the wash and pulse of the sea as the waves roll in, leaving deposits of rubbery kelp and delicate shells. On the other is a steep wall of volcanic rock rising straight up from the beach in streaks of black, gray, brown, green, and rust. An outcropping, the so-called Keyhole Rock, juts onto the beach about halfway along the walk; to me it looks more like a massive fist with fingers curled into a gigantic O. Looking across the harbor, you can see the blinking eyes of the Taiaroa Head lighthouse and perhaps an albatross riding the wind. Straight ahead the sea meets the shifting clouds and a gray sky, turning pink in the late winter afternoon. The rhythm of the sea and feet crunching shells and the immensity of rock, water, and sky suggest another response to my question about the power of prophetic poetry: rhythm and immensity. Perhaps it is the cadences of the language and the strategies which weave the mundane to the Transcendent that enable their messages to lodge in the heart. *How the poems are constructed makes all the difference.*

INTRODUCTION

The Roads Are "Different"

But first, of course, one must read the poems. In my role as a teacher of biblical texts, I've sometimes heard people confess that their attempts to read through the whole Bible were derailed by the prophets. They might have slogged through Leviticus and even caught the highlights of Isaiah, but beyond that the prophetic texts, especially the poetic passages, were either incomprehensible or too austere. In response to this frustration, I venture another analogy from the setting in which I write. I think of the many signs on our travels that warn us "NZ Roads Are Different." Well, yes they are! Not only must visitors adjust to left-side driving, but roads are normally two lanes with S-curves up and down mountains, on the edge of steep cliffs, snaking around the seashore with no shoulder, narrowing to one lane on bridges, sometimes shared with trains, tidal water, sheep and cattle. Nevertheless, they are *roads*, which will—usually!—take the traveler from one place to another. So too "Prophetic Poetry Is Different," and our progress through these poems is more difficult than through the usual exemplars of biblical poetry: Psalms, Proverbs, Song of Solomon, short early songs within narratives, and the one more "normal" prophetic book, Isaiah. Nevertheless, much of the prophetic writing is recognizable as poetry by its elaborate, dense patterning; but we might need to reconsider the way biblical poetry is usually described, and we might need some "road signs" to help us arrive at understanding and appreciation of these rich poems.

I offer these chapters as guides and encouragement to anyone who wishes to explore the prophetic poems of the Bible. I envision these explorers with different motivations and interests. Some might be college or university students in courses on Bible, prophets, poetry, or comparative literature; others might be seminarians or pastors preparing to preach from these texts or lectors preparing to read them; some might wish to meditate on and apply the words of these ancient messengers; some want a deeper understanding of the roots of the prophetic language of Jesus; other explorers simply appreciate great poetry; and some will be looking for guidance from the ancients in the language of moral outrage or hope. Although readers might approach this study from many different directions, I should clarify that my goal is to offer ideas to help the modern audience understand and appreciate biblical prophetic poetry. The study is therefore more literary than historical or theological and addresses the general reader more so than the specialist in Hebrew Bible.[1]

---

1. This study would then differ from Vayntrub's recent scholarly analysis, *Beyond Orality*, which critiques previous studies of biblical poetry for subjectively reflecting their own "self-image of verbal art" and promises to "allow ancient texts to speak for

Parallelism, Voice, and Design

Not a "tools" book that offers a whole set of instruments for understanding prophetic literature in general,[2] this study focuses on specific literary features of prophetic poetry. Each of the three sections of the book examines a particular aspect of the poetry: parallelism, voice, and design. In addition, all chapters attend to another essential element of the poems, the imagery (metaphors and similes), as it relates to the feature under examination. Each section has two parts: first a chapter surveying parallelism, voice, or design with several short examples and then a chapter on a particular prophetic poem as a whole, highlighting that poetic feature—Joel 2 on parallelism, Jeremiah 4 on voice, and Isaiah 24 on design. The intention is therefore not just to describe these important dimensions of Hebrew poetry but to show how they work in the interpretation of whole poems, thereby encouraging readers to make their own way through other prophetic passages of their choosing.

With the understanding that form conveys meaning in poetry, I open with a section on parallelism, which I regard as the basic structural feature of Hebrew poetry. Chapter 2, "Parallelism: Vertical Reading and the Cosmic Slide," proposes a definition of parallelism suited to the complexities of prophetic poetry and supplies numerous examples, most of them from the relatively neglected minor prophets (*minor* because they are short, not unimportant books). Parallelism, I suggest, is fitting for the perspective of the prophets, which slides back-and-forth between attention to specific mundane experience in the fields, marketplaces, city gates, homes, courts, and altars and focus on the transcendent realm. In this chapter I also encourage interpreters of prophetic poetry to construct diagrams of the parallels in the poems, enabling them to read texts both horizontally (line-by-line) and vertically (through the columns of parallels) for a "binocular" view of the poems.[3]

Chapter 3, "The Day of the Lord/Locust: Moving Up and Down the Cosmic Slide in Joel 2," examines the way parallelism works in this dramatic poem about a locust plague in Judah. In this three-act drama, the prophetic poet

---

themselves on their own terms" (vii). I am more inclined to adopt Martin's proposition that "texts don't 'speak.' . . . 'Texts don't mean. People mean with texts'" (*Sex and the Single Savior*, 1).

2. Recent, very helpful "tools" books which could usefully be paired with my study of prophetic poetry are Nogalski, *Interpreting Prophetic Literature* and Goh, *Basics of Hebrew Poetry*. The latter also offers practical criticism of Psalm 1, Ecclesiates 1:3–8, and Job 42:2–6. This study is closer to Couey's *Reading the Poetry of First Isaiah*, which offers insightful study of line, structure and movement, and imagery and metaphor, with analyses of specific poems from First Isaiah.

3. The image of a "binocular" view of biblical poetry comes from Jakobson's description of Peter Boodberg's study of Chinese poetry ("Grammatical Parallelism," 402).

employs parallelism to shift between vivid, sensual description of the experience of an invasion of a locust "army" and cosmic Day-of-YHWH language (*YHWH=the* LORD; see below); between summons to engage in communal ritual practices and report of restored *shalom*; and between sprouting fields and assurance of YHWH's presence. This layered, complex poem illustrates many of the observations on the workings of parallelism offered in Chapter 2 and challenges readers with the depiction of a deity whose agency remains mysterious and of worshipers whose need for assurance of Divine Presence is more vital than their confidence in Divine Beneficence.

Part Two opens with chapter 4, "Hearing Voices in Prophetic Poetry," an introduction to the challenge of identifying unlabeled speakers and discerning their relationship to one another in prophetic poems. Contrary to the common assumption that prophetic texts convey a clear, unmediated word of God (*Thus says YHWH* . . .), many of the poems read like dramatic scripts with some of the voices unlabeled. Determining who is speaking, who is being addressed, and how the voices are interacting involves attentiveness to the words as well as subjective judgments. These judgments have great significance for interpretation of the poems. If the reader hears the voices as harmonious or merged, then the text conveys a singular theme, expressed most emphatically by the divine voice; but if one hears the voices as a polyphony of independent speakers—or even as a cacophony—then the text remains open, challenging the reader or listener to engage the unresolved issues. In this chapter I will lift up three cases for consideration: the interaction of the voices of YHWH and Zion in Isaiah 40–66; the voices of YHWH and the prophet in Habakkuk; and the multiple voices in Jeremiah, with Jeremiah 6 as an exemplar.

Chapter 5, "Reader's Theater for the Traumatized: An Interpretation of Jeremiah 4," proposes an identification of the many unlabeled speakers in Jeremiah 4:5–31 and an interpretation of their interactions, as well as an examination of the parallels within the eighteen sections of the poem marked by changes in speaker, addressee, or specific content. According to this interpretation the unmerged voices of YHWH, Judean watchmen, the prophet, and Lady Zion in the polyphonic poem create a reading drama designed for dealing with the traumas of suffering after the Babylonian devastation of Judah in 586 BCE. The chapter closes with a script version of the poem, which invites performance of the text as a Reader's Theater drama, still relevant for expressing the fury and pain of communal suffering.

Part Three on design begins with chapter 6, "Seeing Shapes in Prophetic Poetry," which proposes that readers engage in the meaning-making activity of a poem through attentive observation of the larger verbal and structural patterns the writer has constructed. As examples I propose three metaphors for describing the shape of particular poems: an architectural metaphor for describing the design of two sections of Isaiah 40; the metaphor of a diptych to describe the balance in Hosea 6:1–6; and the metaphor of sonata form to characterize the complex design of Micah 3.

The companion chapter 7, "Divine Mayhem and Prophetic Rebuke: The 'Fearful Symmetry' of Isaiah 24," identifies a chiastic structure in that fierce poem and suggests a meaning for the design—the prophetic poet's protest against Yahwists' rejoicing over the recent fall of an enemy (probably Moabite) city while ignoring their own culpability in the breaking of an eternal covenant. A final section of the chapter uses my interpretation of Isaiah 24 to leave readers with two questions for discussion. First is the issue of subjectivity in perception of design: Is the design intrinsic to the poem, or do readers perceive design on the basis of their own experience and preparation? Second, if prophetic poets address specific, concrete issues of their own day—as I argue they do—how can those texts continue to be relevant for modern readers?

Ancient Hebrew Prophets and Biblical Prophetic Poets: Messengers and Interpreters All

We do not have access to *the prophets* Isaiah, Jeremiah, Hosea, Joel, or Amos. We do have access to *books* called Isaiah, Jeremiah, Hosea, Joel, and Amos.[4] That is not to say, however, that Hebrew prophets by these names did not exist or deliver messages, or oracles, related to the content of the books called by their names. Ancient Near Eastern sources from Mari in Northern Syria, Nineveh and Babylon and other Mesopotamian cities, Egypt, Moab, and Ammon, as well as the Bible relate the activities and report the words of various functionaries who delivered messages from their gods. Probably the simplest but nevertheless most useful definition of a prophet in the ancient context would be *a messenger of the Divine*, which, I believe, implies these four components highlighted and discussed by scholar Martti Nissinen in a chapter on Ancient Near Eastern prophecy:

1. "the divine sender of the message;
2. the message (the 'revelation');
3. the transmitter of the message (the prophet); and

---

4. Writings which particularly influence my discussion here are Nissinen, "What Is Prophecy?" 17–31; van der Toorn, "From the Mouth of the Prophet," 191–202; and Stulman, "Reading the Prophets," 153–75.

4. the recipient of the message."[5]

The simplicity of the definition leaves open the various ways prophecy was manifest in the ancient Near East. Some prophets were also priests or diviners; some were professionally trained, but others spoke spontaneously; some, but perhaps not all, had ecstatic experiences; some organized in guilds, while others were loners; some had access to power, while others were outsiders; there were both men and women among the prophets. The message of the Hebrew prophets was rarely prediction of the future, but more often exposure of injustice and idolatry, warning of consequences for continued rebellion against YHWH, reaffirmation of covenant stipulations and promises, guidance for restoring communal *shalom*, and expression of hope in defeat and exile.

How did the Hebrew prophets receive these messages? Once again, we do not have access to the prophets themselves but rather to stylized texts *about* prophets receiving divine communications, designed to authenticate the messages. Sometimes the texts simply portray prophets claiming divine authority with the messenger formula, *Thus says YHWH*; and often the prophetic passages rather vaguely report a divine command to speak, as in Jeremiah 7:1–2: *The word that was to Jeremiah from YHWH, saying: "Stand in the gate of the house of YHWH, and proclaim there this word, and say . . . ."* More poetically, some texts portray the prophets responding to an irresistible compulsion, as in these powerful images:

> For Adonai YHWH does nothing
> unless he reveals his counsel
> to his servants the prophets.
> A lion roars;
> who can but fear?
> Adonai YHWH speaks;
> who can but prophesy? (Amos 3:7–8)

> When I say, "I will not mention him [YHWH],
> or speak any more in his name,"
> then there becomes in my heart something like a burning fire
> shut up in my bones;
> I am too weary to contain it,
> and I am not able. (Jer 20:9)

---

5. These are the four components which Nissinen extracts from an earlier definition of prophecy by Manfred Weippert ("Prophetie im Alten Orient," *Neues Bibel-Lexikon* 3:197) in "What Is Prophecy?" 20. Nissinen himself does not offer my simplified definition of a prophet and discusses some critiques of Weippert's definition in his chapter.

Occasionally narratives of prophets tell of special preparations to receive messages, such as Elisha's request for a musician (2 Kgs 3:15) or Ezekiel's isolation and silence (3:24–27). Most dramatically accounts of the reception of prophetic messages describe visions either in prose (for example, stories of Moses in Exod 3–4; Micaiah ben Imlah in 1 Kgs 22; Ezek 1–3; and Zech 1–6) or in poetic accounts (Isa 6, Jer 1), some written in first-person voice.

I want to draw attention to one aspect of the visually rich account of Ezekiel's commissioning vision, the incommunicability of an experience of revelation. True to the usual form of call narratives but rather unusually specific about setting, the vision report begins boldly with the voice of Ezekiel describing a theophany: *In the thirtieth year, in the fourth month, on the fifth of the month, as I was among the exiles on the river Chebar, the heavens were opened, and I saw visions of Elohim* (Ezek 1:1; *Elohim=God*). The vision continues with a fantastically detailed description of *the likeness of* four four-faced, winged living creatures with calves' feet commandeering the wheeled chariot-throne of Elohim, perhaps symbolic of the omnipresence and mobility of YHWH. At the climax of the description is this revelation of the flashing thing at the center of the creatures, translated as literally as possible in this way:

> And above the dome over their heads, like the appearance of sapphire was the likeness of a throne; and above the likeness of the throne was a likeness like the appearance of a human above it. Upward I saw like a gleam of amber, like an appearance of fire as an enclosure for it round about; and upwards from the appearance of his loins and downwards from the appearance of his loins I saw like the appearance of fire, and brightness was his all around. Like the appearance of the bow in the cloud on a rainy day, such was the appearance of the brightness all around. It was the appearance of the likeness of the glory of YHWH. When I saw, I fell on my face, and I heard a voice of one speaking. (Ezek 1:26–28)

Well, this is hardly an example of economy and clarity in writing! But it is a wonderful example of circumlocution, a kind of indirection in language or "beating around the bush," probably designed carefully and deliberately to convey the perception of an indescribably transcendent Deity, whose manifestation is only like *the appearance of the likeness* of amber and sapphire, bows and clouds, fire and brightness, humans and loins. Such indirection also impressionistically expresses the writer's view that ecstatic experiences themselves cannot be described within the logical "boxes" of language; words keep spilling out of those boxes in messy heaps of repetition and indirection. The message from the divine voice which follows this description is the "sound track" for the scene; its context is the mystical revelation. If we grant the claim that Hebrew prophets received divine revelations and auditions as the source of their messages, then their role as interpreters of those messages is just as vital as their role as recipients if their words are to be more communicable than "I heard what sounded something like the sound of the words . . ." In prophetic communication there is always distance between the sender and the transmitter; therefore, the message requires interpretation. The prophetic messenger always interprets the message.

If a prophet is always an interpreter as well as a messenger, there is not such a wide gap between the role of a Hebrew prophet, who likely delivered most messages orally, and the scribes who collected prophetic oracles and narratives, committed them to writing, edited and arranged them, added to them, and in this process interpreted them to address the situation of a new audience. Nissinen calls the work of these scribes *biblical prophecy* to distinguish it from the oral *Ancient Hebrew prophecy* but also to acknowledge that the roles of both the scribes and the oral prophets were part of a process to transmit and interpret divine messages.[6] He offers this important assessment of the relation between the two:

> . . . it does not seem to have been the primary task of the scribes to conserve the words uttered by the [ancient Hebrew] prophets in pristine condition but, rather, to make the messages viable and communicable . . . . A prophecy means nothing unless it is understood, interpreted and applied in a specific socio-religious and linguistic environment, whereby interpretation is not a matter of perverting the original words but making the message significant.[7]

In my study of the poetry of the biblical prophetic books, I will call these anonymous scribal messengers and interpreters *scribal prophets* or *prophetic poets* or use such designations as *the Joel poet* or *the Joel prophet*. This acknowledges that they are, like their sources, both transmitters of divine messages and also creative interpreters, who shape the messages—perhaps passed through several stages of oral and written transmission—into powerful poems intended to move their contemporaries.

---

6. Nissinen, "What Is Prophecy?" 28–31.
7. Nissinen, "What Is Prophecy?" 29.

Notes on Translation: Structure over Smoothness

Unless otherwise indicated, translations are my own from the standard texts of the Hebrew Bible, or *Tanakh,* used by most contemporary biblical scholars, *Biblia Hebraica Stuttgartensia* (BHS) or *Biblia Hebraica Quinta* (BHQ),[8] primarily based on the Leningrad Codex, the oldest complete manuscript of the Bible in Hebrew (1008 to 1009 CE). I refer to this text as the MT, the Masoretic Text, crediting the Masoretes, medieval scholars who preserved and copied ancient Hebrew manuscripts and supplied a system of vowel pointing and accentuation to the ancient consonantal manuscripts in order to assist in reading and interpretation. While I benefit particularly from the decisions of the contributors to *The New Oxford Annotated Bible,* New Revised Standard Version (NRSV),[9] the new and lively translations of Robert Alter,[10] and the textual renditions of numerous commentaries, I offer few notes on my translations of the MT except for cases in which I defend a different reading than the one in the MT or my translation departs radically from most English versions. Even though I work with a Hebrew text, my goal is to encourage readers to take up the prophetic poems on their own in whatever language is most accessible.

I use the transliteration of the Hebrew consonants YHWH, translated LORD or the LORD in most English versions, and the Hebrew *Elohim,* generally translated *God,* for the names of the Israelite deity. Prophetic texts most often refer to YHWH, the personal name of the Israelite god; and the consonantal form of the name conveys the point that the pronunciation is uncertain and unspoken in some religious contexts. Representing the name as *YHWH* rather than LORD avoids the masculine, feudal connotation of the latter; reminds readers of the ancient Israelite perspective of the texts; and conveys the important point that the writer is addressing the deity with a personal name.

My interest in preserving the syntactic parallels within lines accounts for relatively literalistic translations which sacrifice smoothness and idiom for clarity in identifying parallels. The differences between standard English translations and the ones I propose are not usually great but are attempts to honor the creative choices of the Hebrew poets. For example, Joel 2:17, part of a priestly prayer for deliverance from a locust plague, appears this way in the NRSV (with underlining and italics added to highlight corresponding terms):

---

8. Elliger and Rudolph, *Biblia Hebraica Stuttgartensia*; Gelston, *Biblia Hebraica Quinta*, Volume 13, *Minor Prophets.*

9. Coogan et al., *New Oxford Annotated Bible with Apocrypha.*

10. Alter, *The Hebrew Bible,* Volume 2, *Prophets.*

> Spare <u>your people</u>, O Lord,
> and do not make <u>your heritage</u> *a mockery*,
> *a byword among the nations.*

This smooth rendering aligns the semantic and syntactic parallels between *your people / your heritage* and *a mockery / a byword among the nations* and faithfully conveys the general meaning of the petition. The Hebrew text, however, is a bit "messier" and more literally reads with sharper nuance:

> Have pity, O YHWH, <u>upon your people</u>,
> and do not make *your heritage* <u>into a reproach</u>,
> <u>into a byword among the nations.</u>

Here the traditional semantic link between *your people* and *your heritage* is broken by the syntax. In the Hebrew text *your people* is not a direct object like *your heritage* but rather part of a prepositional phrase; so *your people* syntactically corresponds to the other prepositional objects *a reproach* and *a byword among the nations*. Although both translations have a similar meaning, the more literal translation of the Hebrew strikes with greater impact, since the very structure of the text underlines the concern about the vulnerable status of YHWH's people: while they *should* be YHWH's precious heritage, their devastation in the plague threatens to make them instead an object of reproach to their neighbors and an exemplar of a nation abandoned by its god.

Literalistic though they are, my translations often abandon the word order of the Hebrew lines when reproduction of that order renders the English so awkward as to be almost unreadable and certainly not pleasurable. Although word order in Hebrew poetic lines varies considerably and is meaningful, I will usually translate for readability and offer comments on particularly significant points related to order. For example, I translate Jeremiah 4:27b *The whole earth shall become a desolation*, but I comment that the literal order is *A-desolation shall-become the-whole-earth*, with emphasis on first-position *desolation* (šᵉmāmāh) and a link to the following line, beginning with the rhyming *kālāh* (*a full end*) and qualifying YHWH's stark judgment with *But a full end I will not make*.

Reflections on Hewing

> *Therefore I have hewn by the prophets;*
> *I have slain them by the words of my mouth.*
> *And my judgment goes forth as light.* (Hos 6:5)

Besides their difficulty, another reason readers often avoid prophetic poems is the violence of their imagery, sometimes specifically misogynistic or xenophobic. Returning to Aramoana Beach, we might think of the prophetic poems as a restless sea washing up not only beautiful and delicate shells but also great heaps of bladdery kelp. In vivid metaphors and similes, prophetic poems portray YHWH not only as a watchful shepherd, a caring mother, a benevolent father, a loving husband, or a fountain of living water but also as an abusive husband who strips and isolates wife Israel, a wild animal devouring the heart of carcass Israel, a rapist attacking Lady Jerusalem, an enraged deity twisting the whole surface of the earth, and a fierce warrior cutting down his foes. The Moabites are swimmers in a manure pile, the Edomites become drunk on the blood of their enemies, Lady Babylon is exposed and ridiculed, and Judeans sing over the piles of corpses in the streets of Nineveh. With images and experiences of abuse, rape, war, degradation, and other forms of violence and inhumanity so real and familiar to us in our lives, we might wish to turn away from poems with this kind of imagery, regardless of our realization that metaphors and similes are not literal descriptions and that the writers and first audiences were a devastated and colonized people.

This is a very important and complex subject for thorough treatment, which others have offered with thoughtfulness and competence.[11] It is not my topic here, but I would be remiss in failing to acknowledge the issue, particularly since the examples I select include many ferocious texts, chosen because they receive relatively little attention in the secondary literature and because they nevertheless represent luminous and powerful poetry. Readers disturbed by the brutal force of some of the poems might reasonably decide to turn away from them, but a better option might be to expose and wrestle with the violence of the language.

Acknowledging the "thin blade of difference between real swords and words about 'sharp-edged iron things,'"[12] I would nevertheless suggest that these fierce prophetic texts are not designed to promote physical violence but rather to express divine and human outrage. Consider, for example, Hosea 6:5 above, which imagines YHWH as a warrior wielding a sharp sword or perhaps a mace to slay the people of Israel. Having viewed too many reports of literal sword-slayers and gun-and-knife-wielders claiming to act under a divine mandate, we might justifiably be repelled by this metaphor. But before

---

11. See, for example, O'Brien and Franke, *Aesthetics of Violence*; O'Brien, *Challenging Prophetic Metaphor*; Claassens, "God and Violence," 334–47; and especially Sherwood, "'Darke Texts Needs Notes,'" 47–74.

12. Sherwood and Bekkencamp, "Introduction: Thin Blade of Difference," 1. The phrase "sharp-edged iron thing" is from Edwin Morgan's play *A.D.*

we summarily reject the image, we should clarify that the "weapon" in the hand of YHWH is the prophets, aligned closely to YHWH by the parallel *the words of my mouth*. The hewing and slaying happen in the form of fierce words of outrage against unfaithfulness that do indeed have the power to destroy a people but also a goal to establish justice that *goes forth as light*.

As much as these violent words might shock and repel us, attending to the powerful language of prophetic poetry might also restore our own capacity for outrage in the face of intractable injustice or spiritual ennui. In his "Prayer for Peace" during the Vietnam War (1971), Abraham Heschel exposed complacency in these words: "We are a generation that has lost the capacity for outrage."[13] At first thought that does not seem to be true of our own day, which has witnessed numerous expressions of outrage in violent actions and hateful words. Maybe we need to clarify Heschel's statement by adding some qualifiers: We seem to have lost the capacity for *transformative communal* outrage, conveyed through fierce words that are not simply trivial, self-pitying, obfuscating, or self-serving. Reading and studying the forceful, often shocking language of prophetic poetry might revive the capacity for transformative outrage expressed in powerful words, not swords. At other times, though, the best response from readers in a privileged position might be silence that lasts long enough for attentive listening to the voices of rage and pain from these ancient sufferers.

To continue reflecting on Hosea 6:5, I am intrigued by that word *hew* (חָצַב *ḥāṣab*). Parallel to *slay* here, it clearly denotes the action of obliterating with a sword, or possibly a mace, as in the image of YHWH bludgeoning or cutting in pieces the sea monster Rahab in Isaiah 51:9. The verse from Hosea depicts YHWH using the sharp, forceful words of the prophets to slice through Israel's self-deceptions, callousness, and complacency. But prophetic texts are not simply collections of independent acerbic images. To return to the earlier analogy, both the delicate shells and bladdery kelp are carried and deposited by a restless sea; the images exist in a rich poetic context, the structures of the poems. The prophetic poets who wrote their texts rooted in the words of the ancient Hebrew prophets were craftsmen who shaped the words into intricate structures with driving cadences that work on the heart as forcefully as the vivid images.

To imagine the work of these poets, I want to play with the other meanings of that word *hew* in contexts related to stone work. Sometimes *hew* appears in the references to the artistry of a mason: *Wisdom has built her house; / she has hewn her seven pillars* (Prov 9:1). First Chronicles portrays David giving orders for resident aliens to become *hewers* of stone for the temple (1 Chr 22:2); and likewise Solomon employs 80,000 *hewers* for

---

13. Heschel, "Prayer for Peace," 231.

its construction (1 Kgs 5:29). Here is another kind of *hewing*: Lady Wisdom and the royal employees forcefully and artfully shape stone for the most valued of buildings. Sometimes the verb refers to the digging of a cistern in the rock to hold water essential for the support of life. King Uzziah of Judah, *a lover of the soil*, hewed many cisterns to supply water to his cattle, plowmen, and vinedressers in the countryside (2 Chr 26:10). The term is also used for the forceful effort to mine precious metal from rock, as when YHWH promises Israel a land *from whose hills you may hew copper* (Deut 8:9). A mining metaphor functions to express the connection between the post-exilic remnant of Israel and their ancestors:

> Listen to me, you who pursue righteousness,
> you who seek YHWH:
> Look to the rock from which you were *hewn,*
> and to the quarry from which you were dug.
> Look to Abraham your father,
> and to Sarah who bore you. (Isa 51:1–2b)

In another context *hew* refers to the forceful effort to cut words into stone, as when the passionate Job longs for his own words defending his innocence and integrity to be eternally preserved, as if *with a pen of iron and lead [they were] forever hewn in a rock* (19:24). What these meanings share with the reference to wielding a sword or mace is the connotation of carefully directed effort or force applied to overcome some kind of resistance—the resistance of flesh or of stone.

If I might take that phrase *hewn by the prophets* from its original context of the metaphor of slaying with a weapon and color it with the other contexts for *hewing*, we might think of the prophetic scribe's intellectual and artistic force shaping from language an intricately wrought poem. The scribal work of shaping and writing down a poem, while intended to meet the immediate needs of a contemporary audience, nevertheless preserves the words, as if they were *with a pen of iron and lead / forever hewn in a rock*. We might imagine the poem as a vessel containing life-sustaining words— whether of judgment, pain, outrage, aspiration, or hope—constructed forcefully out of shapeless everyday experience. Playing with the image even further, we might think of the poem as a quarry from which *readers* are the hewers, mining with patience and effort what is precious—though often hard and disturbing—and what connects them to their spiritual ancestors. I offer these chapters with considerable fascination for the poems which have been *hewn by the prophets* and with encouragement for readers to expend the effort to find in them what is life-transforming through careful attention to their images, structures, voices, and shapes.

Part I

Parallelism

2

Parallelism

Vertical Reading and the Cosmic Slide

RHYTHMIC PARALLEL PHRASING IS characteristic of the most archaic poetry inscribed on clay tablets; but it is familiar to modern audiences as well. In fact, two of the most notable speeches in contemporary American history employ parallel phrasing masterfully in language similar to the prophetic texts of the Hebrew Bible. Consider the conclusion of Martin Luther King's speech at the Lincoln Memorial in Washington, DC, in August 1963. We can easily line up the parallel phrases in this way:[1]

So	let freedom ring	from the prodigious hilltops	of New Hampshire.
	Let freedom ring	from the mighty mountains	of New York.
	Let freedom ring	from the heightening Alleghenies	of Pennsylvania
	Let freedom ring	from the snow-capped Rockies	of Colorado.
	Let freedom ring	from the curvaceous slopes	of California.
But not only that.	Let freedom ring	from Stone Mountain	of Georgia.
	Let freedom ring	from Lookout Mountain	of Tennessee.
	Let freedom ring	from every hill and molehill	of Mississippi,
		from every mountainside,	
	let freedom ring!		

With each anaphoric *let freedom ring* we can hear the bell tolling. Reading vertically through the list of states, we move in a great circle from the Northeast to the West to the South, surveying the whole Union. The unparalleled

---

1. King, *I Have a Dream*, 105. The arrangement in columns is mine.

introductory phrase, *But not only that,* clearly signals the transition from celebration to challenge, from the lofty mountains down to the lowly molehills. Introducing a shift in emphasis from geography to history in specific references to Stone Mountain and Lookout Mountain, the phrase pulls the troubling legacy of confiscation of native lands, the Civil War, and the Ku Klux Klan into the survey of the American landscape. King's strategic inversion of phrasing in the summarizing line concludes his summons on the tolling phrase *let freedom ring,* now understood with challenge and urgency.[2] The parallel phrasing here is not only rhetorically stirring but also conceptually appropriate to the themes of King's speech: the indivisibility of freedom, the necessity of facing the shadow side of American history as well as embracing its grandeur, and the inescapable urgency of the moment.

Even more challenging are the lashing parallels from preacher Jeremiah Wright's infamous sermon at Trinity United Church of Christ in Chicago in April 2003. To follow the rhetorical strategy and progression of thought and to catch the rhythm in the climax of the sermon, we can diagram the parallels in this way:[3]

And the United States of America government:

when it came to treating her citizens of Indian descent fairly,		she	failed.
She put them	*on reservations.*		
When it came to treating her citizens of Japanese descent fairly,		she	failed.
She put them	*in internment prison camps.*		
When it came to treating the citizens of African descent fairly,		she	failed.
She put them	*in chains.*		

The government	*put them*	*on slave quarters,*
	put them	*on auction blocks,*
	put them	*in cotton fields,*
	put them	*in inferior schools,*

---

2. In his chapter "Marking Closure," Rendsburg traces a similar concluding strategy in biblical verse (*How the Bible Is Written,* 269–98).

3. The text of the speech is from a transcription by Sharp, "Hewn by the Prophet," 71. I have also checked the transcription with the wording in *Bill Moyers Journal: The Reverend Jeremiah Wright Speaks Out,* videorecording. The arrangement of phrases in the columns is mine; italics are added not for emphasis but for clarity in reading the chart. For interesting discussion of Wright's sermon, see the Moyers video, Sharp's chapter, and Walker and Smithers, *The Preacher and the Politician.*

	put them	*in substandard housing,*
	put them	*in scientific experiments,*
	put them	*in the lowest-paying jobs,*
	put them	*outside the equal protection of the law,*
	kept them	*out of their racist bastions of higher education,*
	and locked them	*into positions of hopelessness and helplessness.*

The government	gives	them	the drugs,	
	builds		bigger prisons,	
	passes		a three-strike law,	
	and then wants	us		to sing

	God bless America.	
No, no, no!	Not "God bless America,"	
	"God damn America" —that's in the Bible—	
		for killing innocent people!
	God damn America	for treating her citizens as less than human!
	God damn America	as long as she tries to act like she is God
		and she is supreme.

Through parallel phrasing, Wright links the oppression of Native, Japanese, and African Americans and renders the promise of "liberty and justice for all" a lie. His rhythmic recital of crimes against African Americans not only retells American history with its shameful underside exposed, but it also connects past and present so that the contemporary violence of racism in housing, employment, education, and the legal system is linked to the chains and auction blocks of slavery. Unacknowledged crimes (abusive scientific experiments, racist educational institutions, drugging) appear with the assurance of undeniable accusations against the government. Toward the conclusion of the invective, past tense verbs of confinement—*put, kept, locked*—give way to present tense verbs of diabolical offering—*gives, builds, passes*; and third person recital turns to the first person *us* as Wright identifies with his original audience. Parallel phrasing and repetition enhance the shock of the final blessing-turned-curse and expose the unparalleled, bold claim, *that's in the Bible*. How is *God damn America* in the Bible? we might ask. How is this modern Jeremiah reading scripture? Is this *our* history? Is this *our* Bible? Like his ancient namesake, this contemporary Jeremiah leaves his audiences reeling—whether in cathartic release, enraged protest, or disturbed thought.

That's in the Bible

Leaving open how the message of either speech relates to the Bible, we easily recognize the rhetoric as the language of prophetic poetry, etched into the consciousness of both preachers. This is, for example, the same kind of language Zephaniah 1:15–16 employs to announce YHWH's impending judgment against the unfaithful of Jerusalem:[4]

>That day is   a day of wrath,
>
>   a day of distress and anguish,
>
>   a day of ruin and devastation,
>
>   a day of darkness and gloom
>
>   a day of clouds and thick darkness,
>
>   a day of trumpet blast and battle cry
>
>   against the fortified cities,
>
>   against the lofty battlements.

The preachers' speeches find inspiration in parallel structures like those through which Amos 9:2–4 conveys YHWH's inescapable wrath against the socially unjust leaders of Israel:

> Though they dig   into Sheol,
>   *from there*   my hand   will take   them;
>
> though they climb   to heaven,
>   *from there*   I   will topple   them;
>
> though they withdraw   to the top of Carmel,
>   *from there*   I   will search out
>   and take   them;

---

4. Translation based on the NRSV in this case, except for verb tense, which the NRSV renders as future. The Hebrew has a verbless clause, which I render as present.

though they hide	from my sight at the floor of the sea,		
from there	I	will command	*the sea serpent,*
	and it	will bite	them;
though they go	into captivity before their enemies,		
from there	I	will command	*the sword,*
	and it	will slay	them.

When modern speakers intend to "sound biblical" and to align their messages with the words of the ancient prophets, their voices modulate to the rhythms of this kind of parallel phrasing, or *parallelism*, sometimes reinforced by anaphora and other verbal repetition, as in the examples above. Parallelism in the language of the Hebrew prophets is clearly discernible, even in translation; but it is not so easy to define, and its workings are often subtle and complex. Nevertheless, I will argue, readers who make the effort to examine parallelism in prophetic texts—who learn to read vertically through the columns as well as line-by-line—will be repaid with deeper understanding and appreciation of these dense, often enigmatic texts.

From Paragraphs to Lines to Charts

Before turning to a definition of parallelism, the subject of this chapter, we might consider a practical example of the benefits of reading and examining a particular prophetic text as poetry. Some Christian churches use a standard set of biblical readings, the Revised Common Lectionary, for their worship services. Often the texts for the day—a section of the Hebrew Bible, a psalm, an epistle from the New Testament, and a gospel reading—will be printed in the church bulletin for worshipers to follow as a lector reads or musicians chant the words. From a laudable concern for the environment, bulletins will often display poetic texts as running paragraphs to economize on print space. For example, Isaiah 58:1–10, a section of one lectionary reading, would appear this way in the words of the New Revised Standard translation, here printed without poetic line divisions:

> [1]Shout out, do not hold back! Lift up your voice like a trumpet! Announce to my people their rebellion, to the house of Jacob their sins. [2]Yet day after day they seek me and delight to know my ways, as if they were a nation that practiced righteousness

and did not forsake the ordinance of their God; they ask of me righteous judgments, they delight to draw near to God.

³"Why do we fast, but you do not see? Why humble ourselves, but you do not notice?" Look, you serve your own interest on your fast day, and oppress all your workers. ⁴Look, you fast only to quarrel and to fight and to strike with a wicked fist. Such fasting as you do today will not make your voice heard on high. ⁵Is such the fast that I choose, a day to humble oneself? Is it to bow down the head like a bulrush, and to lie in sackcloth and ashes? Will you call this a fast, a day acceptable to the Lord? ⁶Is not this the fast that I choose: to loose the bonds of injustice, to undo the thongs of the yoke, to let the oppressed go free, and to break every yoke? ⁷Is it not to share your bread with the hungry, and bring the homeless poor into your house; when you see the naked, to cover them, and not to hide yourself from your own kin? ⁸Then your light shall break forth like the dawn, and your healing shall spring up quickly; your vindicator shall go before you, the glory of the Lord shall be your rear guard. ⁹Then you shall call, and the Lord will answer; you shall cry for help, and he will say, Here I am. If you remove the yoke from among you, the pointing of the finger, the speaking of evil, ¹⁰if you offer your food to the hungry and satisfy the needs of the afflicted, then your light shall rise in the darkness and your gloom be like the noonday.

A skilled lector might be able to capture the poetic rhythms of the passage; however, while readers and listeners can discern the fundamental message of the text graphically displayed as prose, they will often experience the reading as redundant and lacking in beauty and power. Sometimes the reading will seem to move too slowly, as impatient listeners wonder why the writer must reinforce the line *Announce to my people their rebellion* with *to the house of Jacob their sins*, and *Yet day after day they seek me* with *and delight to know my ways*. At other times the reading will move too quickly for listeners to appreciate the impassioned listing of actions of care and justice which YHWH demands or to linger on the rich imagery of heads bowed like bulrushes, bonds and yokes and thongs, or light and gloom.

The graphic display of the lines as verse, as in the NRSV, guides the lector and listener or reader to hear Isaiah 58:1–10 as poetry, with the cadence and web of associations contributing to the meaning of the text:

¹Shout out, do not hold back!
   Lift up your voice like a trumpet!
Announce to my people their rebellion,

to the house of Jacob their sins.
²Yet day after day they seek me
 and delight to know my ways,
as if they were a nation that practiced righteousness
 and did not forsake the ordinance of their God;
they ask of me righteous judgments,
 they delight to draw near to God.
³"Why do we fast, but you do not see?
 Why humble ourselves, but you do not notice?"
Look, you serve your own interest on your fast day,
 and oppress all your workers.

⁴Look, you fast only to quarrel and to fight
 and to strike with a wicked fist.
Such fasting as you do today
 will not make your voice heard on high.
⁵Is such the fast that I choose,
 a day to humble oneself?

Is it to bow down the head like a bulrush,
 and to lie in sackcloth and ashes?
Will you call this a fast,
 a day acceptable to the Lord?

⁶Is not this the fast that I choose:
 to loose the bonds of injustice,
 to undo the thongs of the yoke,
to let the oppressed go free,
 and to break every yoke?
⁷Is it not to share your bread with the hungry,
 and bring the homeless poor into your house;
when you see the naked, to cover them,
 and not to hide yourself from your own kin?
⁸Then your light shall break forth like the dawn,
 and your healing shall spring up quickly;
your vindicator shall go before you,
 the glory of the Lord shall be your rear guard.
⁹Then you shall call, and the Lord will answer;
 you shall cry for help, and he will say, Here I am.

If you remove the yoke from among you,
 the pointing of the finger, the speaking of evil,
¹⁰if you offer your food to the hungry
 and satisfy the needs of the afflicted,

> then your light shall rise in the darkness
> and your gloom be like the noonday.

If the passage is printed in this way, the lector and the audience are likely to feel the power of the text in the pulse of its rhythms and clarity of associations. Instead of concluding that the passage is redundant, readers and listeners will appreciate rhythm, intensification, and specification as the lines unfold. They will hear that the prophetic leader whom YHWH is commissioning must not only shout unrestrainedly, but his or her voice must summon the community to action, as a trumpet summons to war or worship (v. 1). The people not only *seek* YHWH in worship, but they (ironically, as it turns out) *take delight* in knowing the ways of YHWH (v. 2). The metaphor *to undo the thongs of the yoke* is specified as meaning *to let the oppressed go free* (v. 6). Readers who discern Isaiah 58 as poetry will hear the correspondences among these lines and phrases and perhaps even perform the poetry as a rhythmic chant inviting listeners into the world of the poem, which convicts enthusiastic worshipers of hypocrisy but also promises vibrant communal life to those who devote themselves to care for the vulnerable. They will not only discern the message but also feel its power.

We readers who have Isaiah 58:1–10 before us as a written poetic text can also prepare for an even richer experience with the poem if we construct diagrams of the parallels as an analytical tool before we return to reading the lines of the poem as a whole. Lining up parallel phrases, we might diagram the poem in this way:

¹Shout out,

do not hold back!

Lift up your voice   like a trumpet!

Announce   to my people   their rebellion,

                                             to the house of Jacob   their sins.

²Yet day after day they   seek   me

                              and delight to know   my ways,

as if they were a nation that   practiced   righteousness

                                  and did not forsake   the ordinance of their God;

they	ask		of me	righteous judgments,
they	delight to draw near		to God.	

³"Why do we   fast,   but you do not see?
    Why   humble ourselves,   but you do not notice?"

Look, you   serve   your own interest on your fast day
               and oppress   all your workers.

⁴Look, you   fast   only to quarrel
                                               and to fight
                                               and to strike with wicked fist.

Such fasting as you do today
will not make your voice heard on high.

⁵Is such   the fast that I choose,
                a day   *to humble oneself*?
Is it   *to bow down* the head like a bulrush,
                                               and *to lie* in sackcloth and ashes?

Will you
     call this   a fast,
                a day acceptable to the Lord?

⁶Is not this   the fast that I choose:
                                             to loose the bonds of injustice,
                                             to undo the thongs of the yoke,
                                             to let the oppressed go free,
                                             and *to break* every yoke?

⁷Is it not   *to share* your bread with the hungry,
                                               and *[to] bring* the homeless poor into your house;

			when you see the naked,	
			to cover them,	
			and *not to hide* yourself	
			from your own kin?	

⁸Then   your light   shall break forth   like the dawn,
              and your healing   shall spring up   quickly;

your vindicator   shall go before you,
the glory of the Lord   shall be your rear guard.

⁹Then   you shall call,   and the Lord   will answer;
              you shall cry for help,   and he   will say, Here I am.

If you remove   the yoke   from among you,
                    the pointing of the finger,
                    the speaking of evil,

¹⁰if you   offer   your food   to the hungry
              and satisfy   the needs   of the afflicted,

then   your light   shall rise   in the darkness
              and your gloom be   like the noonday.

Diagramming the parallels enables us to read the text two-dimensionally, as the poet constructed it. Not only do we read line-by-line, but we also notice the associations of words in the same column within a section. For example, reading through the columns of verses 5–7, we first notice in the parallels among *Is such / Is it / Will you call this / Is not this / Is it not* that this section consists of a series of five related rhetorical questions through which YHWH draws the audience into the message and implies that their assent to YHWH's viewpoint is the only logical response. The subject column, with alternating *fast* and *day*, thrice qualified by *that I choose / acceptable to the* Lord */ that I choose*, holds all the lines of verses 5–7 together as considerations of a singular topic, the nature of a true fast day. Most important, the column of infinitive verb phrases links the three usual practices on a fast day, *to humble oneself / to bow down the head like a bulrush / to lie in sackcloth and ashes*, with the impassioned list of eight infinitive phrases describing the specific kind of religious observance YHWH desires more than these: *to loose the bonds of injustice / to undo the thongs of the yoke / to let the oppressed go free / to break every yoke / to share your bread with the hungry / [to] bring the homeless poor into your house / when you see the naked, to cover them / not to hide yourself from your own kin*. An echo of the three other infinitive phrases from verse 4 revealing the actions of the Israelites on their fast day—*to quarrel / to fight / to strike with wicked fist*—suggests that this is not simply an anti-ritual rant, but rather an indictment of hypocrisy.

Unless we charted the parallels, we would probably not notice the intricate structure of verse 2, which sharpens the perception of the opening enigma of the poem:

²*Yet day after day they   seek   me*
                    and delight to know   my ways,

       as if they were a nation that   practiced   righteousness
                             and did not forsake   the ordinance of their God;

       they   ask   of me   righteous judgments,
       they   delight to draw near   to God.

I have italicized the first and second and fifth and sixth lines so that we can recognize the parallels among these four lines, which have been interrupted by the dependent clause comparing Israel to a nation which does righteousness (a more neutral comparison in the Hebrew, which simply begins, *like a nation* rather than *as if they were a nation*). In the parallel verbs and objects the Israelites are characterized very positively as not only seeking YHWH and YHWH's ways and asking for righteous judgments but also exhibiting great enthusiasm in their worship (*delight to know, delight to draw near*). Thus we perceive the sharpness of the initial enigma: why is the prophetic voice called to denounce the rebellions of Israel (v. 1) when the Israelites are such ardent devotees pursuing the right objects: YHWH, YHWH's ways, and righteous judgments? The rest of the poem addresses that question and challenges any listener who fits the description of the enthusiastic worshipers in Isaiah 58:2.

Diagramming the parallels and reading through the columns also helps us appreciate some of the simpler associations among paired words or images. We notice, for example, that the common image of light in the generalized promise *Your light will break forth* is specified as *healing* which will spring forth, appropriate for a community which has been destroyed in war and suffers internal division and strife. The image of the yoke, linked to oppression, perhaps of debtors or victims of a corrupt legal system in verse 5, is expanded to include shaming, accusations, and slander through the parallels between *yoke / pointing of the finger / and speaking of evil* in verse 9. There is so much more to discover in a two-dimensional reading of this rich poem, but I hope these examples might be sufficient to encourage readers of prophetic poetry to linger over each poem, perhaps copying the lines and then using computer tabs or colored markers to chart the parallels before returning to a line-by-line reading of the poems.

Vertical Reading

An explanation of *vertical reading*, which I have introduced in the examination of Isaiah 58, starts with the observation, shared by most scholars of Hebrew poetry, that understanding parallelism is the key to appreciating this ancient writing.[5] This is not to claim that parallelism is unique to Hebrew poetry, for we can readily supply examples in other ancient poetry and even from modern American orators like King and Wright, as we have seen. Nor does parallelism necessarily distinguish poetry from prose, since we can find examples of parallel phrasing in prose as well, although it is usually not as pervasive as in poetry. While parallelism is not the definitive aspect of Hebrew poetry, I will join other interpreters in the claim that examining how parallelism works in a biblical poem is essential to understanding and appreciating it.

I define *parallelism* in Hebrew poetry as *the relationship in both form and meaning among lines which are usually adjacent or among the words, phrases or clauses within a single line.* That definition seems vague; but every word—even the preposition *among*—represents a stance in a debate about parallelism in biblical poetry. In this chapter I will introduce the broad contours of the discussion, enough for readers to understand the choices I have

---

5. Dobbs-Allsopp disagrees with this judgment in his recent book *On Biblical Poetry*. He argues that the line, not parallelism, is the distinctive constitutive element of Hebrew verse.

made among multiple options. Quickly I will turn to illustrations of each aspect of the definition, usually from the relatively neglected minor prophets, the shorter prophetic books in the Hebrew Bible, where parallelism is not typically as neat as in Isaiah.

The diagrams of prophetic passages which I offer are essentially maps of the parallels, guiding the reader on a two-dimensional journey through a poem. Words serving the same syntactic function in their respective lines appear in the same column, as in all the examples above. Therefore one can read the lines horizontally—phrase-by-phrase as the sentences unfold in translation—and vertically through the columns, examining the meaning of the correspondence among words in the same column.

If we set aside the traditional idea of the bicolon (two-line unit) or the tricolon (three-line unit) as the basic building blocks of biblical poetry—as I will argue we should in the case of prophetic poetry—there is no one correct way of recognizing poetic units. Parallelism might extend through two or three lines but equally might draw more than a dozen lines into a unit, as we have observed in the grouping of fifteen lines with rhetorical questions about the fast YHWH desires in Isaiah 58:5–7. There are some guidelines for recognizing a new section of parallels; change of grammatical subject, shift in speaker or addressee, or new semantic content might signal a new section. But interpreters really must "feel their way" through a poem, experimenting with various options and making the case for the strength of their decisions. As the astute interpreter Luis Alonso Schökel advises, "What has been written with imagination, must also be read with imagination . . . ."[6] Charting parallels is *flexibly* systematic, allowing various options and always aimed toward imaginative two-dimensional reading of a poem. (Hebrew readers have the advantage of appreciating a third dimension—sound—to add to the richness of their reading.)

The Cosmic Slide

The spatial image of vertical reading of parallel lines is suited to the fundamental logic of prophetic thinking. Parallelism is not only a rhetorical technique to persuade audiences, an aesthetic device to express emotions and inspire shock or admiration, but also a cognitive strategy to convey ideas.[7] Biblical prophets claim to offer a "God's-eye-view" of concrete events in their own communal experience. In his classic study of prophets,

---

6. Alonso Schökel, *Manuel of Hebrew Poetics*, 104.

7. See the very fine discussion of the cognitive approach to metaphor (not parallelism) in Jindo, *Biblical Metaphor Reconsidered*, 1–53.

Abraham Heschel describes prophets' understanding of their mission in this way: "Indeed, the main task of prophetic thinking is to bring the world into divine focus."[8] Robert Alter explains why poetry is the most effective means of connecting the concrete, historical world with the divine realm:

> Poetry . . . is not just a set of techniques for saying impressively what could be said otherwise. Rather, it is a particular way of imagining the world—particular in the double sense that poetry as such has its own logic, its own ways of making connections and engendering implications, and because each system of poetry has certain distinctive semantic thrusts that follow the momentum of its formal dispositions and habits of expression. In prophetic verse, I think this momentum of the poetic medium is most strikingly evident in the poetry of monitory prediction. The repeated move here from the immediate context to a horizon of ultimate possibility is emphatic and quite awesome.[9]

Alter calls this move the "semantic skid from the historical to the cosmic."[10] I will call it the "cosmic slide," suggesting that the move between the cosmic and the historical is not only semantic but also has a formal counterpart in parallelism, the way the prophetic message is conveyed. Although parallelism can function for various purposes, it is eminently suited to allow the prophet's focus to slide up and down between the concrete, everyday world and the realm of the divine. Through parallelism, for example, the prophet can link a locust plague to a heavenly army, blossoming vines and fertile fields to YHWH's favor, impending military invasion to YHWH's wrath, devastation in war to a return to pre-creation chaos. A diagram of the parallels in a text maps out a vertical reading that exposes a prophet's movement up and down the slide connecting the concrete and the cosmic.

Parallelism: A Relationship among *Lines*

As F. W. Dobbs-Allsopp does in his recent book *On Biblical Poetry*, I will use the familiar term *line* to refer to syntactic-semantic units of Hebrew poetry, rather than *colon/cola, verset/verse,* or *stich/stichos,* which derive from comparisons to Greek and Latin verse and appear in many studies addressed primarily to biblical specialists.[11] Occasionally, however, I will refer to the bicolon (two-line unit) or tricolon (three-line unit) because these terms are

---

8. Heschel, *Prophets*, 29.
9. Alter, *Art of Biblical Poetry*, 189.
10. Alter, *Art of Biblical Poetry*, 192.
11. See the discussion of terminology in Dobbs-Allsopp, *On Biblical Poetry*, 20–29.

well-established in general discussions of biblical poetry. In his thorough analysis of the line structure of Hebrew poetry, Michael O'Connor argues that a line of Hebrew poetry can be described on the basis of certain syntactic constraints and numbers of words, stresses, and syllables.[12] Based on his view of the originally oral nature of Hebrew poetry, still evident in written verse, the constraints relate to the limitations of the memory of the listeners.[13] Although variable, the Hebrew poetic line is a syntactic and semantic unit that, in Dobbs-Allsopp's words, usually "consists of five to twelve syllables, three to five words, and two to four stresses, and thus can be sung or recited comfortably within the normal two-second capacity of working memory."[14] Readers in English translation will not see this, but consideration of Amos 1:2 in Hebrew transcription, transliteration, and translation might convey some sense of the typical shape of a line. Because Hebrew words often include suffixes, prefixes, and attached prepositions or conjunctions, English translations frequently require two or three words to render one Hebrew word. I will show this in the chart below by using hyphens to connect all English words which are constituents of one Hebrew word. Syllable counts are based on the pronunciation guide from the system of vowel pointing supplied by the medieval scholars and scribes, the Masoretes.

יהוה מִצִּיּוֹן יִשְׁאָג	YHWH miṣṣiyôn yišʾāg	YHWH/ from-Zion/ roars	3 words/ 7 syllables
וּמִירוּשָׁלַם יִתֵּן קוֹלוֹ	ûmîrûšālaim yittēn qôlô	and-from-Jerusalem/ he-utters/ his-voice	3 words/ 10 syllables
וְאָבְלוּ נְאוֹת הָרֹעִים	wᵉʾābᵉlû nᵉʾôt hārōʿîm	then-mourn/ the-pastures/ of-the-shepherds	3 words/ 9 syllables
וְיָבֵשׁ רֹאשׁ הַכַּרְמֶל	wᵉyābēš rōʾš hakkarmel	and-withers/ the-top/ of-Carmel	3 words/ 7 syllables

---

12. O'Connor, *Hebrew Verse Structure*.

13. Vaybtrub's *Beyond Orality* offers a thoughtful challenge to the usual view that written biblical poetry has oral roots. She begins her study with Edward Greenstein's observation that almost all biblical verse is presented as a character's speech by a narrative framework, but scholars fail to critically examine the claims of that framework. Hence "orality is imagined ... as an earlier stage of literary composition" (8). This is a challenge worth considering; but I nevertheless think that the tradition of prophets delivering messages orally as a basis of many of the written prophetic poems has cogency, as does the theory of an oral basis of liturgical poetry.

14. Dobbs-Allsopp, *On Biblical Poetry*, 50.

Amos 1:2 exemplifies typical poetic lines, but there is little regularity in lineation; and for special effects the poet might lengthen or shorten lines, sometimes even outside the typical constraints listed above. For example, the opening lines of Nahum 3:3 celebrating the fall of Nineveh, capital of the Assyrian empire, achieve a heightened mood of imagined on-the-scene intensity with a series of two-word lines.

פָּרָשׁ מַעֲלֶה	pārāš ma⁽ᵃ⁾leh	horseman/ charging	2 words/ 5 syllables
וְלַהַב חֶרֶב	wᵉlahab ḥereb	flame-of/ sword	2 words/ 5 syllables
וּבְרַק חֲנִית	ûbᵉraq ḥᵃnît	flash-of/ spear	2 words/ 5 syllables
וְרֹב חָלָל	wᵉrōb ḥālāl	mass-of/ slain	2 words/ 4 syllables
וְכֹבֶד פָּגֶר	wᵉkōbed pāger	heap-of/ corpses	2 words/ 5 syllables

Like English free verse, Hebrew lines do not have regular meter, although the arrangement of stressed and unstressed syllables, pauses for line breaks at the ends of phrases, and patterns of verbal and structural repetition create powerful rhythms. Common suffixes might produce rhymes, which are sometimes semantically significant; but lines are usually not associated through rhyme.

Although some medieval Masoretic manuscripts and Qumran scrolls used special formatting to display Psalms, Proverbs, Job, and a few songs from other biblical books as poetry, early manuscripts of Hebrew prophetic books did not display the texts as verse lines, with the notable exception of the small section Isaiah 61:10—62:9 in the great Isaiah scroll (1QIsaᵃ) from Qumran (second century BCE).[15] Those who study prophetic poetry must always recognize the innovative scholarship of Oxford Professor of Poetry, Robert Lowth, whose thirty-four lectures on biblical poetry, first delivered in Latin between 1741 and 1751, and his translation and commentary on Isaiah (1778) developed a way of describing biblical poetry and a system of displaying prophetic texts in verse lines rather than prose. We will return to Lowth in the next subsection on poetry as a *relationship* because his line divisions were based on his perception and description of parallelism as a relationship between lines. For now we should simply recognize that the reason the standard Hebrew texts used for study today, *Biblia Hebraica Stuttgartensia* and *Biblia Hebraica Quinta*, and modern English translations (NRSV, New International Version, etc.; as distinct from the King James Version) graphically display much of the prophetic corpus as lines of poetry

---

15. For a survey of manuscript history, see Dobbs-Allsopp, *On Biblical Poetry*, 29–42.

is due in part to the persuasiveness of Lowth's lectures and writings on the poetry of the Hebrew Bible.

Because I am most interested in examining relationships among parallel words and phrases, the examples I will offer throughout this study will usually take the form of diagrams, which line up syntactically corresponding terms but sometimes obscure the poetic lines. Generally a graphic line in the diagrams conforms with a poetic line, although there will be spaces between words or phrases to create columns, as we have seen above in the diagrams of Isaiah 58. So, for another example, the lines of Joel 1:2,

> Hear this, O elders;
> give ear, all inhabitants of the land!
> Has such a thing happened in your days.
> or in the days of your ancestors?

would appear like this in a chart of parallels:

| Hear | this, | O elders; |
| give ear, | | all inhabitants of the land! |

| Has such a thing happened | in your days |
| | or in the days of your ancestors? |

However, the lineation in diagrams will not conform to poetic lines in the case of parallel phrases within a line, as in Micah's four-line verse on YHWH's expectation of all humans:

> He has told you, O mortal, what is good,
> and what YHWH seeks from you:
> only to do justice and to love *ḥesed* [fidelity to covenant, kindness]
> and to walk humbly with your God. (6:8)

In a diagram of parallels, which displays all corresponding terms in the same column, this verse requires five graphic lines to highlight the three separate, parallel demands from YHWH:

> He has told you,
>> O mortal,   what is good
>>> and what YHWH seeks
>>>> from you:
>>>>> only to do justice,
>>>>>
>>>>> to love *ḥesed*,
>>>>>
>>>>> and to walk humbly with
>>>>> your God.

Other cases in which the charts of parallels might obscure poetic line structure are those in which the chart requires an additional line in order to display an important change of word order in the Hebrew text. For example, Joel 2:3 describes the devastation of the locust plague in this way:

> Like the Garden of Eden is the land before it,
> and after it a desolate wilderness.

A chart of the parallels requires three lines to display the stark contrast between *the Garden of Eden*, with which the text opens, and *a desolate wilderness*, with which it closes:

> Like the Garden of Eden   is the land   before it,
>> and after it
>
> a desolate wilderness.

The charts are analytic tools to help readers explore relationships among parallels. Although I understand that these diagrams might obscure the line structure of the poems, readers can become accustomed to viewing a poem both horizontally and vertically as they proceed through the diagrams.

Parallelism: The *Relationship*

The definition I propose begins with the intentionally open description of parallelism as a *relationship* in both form and meaning among lines, clauses, phrases, or words. But what kind of relationship? Any discussion of that question must credit Lowth's much-quoted definition of parallelism in his commentary on Isaiah, first published in 1778:

> The correspondence of one verse, or line, with another, I call Parallelism. When a proposition is delivered, and a second is subjoined to it, or drawn under it, equivalent, or contrasted with it, in sense; or similar to it in the form of grammatical construction; these I call Parallel lines, and the words or phrases, answering one to another in the corresponding lines, Parallel terms.[16]

In his earlier *Lectures on the Sacred Poetry of the Hebrews* (first in Latin in 1753), Lowth classified the relationship between parallel lines as synonymous, antithetic, or synthetic ("sentences [which] answer to each other . . . merely by the form of construction"[17]). Although his definition also recognized grammatical correspondences between adjacent lines, important for my study of parallelism, it is Lowth's semantic classifications which became the basis for subsequent discussions of parallelism and still influence introductions to biblical poetry, despite the acknowledged critiques that parallel terms are never precisely synonymous, that contrast also involves some kind of equivalence, and that "synthetic" is too broad to designate a specific category.[18]

One solution to the inadequacy of Lowth's classification of parallel lines into these three types is to multiply the categories, particularly refining the definition of synthetic parallelism. For example, Stephen Geller offers twelve categories of relationships between parallel lines in his study, *Parallelism in Early Biblical Poetry*.[19] Rejecting this solution or any other attempt to classify different types of parallels, James Kugel concludes, "Biblical parallelism is of one sort, 'A, and what's more, B,' or a hundred sorts; but it is not three."[20] He explains his argument in this way:

> Furthermore, as even our brief survey of parallelism suggests, there are quite a few lines in which B [the second part of a bicolon, or two-line unit] is clearly a continuation of A [the first part of the bicolon], or a going-beyond A in force or specificity. And this, it is suggested, corresponds to the expectations the ancient Hebrew listener, or reader, brought to every text: his ear was attuned to hearing 'A is so, and *what's more*, B is so.' That is, B was connected to A, had something in common with it, but was not expected to be (nor regarded as) mere restatement.[21]

16. Lowth, *Isaiah*, 12–13. We should note that Lowth was not the first to notice parallels in biblical texts. See Vayntrub, *Beyond Orality*, 38.

17. Lowth, *Lectures on the Sacred Poetry of the Hebrews*, 48–49.

18. For a summary of critiques of Lowth, see Fokkelman, *Reading Biblical Poetry*, 26–27.

19. Geller, *Parallelism in Early Biblical Poetry*, 31–42.

20. Kugel, *Idea of Biblical Poetry*, 58.

21. Kugel, *Idea of Biblical Poetry*, 8.

Similarly, Robert Alter argues that semantic parallelism is a distinct phenomenon usually involving various types of intensification or specification of one line in the next, but categorization is of little value:

> In the abundant instances, however, in which semantic parallelism does occur in a line, the characteristic movement of meaning is one of heightening or intensification . . . , of focusing, specification, concretization, even what could be called dramatization. There is, of course, a certain overlap among these categories, but my concern is to point to the direction in which the reader can look for meaning, not to undertake an exercise in taxonomy. The rule of thumb, then—and in all of what follows I shall be talking, necessarily, about rule of thumb, not invariable law—is that the general term occurs in the first verset [the first line of a bicolon] and a more specific instance of the general category in the second verset.[22]

After an initial survey of various types of relationship between parallel lines, David Clines concludes with an argument for the unpredictability of the association:

> Within the couplets that we have examined here, we can affirm, *the relationship of the two lines is unpredictable*. . . . The relationships of A and B are so diverse that only some statement such as 'A is related to B' will serve as a valid statement about *all* parallelistic couplets. . . . Because the relationship of the two lines within the couplet is not predetermined, the reader is more fully engaged in the process of interpretation, a more active participant in the construction of meaning, than when a text presents itself in more straightforward linear fashion.[23]

Since each relationship between the parallel lines is unique, Clines summarizes, "that relation . . . is a dynamic one which cannot be mechanically delineated, but which often yields itself only to patient exegetical probing, each couplet in its own right."[24]

Adopting Clines's viewpoint, I will define parallelism generally as a *relationship* in form and meaning without offering any classification of types of parallels. I agree with Clines's final assessment that what makes biblical poetry so compelling is the reader or listener's engagement in examining each set of parallel lines for its unique, often surprising relationships.

---

22. Alter, *Art of Biblical Poetry*, 20.
23. Clines, "Parallelism of Greater Precision," 94–95.
24. Clines, "Parallelism of Greater Precision," 96.

However, my study will differ from Clines and many other analysts of Hebrew poetry in challenging the assertion that the bicolon or couplet (and occasional tricolon) is the basic building block of all biblical poetry.[25] Therefore, even the openness of Clines's formulation "A is related to B," I will argue, might apply well to some poetry of the Hebrew Bible but will not be suitable for an examination of *prophetic* poetry, in which two- or three-line units are not necessarily the norm.

Before turning to that argument in another section below, we can consider some benefits of probing each set of parallels without the intention to categorize them. Although stereotypical word pairs do appear as parallel terms in prophetic poetry (e.g., dust / ground; YHWH / Elohim; hear / give ear; heavens / earth), associations among parallel terms are often unconventional, offering meaningful assertions about the relationship among persons, actions, and ideas. For example, Hosea 6:5, considered in the introductory chapter, tightly links the prophets with YHWH's own words:

| Therefore | I have hewn | by the prophets; |
| | I have slain them | by the words of my mouth. |

The relationship between the parallels suggests that the prophets receive their authority and messages directly from YHWH and that their indictments have the same deadly efficacy as YHWH's own sword-words of doom. In another unconventional pair of lines, Hosea 14:3 (Heb. 14:4) conveys the Israelites' repentance of foreign alliances:

Upon horseback	we will not ride.
	We will no longer say, "Our God"
to the work of our hands.	

The parallels associate two types of misplaced trust—dependence on military might as a savior and idolatrous worship—probably linked together in alliances with other nations.

Sometimes the association among parallel lines is not simply unconventional but puzzling or even shocking, and the audience is left either

---

25. While Dobbs-Allsopp recognizes that parallelism can extend beyond the two- or three-line unit, he concludes that "the higher reaches of iteration's additive horizon are mostly left unrealized in biblical forms of poetic parallelism" (*On Biblical Poetry*, 69); and "ordinarily these larger grouping [of parallel lines] break down into combinations of couplets and triplets..." (83).

pondering the relationship or reeling from the blow. Zephaniah 1:7b introduces a peculiar image of YHWH performing a sacrifice, rather than humans making an offering *to* YHWH. The already enigmatic image becomes shocking when one considers the parallels:

YHWH	has prepared	a sacrifice,
	has consecrated	his guests.

The juxtaposition of *a sacrifice* with *his guests* invites the terrifying recognition that the guests, the people of Jerusalem, *are* perhaps the sacrifice.[26] That suspicion is confirmed in the following lines, which describe YHWH's punishing fury against the idolatrous, the violent, and the complacent, a portrait which ends with another wrenching parallel between *their blood . . . poured out like dust / and their intestines*[27] *like dung* (v. 17).

Micah 4: 6–7 offers another unusual association among parallels, which presents a puzzle to the reader:

On that day—saying of YHWH—

I will gather	the lame;	
I will assemble	the banished—	
	those whom I have injured.	
I will make	the lame	a remnant
	and the cast-off	a great nation.

Readers of prophetic poems are accustomed to the depiction of YHWH as the champion of the afflicted and the outcast, presented as the objects of divine

---

26. Several commentaries also recognize the significance of the parallelism. For example, Sweeney writes: "In the case of v. 7bα, the two subclauses, 'for YHWH has prepared a sacrifice' . . . , and 'he has sanctified his invitees' . . . , constitute parallel statements in that they relate YHWH's preparation of two parties that are essential to the sacrifice, that is, the sacrifice itself and those who are to attend the sacrifice. Indeed, as the passage develops, the distinction between these two parties seems somewhat blurred, as those who are invited to observe or attend to the sacrifice are indeed those who are themselves to be sacrificed" (*Zephaniah: A Commentary*, 78).

27. Translation of Hebrew לְחֻם, occurring only here and in Job 20:23, is uncertain. See the brief discussion in Berlin, *Zephaniah: New Translation*, 91. Berlin translates "fleshy parts"; Sweeney renders the word "guts" (*Zephaniah: A Commentary*, 73); and others have "bowels."

care in the first and last pairs of this set of lines, and in this context probably a reference to survivors of invasion. The puzzling interruption in the list of objects, *those whom I have injured*, stands out like the answer in a multiple choice question: Which of the following does not fit? Perhaps the stand-out object in association with the others in the column suggests that YHWH is repenting of the harm which YHWH has sent to Judah, which sweeps up the vulnerable population along with the wicked leaders.

As Kugel, Alter, Clines, Adele Berlin and others emphasize, parallels often serve the purpose of clarification or intensification.[28] We can point to many examples of that function in prophetic literature. Not simply decorative ways of renaming a subject, parallel terms contribute important nuance to the most general words. For example, Joel 1:13 does not simply provide elaborate titles for priests in the parallel addressees:

Gird yourselves and wail,	O priests.
Howl,	ministers of the altar.
Come, spend the night in sackcloth,	ministers of my God.

Ministers of the altar specifies the particular function of the priests which is most relevant to the context of Joel 1; they are to gather the congregation to the altar in Jerusalem for a grand service of communal mourning in the face of a devastating plague. In the final parallel phrase characterizing the priests as *ministers of my God*, Joel specifies that the altar is the focal point of the presence of his God. Despite YHWH's assault on Judah through drought and locust plague, the God who acts in both destruction and renewal still meets the community at the altar through the ministrations of the priests. In the context of the devastating plague, Joel might also wish to suggest that the priests remind God that since the altar belongs to YHWH, the absence of grain, wine, oil, and animals to offer there is YHWH's problem as well as Judah's.

In a similar use of parallelism, Habakkuk 1:14 compares humans to the fish of the sea and then specifies the comparison with an elaborate parallel to *fish*:

You have made	humanity	like the fish of the sea,
		like swarming creatures who have no ruler.

---

28. See, for example, Kugel, *Idea of Biblical Poetry*, 1–95; Alter, *Art of Biblical Poetry*, 1–28, 75–103; Clines, "Parallelism of Greater Precision," 77–96; Berlin, *Dynamics of Biblical Parallelism*, 64–102, 127–41.

Swarming creatures who have no ruler is not simply a decorative way of describing fish. Rather, the prophet suggests, humans of the smaller nations are vulnerable to the "nets" of the powerful Chaldean "fishermen" in the poem because they act en masse without thought or purpose or organization under able rulers. According to the accusatory prophet, the Creator is ultimately at fault for making such unimportant and helpless creatures as humans, who certainly do not rule over creation, as in Genesis 1, but have the same status as the most basic swarming things.

As poetic lines unfold, a prophet can also create parallels to clarify assertions or images that are vague or puzzling. The Zephaniah poet admonishes his audience to *seek YHWH*, but his readers or listeners might not know what that means: Consult oracles? Perform sacrifices? Celebrate festivals? Through the parallels he clarifies (2:3):

Seek YHWH,

    all humble of the earth,

        who do his law.

Seek righteousness;

seek humility.

Although the audience must still consider what righteousness and humility mean in each concrete decision, their focus is now on the actions and attitude which the Zephaniah poet prescribes.

Prophets also employ parallelism to clarify metaphors, as in the poet's development of the image of Mother Israel as the adulterous woman in Hosea 2:5 (Heb. 2:7):

For their mother	has acted promiscuously;			
the one who conceived them	has acted shamefully.			
For she	has said: "I will go after	my lovers,		
		those who give me	my bread	and my water,
			my wool	and my flax,
			my oil	and my drink."

The parallel lines proceed as answers to questions asking for explanation. Q: How has Mother Israel acted promiscuously? A: She has said, "I will go after my lovers." Q: Who are the lovers? A: They are the ones whom she credits with the products of the land (i.e., the Baʿalim, local manifestations of Canaanite god Baal here).

Another example of parallelism clarifying a metaphor appears in Zephaniah 1:12, which begins with a clear image of YHWH as a night watchman searching Jerusalem for criminals but then shifts to a more enigmatic metaphor characterizing the Jerusalemites for whom YHWH searches:

At that time	I will search	Jerusalem	with lamps,
	and I will punish	the people who congeal on their dregs	
		those who say in their hearts,	
		"YHWH will do no good,	
		and he will do no harm."	

The metaphor compares the reprobate of Jerusalem to grape juice fermenting so long on the skins and pits that it congeals before it is drained as wine and is therefore ruined as a product. If the prophetic poet offers no clarification, the reader or listener might conclude that his harsh words target drunkards or the lazy in Jerusalem. But the parallel specifies the image and moves interpretation in another direction. Like wine that sits too long and congeals to spoiling, so are *those who say in their hearts: / "YHWH will do no good / and he will do no harm."* It is not laziness or drunkenness which is the target of the threat but the spiritual ennui of those Jerusalemites, who become complacent because they believe YHWH does not act. Their attitude is particularly ironic in the context of the whole chapter, which depicts a furiously active YHWH sweeping away, cutting off, searching, punishing, and sacrificing. In fact, YHWH is the only effective actor in the entire poem except for a lone warrior who shrieks at the approach of the great and terrible Day of YHWH (1:14).

Prophetic poets also use parallelism for intensification, a function of the device we will have occasion to observe frequently in the analysis of specific prophetic poems. For the present, consider the clear example in Hosea 2:8 (Heb. 2:10):

She did not know		
that it was I	who gave to her	
		the wheat and the wine and the oil;
	who lavished upon her	silver
		and gold, which they made into Baal.

The first verb phrase, *gave to her*, is ordinary gift language, but *lavished/made great upon her* connotes abundance or even overindulgence. Similarly, the first objects, wheat and wine and oil, denote the usual economy of the land, while silver and gold are luxuries. Following these words on YHWH's lavish attention toward Israel, the final modifying clause hits with cruel irony—the Israelites made YHWH's extravagant gifts into an image of Baal.

Parallels can also serve to suspend clarifying information until the end of a sequence of lines in order to conclude with maximum impact, as in Habakkuk 3:2:

YHWH,	I have heard	your reputation [=your report].	
YHWH,	I have stood in awe of	your work.	
Within [our] years	revive it;		
within years		may you make known.	
In rage		may you remember	to have compassion.

Initially we want to know what work of YHWH inspires awe in the prophet. What particular work is "it" which the prophet implores YHWH to revive in the third line? That question arises again in the next line, where the poet suspends the expected object of *may you make known*.[29] What does he wish YHWH to reveal? Only in the final line in the unparalleled infinitive, *to have compassion*, does the petition become clear.[30] At the same time that YHWH vents fury, the prophet implores YHWH to remember "the work" of compassion. The occurrence of only two unparalleled words (*revive-it*

---

29. While some manuscripts add an object suffix, I am reading the MT as stylistically significant without the object.

30. In this case the English translation of the Hebrew makes the point about suspending the object even clearer. In Hebrew the word order is: *In-rage to-have-compassion may-you-remember*. The Hebrew order makes an impact in the juxtaposition of the words *rage* and *compassion*.

and *to-have-compassion* are single words in Hebrew) in a section with tight parallels draws the lone words together into the recognition of the central plea: revive compassion.

As Robert Alter discusses in his chapter, "From Line to Story,"[31] the sequence of parallel terms can also create a mini-narrative. Rather than lingering on an idea to intensify and clarify it, a poet can cast a scene through the parallels. For example, in a short sequence from Obadiah 16 we view the nations becoming drunk on their vengeance toward Edom, or perhaps even more graphically on the blood of Edom:

For just as	you [Edom]	have drunk		on my holy mountain,
	all the nations	will drink continuously.		
	They	will drink		
		and gulp down		
		and become as they have never been.		

Reading through the column of verbs, we can picture the warriors lifting great bowls, swallowing the "wine" in gulps, and staggering in drunkenness.

In Hosea 13:7–8 the poet imagines a horrific scene of YHWH as a terrifying beast tracking and devouring the Israelite prey. Although the similes compare YHWH to different animals, the parallel verbs in sequence—*lurk, meet, rend, devour*—construct a unified scene of carnage:

I	will become		to them	like a lion.
				Like a leopard
I	will lurk		beside the way.	
I	will meet	them		like a bereaved bear.
I	will rend	the covering of their heart.		
I	will devour	them	there	like a lioness.
An animal of the field	will rip	them.		

---

31. Alter, *Art of Biblical Poetry*, 29–73.

The final line stands apart from the sequence in several ways. First, it retreats to envision an earlier stage of the attack when the animal rips open the prey before devouring it. Furthermore, if the Masoretic Text is correct, the comparison in that final line—*an animal of the field will rip them*—is not signaled by *like*, as is the case with the other animal images.[32] It is the only metaphor among the similes. Also, since the metaphor includes the finite verb *rip*, the line links more closely with the independent clauses rather than the prepositional phrases introduced by *like*, as the diagram indicates. Grammatically, then, *an animal of the field* parallels *I* in the other lines, and the comparison between YHWH and the rending beasts assumes more direct force than the images mediated by *like*. To claim that YHWH *is* the wild animal hits with even greater shock than saying YHWH is *like* the wild beasts. Though the verb retreats to narration of an earlier stage of the attack, pulling the scene out of sequence, the graphic verb *rip* carries more emphatic weight than the common term *devour* (or *eat*, the frequent אָכַל in Hebrew) and therefore better suits the terrifying conclusion of the lines. The point here is that prophetic poetry demands much from the reader or listener. Since parallels are not mere restatements, embellishments, or traditional associations to aid in memorizing or composing poetic lines, the prophet's audience—ancient or modern—is challenged to ponder meaning in each individual case.

Parallelism: Relationship in *Both* Form and Meaning

The definition I propose suggests that parallelism is a relationship in *both* form (syntax) and meaning (semantics) among poetic lines or parts of lines. This differs from Lowth's classic study, in which he defined parallelism as an equivalence or contrast *either* "in sense" *or* "in the form of grammatical construction,"[33] and from many modern commentaries, which distinguish between semantic and syntactic parallelism as separate

---

32. Translators usually insert the comparative *like* or *as*, which does not appear in Hebrew. In a very fine discussion of Hosea 13:6–8, Harold Fisch translates the line simply as *the wild beast shall tear them*. He also notes the word plays on a form of *'ehyeh, I will be,* traditionally associated with the divine name YHWH, and *'āšûr/'aššûr* (I will lurk/Assyria): "But *'Ehyeh* has now become a beast of prey . . . . The actual source of danger is hinted at in verse 7 in the powerful paronomasia of *'āšûr* (I will lie in wait) and *'aššûr* (Assyria). The Assyrian threat has been lurking behind all these oracles, literally 'lying in wait' for Ephraim (5:13, 7:11, 10:6). . . . But behind the face of the leopard is *'Ehyeh* himself. It is he, the shepherd, who has become the devourer" ("Hosea: A Poetics of Violence," 152).

33. Lowth, *Isaiah*, 12–13.

types.³⁴ As evident in the examples I have already offered, I do not mean that syntactic form is *identical* in each of the parallel lines, nor do I mean that every word in a line has a match in the lines parallel to it. But my charts usually match words fulfilling the same syntactic function in their respective lines: verbs match with verbs, subjects with subjects, objects with objects, and verbal modifiers with verbal modifiers.

If there is no grammatical matching of semantically related lines, I will consider the lines non-parallel. For example, Habakkuk describes the haughty Chaldean army in this way:

> He mocks at kings;
> rulers are an object of laughter to him. (1:10)³⁵

Even though the lines are closely related semantically, I will not regard them as parallel because the semantically related terms—*kings / rulers* and *mocks / laughter*—do not line up syntactically. In fact, my concept of parallelism is *primarily* syntactical in the sense that it calls for lining up grammatical correspondences *first* and then examining the semantic relationship among the parallels.³⁶ Proceeding in this way, the interpreter is more likely to notice and contemplate the unusual correspondences frequent in prophetic poetry, associations that would go unnoticed if one were looking only for words obviously related in meaning.

This procedure differs not only from poetic analyses which emphasize and search primarily for the semantic connections between lines, but it also parts company with those who use the insights of generative grammar to construct transformations of lines in order to examine their deep

---

34. See, for example, Berlin, who offers separate chapters on "The Grammatical Aspect" and "The Lexical and Semantic Aspect" in her influential study, *Dynamics of Biblical Parallelism*.

35. Note that the NRSV alters the text so that the lines match both semantically and syntactically: "At kings they scoff, / and of rulers they make sport." This kind of alteration is typical of English translations.

36. This understanding is in agreement with that of the biblical scholars influenced by linguistic studies. Greenstein, for example, understands parallelism to be "the repetition of a syntactic pattern" ("How Does Parallelism Mean?" 44). O'Connor also defines parallelism as "the repetition of identical or similar syntactic patterns in adjacent phrases, clauses, or sentences" ("Parallelism," 877). In an earlier poetic study Collins argues, "A poet's syntax is the most fundamental aspect of his effort to produce the ordered unity of words which is his poem" (*Line-Forms in Hebrew Poetry*, 11). Collins studies the syntactic constructions in prophetic poetry but does not consider the grammatical correspondence between lines to be parallelism.

structure.³⁷ To explain this difference, I can turn to Edward Greenstein's discussion of Psalm 105:17:

> He (God) sent a man ahead of them;
> Joseph was sold as a slave. (Greenstein's translation)

Beginning with the obvious semantic connection between the two lines, Greenstein concludes, "On the surface the two lines differ in syntactic structure. However, if one removes the passivization involved in the second line, a case of parallelism materializes."³⁸ With Greenstein's transformed second sentence the parallel in both form and meaning is clear:

He [God]	sent	a man	ahead of them;
[he]	sold	Joseph	as a slave.

My charts of parallels, however, consider the surface structure of the lines the writer has constructed rather than the deep structure of transformed lines. In the case of the example above, I would argue that the original formulation of Psalm 105:17 consists of two non-parallel lines—one with an active verb and God as the subject, another with a passive verb and Joseph as the subject. Since the poet made the decision to formulate the second line with a passive construction, readers gain insight by asking why the psalmist might have chosen to write *Joseph was sold as a slave* rather than the neater and more dynamic construction, *he sold Joseph as a slave*. We could argue that the passive construction serves an important function here. In the story of Genesis to which the psalm presumably refers, God *does not* sell Joseph as a slave, but rather the brothers do. While the real agent in the story *is* God, as Greenstein's transformed sentence recognizes, the psalmist's original construction implies the presence of the brothers of the Genesis story, whose attempt to get rid of Joseph does not entirely disappear from the poetic account but is rendered ineffectual in the passive construction of Psalm 105. The non-parallel lines of the psalm, then, suggest a contrast between the agency of God, who *sent a man ahead of [the Israelites]*, and the brothers, who serve as passive instruments of the divine will. In general, my understanding of parallelism remains with the surface structure because that is the structure the poet offers us, and our interpretive task is to consider why the writer might have formulated lines the way he did, even if those lines are not parallel or if the semantically corresponding terms are not also grammatically parallel.

37. Collins, *Line-Forms*; Greenstein, "How Does Parallelism Mean?"; Geller, *Parallelism in Early Biblical Poetry*; Berlin, *Dynamics of Biblical Parallelism*.

38. Greenstein, "How Does Parallelism Mean?" 48.

In prophetic poetry there are numerous lines in which semantically and syntactically corresponding terms run in different directions. Micah 6:2cd offers a relatively uncomplicated case:

A)   For YHWH (has) a contention against his people [nominal clause in Hebrew],

       and with Israel he will argue.

Transforming one of the lines would yield neat parallelism which brings syntax and semantics together:

B)   For YHWH has   a contention   against his people,

                             an argument   with Israel.

—or—

C)   For YHWH   will contend   with his people,

                                        and with Israel

      he   will argue.

Rather than focusing on the deep structure of the transformed lines, however, we might ask why the poet wrote the lines as he did. Perhaps he chose A rather than B because he wished to shift from the noun *contention* to the semantically corresponding verb *argue* in order to offer a more effective introduction to the following set of lines, which begin with the words of YHWH's indictment against Israel, *O my people, what have I done to you?* Of course the poet could have chosen the neatly parallel lines of C, where both semantically corresponding terms, *contend* and *argue,* are verbs suitable for introducing YHWH's speech that follows. But he might have written A instead of C as a smooth transition from the previous lines, in which the noun *contention* appears:

     Hear, O mountains, the contention of YHWH,
     O enduring foundations of the earth. (Micah 6:2ab)

Although we can only offer suggestions, pondering the writer's choice opens our eyes to the smooth, skillful transition between the lines he has given us in Micah 6:2cd and those which precede and follow them.

The poet's choice to write non-parallel lines might be important not simply for smooth transitions but also for expression of themes. In Micah 5:9 (Heb. 5:8) the prophet conveys YHWH's promise of Israel's victory:

> Your [i.e. Israel's] hand will rise up over your foes,
> and all your enemies will be cut off.

How much neater this would have been if the poet had constructed lines in which the semantic pair *your foes* and *all your enemies* were both objects of verbs denoting Israel's victorious activity, such as:

> Your hand will root out your foes,
> and you will cut off all your enemies.

So why did the writer shift to the passive construction in the second line? Asking this question about the non-parallel lines in Micah 5:9 (Heb. 5:8) invites the reader to observe the connection between these lines and the following section of the poem (5:10–15 [Heb. 5:9–14]), YHWH's passionate raging against all military installations and idols, where the verb *cut off* occurs four times with YHWH as subject:

> It shall happen on that day—saying of YHWH—
>
> I will *cut off* your horses from your midst,
> and destroy your chariots,
> and *cut off* the cities of your land,
> and cast down all your fortifications,
> and *cut off* sorceries from your hand.
> And you will have no soothsayers.
>
> I will *cut off* your idols
> and your pillars from your midst.
> You will no longer bow down
> to the work of your own hands.
>
> I will root out your Asherim from your midst,
> and exterminate your cities.
> I will take vengeance in anger
> and in wrath
> [on] the nations which do not listen.

The passivization of the line *and all your enemies will be cut off* (v. 9 [Heb. v. 8]), therefore, shifts the identity of the active agent from Israel in the previous line, *Your hand will rise up over your foes*, to YHWH, who is clearly the one responsible for cutting off the foe, specified in an impassioned list of ten objects, both within and outside of Judah.

Habakkuk 1:3 invites another discussion about the relation between semantic and syntactic correspondences. Here the prophet offers a semantically rich vocabulary of terms for evil as he expresses his complaint to YHWH:

Why do you	make me see	*trouble*
	and look upon	*toil?*

Havoc		
and *violence*		before me—
Strife		appears
and *contention*		arises.

As the chart reveals, the writer chooses to shift the syntactic function of the semantically corresponding terms in italics. *Trouble* and *toil* are direct objects; *havoc* and *violence* are subjects in a nominal construction; and *strife* and *contention* are subjects of active verbs. The effect is of a gradual personification of wickedness in its many forms. Initially Habakkuk complains that YHWH is responsible for evil, or at least for the prophet's perception of it; but once unleashed, wickedness takes on a life of its own, arising and acting as an independent agent. Already implied is Habakkuk's complaint, developed later in the book, that YHWH has lost control over the violence of the wicked.

Using a similar strategy, Hosea presents a subject-object shift in semantically related terms in lines which I would consider non-parallel:

My people inquire of his wood,
and his rod declares [oracles] for him. (4:12)

The two designations of idols, *his wood* and *his rod*, are semantically corresponding terms, but the first is an object of the prepositional phrase telling either from whom or with what instrument the people seek oracles. In the second line the diviner's instrument or the god image becomes the personified subject, and the prophet's satire becomes sharper.

Readers who consider the tension between semantic and syntactic relationships in Habakkuk 2:19–20 will be rewarded with a deeper understanding of that prophet's more nuanced critique of idolatry. Simply translating the lines as literally as possible, we can render them this way:

> Woe to the one who says to the wood, "Wake up!"
> "Rouse yourself!" to silent stone.
> Can it teach?[39]
> See—it is sheathed in silver and gold,
> and [there is] no spirit/breath within it [literally, all spirit/breath (is) not within it],
> But YHWH (is) in his holy temple.
> Hush before him, all the earth!

One who focuses initially on semantic relationships would probably divide the last five lines in this way:

> Can it teach?
> See—it is sheathed in silver and gold,
> And [there is] no breath within it.
>
> But YHWH (is) in his holy temple.
> Hush before him, all the earth!

Of course this understanding makes perfect sense and is consistent with the satires of idolatry in other biblical passages, notably Isaiah 44 and 46. Such texts dismiss the challenge of idolatry by conceptualizing the god image literally so that the god is no more than the statue which symbolizes its presence.[40] They seem to say: Who would be so dimwitted as to venerate a "god" of wood and stone and silver and gold, who cannot speak or teach and has no breath? But we might ask: Did the Babylonians really believe that the image was identical to the god? Did the Israelites really think the Babylonians believed this? Were the Israelites distinctive in having no gold and silver and wood and stone symbols for their god YHWH? If the answer is yes to these questions, then it is easy to argue the superiority of Israelite religion, and it is very hard to imagine how Babylonian religion would have posed any challenge to an Israelite. Why the need for the fierce polemics

---

39. The line consists simply of a masculine singular independent pronoun and the imperfect form of the verb *teaches*. In context the line makes most sense if we consider it a rhetorical question, as most translators do: "Can it teach?"

40. See the insightful discussion of prophetic "misreading" of Babylonian idols in Aaron, "Idolatry: The Most Challenging Metaphor," 125–56.

against idolatry? Returning to the lines from Habakkuk with attention to the grammatical correspondences, we might conclude that the prophet recognizes and struggles with the challenge of idolatry more deeply than the usual satire does. If we chart the grammatical correspondences before examining the semantic relationships, the two nominal clauses in the third and fourth lines match up with interesting possibilities for meaning:

Can it [=the idol] teach?
See, it is sheathed in silver and gold [not grammatically parallel, but same subject].

And any spirit   (is)   not within it [=(There is) no spirit within it].
But YHWH   (is)   in his holy temple.

Hush before him, all the earth!

Grammatically the two lines on absence of spirit in an idol and presence of YHWH in the temple relate most closely: both consist of subjects joined with prepositional phrases introduced by *in/within* (ב in Hebrew). Charting the lines together suggests a contrast between an idol, which the prophetic poet asserts has no spirit in it, and the temple, in which YHWH dwells. Perhaps the prophet is introducing some nuance to his own depiction of idolatry. In the previous lines he critiques idolatry in the stereotypical fashion of the satires, reducing the Babylonian gods to their material images. But perhaps he subtly acknowledges the Babylonian worshipers' realization that the idol is not the god itself but a symbolic embodiment of the presence or spirit of the invisible god. Perhaps the prophet realizes that the same critiques he has just delivered about the idol—it does not teach; it is made of stone and wood and silver and gold—also apply to the Jerusalem temple, the chief Israelite symbol of the presence of YHWH. If so, the idol is the functional equivalent of the Israelite temple. The strength of this argument against idolatry then rests on acceptance of the conviction that the Babylonian gods, while they might exist, do not dwell in their images, as the Babylonians claim they do; while YHWH *does* dwell in YHWH's physical symbol, the temple. Even that assertion is qualified by the conclusion of the book of Habakkuk, which depicts YHWH ranging freely over the earth, treading on the mountains and trampling the sea, as well as dwelling in the holy temple.

Relationship *among* Lines: Lists

Even the word *among* in the proposed definition—*parallelism is a relationship in both form and meaning among lines or among words, phrases, or clauses within a single line*—requires defense. The choice of preposition *among*, rather than *between*, suggests that the bicolon, the two-line unit, is not the basic building block of parallelism in prophetic poetry. This assertion runs contrary to a major contention of most analysts of biblical poetry. Those studies, however, focus primarily on Ugartitic texts, early Hebrew poetry, Psalms, Proverbs, and Isaiah—poetry in which the lines are often arranged neatly into parallel bicola and the occasional tricolon. As I have already suggested in many of the examples above, parallels in prophetic poetry often extend beyond the bicolon and tricolon, so that those two-line and three-line units cannot be the most meaningful divisions for this kind of poetry.[41] This is especially the case as the prophetic poetry moves further from its oral roots to become a scribal product amenable to more careful scrutiny of larger units.

The inadequacy of defining parallelism as a relation of bicola or tricola is clearest in the case of impassioned lists occurring frequently in prophetic poetry. Perhaps more than any other characteristic of poetry, it is these lists which contribute to what Heschel calls the "luminous and explosive" language in the prophets.[42] Not unique to prophetic poetry, however, this feature appears occasionally in other poems, notably in Psalms of praise, as in Psalm 146:7c–9b:

YHWH	frees	the prisoners;
YHWH	opens [the eyes of]	the blind;
YHWH	raises	those bowed down;
YHWH	loves	the righteous;

---

41. Because prophetic passages are often not in "terse, binary sentence" form, Kugel does not consider them to be poetry at all but a kind of "'middle ground' in which terse, binary sentences . . . blend in with longer, less easily characterized sentences" ("Poets and Prophets," 4). In a critique of Kugel's earlier book on parallelism, Landy recognizes Kugel's insistence on the binary structure of poetic units as a limitation of his study: "This leads to my last major criticism of Kugel: he entirely ignores larger units. Poetry often marks itself by its intricate structures. Correspondences develop between lines and between parts of a poem, unifying it and breaching the autonomy of the closed line" ("Poetics and Parallelism," 74). Couey, *Reading the Poetry of First Isaiah*, 122–7, discusses lists.

42. Heschel, *Prophets*, 6, 8.

YHWH	watches		sojourners;
			orphan and widow
he	upholds.		

Although prophets also create lists to express exuberance, more often such extended sets of parallels convey the totality of devastation, the relentlessness of human treachery, the intensity of YHWH's anger, or the limitlessness of divine power. Consider the exhaustive indictment of Edom for crimes against Judah on the day of Jerusalem's fall to the Babylonians, according to Obadiah 12–14:

You should not have looked

          on the day of your brother,

          on the day of his calamity.

You should not have rejoiced
  over the sons of Judah

          on the day of their perishing.

You should not have bragged

          on the day of distress.

You should not have entered
  into the gate of my people

          on the day of their misery.

You yourselves should not have looked
  on his disaster

          on the day of his misery.

You should not have stretched out [your hand]
  over his wealth

          on the day of his misery

You should not have stood . . . to cut off his
  fugitives at the junction.

You should not have delivered up his survivors

          on the day of distress.

While one could describe this list as a string of parallel bicola,[43] with every other line beginning *on the day of*, the more important observation, I would argue, is the extended parallelism among all the lines. Whether or not the list accurately depicts the treachery of Edom at the fall of Jerusalem to the Babylonians,[44] it vividly expresses the poet's rage over the perceived betrayal of a neighbor who should have been a brother. The parallel lines move from vague reprimands (*You should not have looked/rejoiced/bragged*) to the more specific accusations of invasion, plunder, and capture of survivors to hand them over to the Babylonians. The anaphoric *you should not* and *on the day of*, with the repetition of *distress* and *misery*, lock the lines together with incantatory power that barely contains the rage. Anger finally spills out of the tightly bound lines to convey an ominous threat, which picks up the key phrase *the day of* to formulate an expression of the *lex talionis*:

> For the Day of YHWH is near
> against all the nations. (Obad 15)

Edom's actions on the day of Judah's misery, warns the prophet, will come to judgment on that great and terrible Day of YHWH:

> Just as you have done, it will be done to you.
> Your recompense will turn on your own head. (Obad 15)

Habakkuk 3:10–11 employs a list of responses of personified nature to convey awe at YHWH's theophany as YHWH comes both to destroy and to deliver. (I will number the lines for the sake of discussion.[45])

1)	Mountains	saw	you	
		and writhed;		
2)	a torrent of water	passed over;		
3)	Deep	sent forth	his voice	on high.

---

43. Dobbs-Allsopp recognizes such extended groupings of lines in *On Biblical Poetry* but emphasizes the essential binary form of these sets of parallels (76–80).

44. Some modern scholars question the historicity of the depiction of Edom's treachery during Judah's fall to Babylon. See, for example, O'Brien, "Edom as (Selfish) Brother," 153–73.

45. This translation reads lines 3–5 closer to the LXX than the MT. The line division in Hebrew would then be:

נָתַן תְּהוֹם קוֹלוֹ רוֹם \ יָדֵיהוּ נָשָׂא שֶׁמֶשׁ \ יָרֵחַ עָמַד זְבֻלָה. This makes sense of the singular verb in the last line and the lack of a coordinating conjunction between *sun* and *moon* and distributes the number of syllables more evenly in each line than in the rendering of the MT. No emendation in wording is required.

4) The sun	lifted up	his hands;	
5) the moon	stood still		on the lofty height
6)			at the light of your arrows going past,
7)			at the gleam of your lightning spear.

Those who view the fundamental structure of all biblical poetry as binary or ternary might configure these poetic lines as three sets of bicola or tricola: 1–3, 4–5, and 6–7. However, such a grouping of the lines would diminish the effect of the full list of parallel subjects and verbs, with the thoroughgoing personification of nature throughout the first five lines, and the relationship of all of those lines to 6–7. All the natural realms, which themselves inspire human awe—mountains, torrential streams, the mysterious saltwater Deep, the sun, and the moon—writhe, boom, raise their hands, or are paralyzed in their tracks at the storm theophany of YHWH.

Frequently the prophets create impassioned lists in their representations of YHWH's fierce wrath. Perhaps nowhere does a prophet convey that fury with such intensity as in Zephaniah 1, which opens with YHWH's angry tirade. Here I chart the parallels in almost the same manner as Ivan Ball does in *A Rhetorical Study of Zephaniah*:[46]

I will utterly	sweep away	everything		from the face of the earth, *says YHWH.*
I will	sweep away	humans and animals;		
I will	sweep away	the birds of the air		
		and the fish of the sea		
		and the stumbling-blocks with the wicked.		
I will	cut off	humanity		
				from the face of the earth, *says YHWH.*
I will	stretch out	my hand		against Judah

---

46. Ball, *Rhetorical Study of Zephaniah*, 52–54, 61.

			and against all the inhabitants of Jerusalem.
I will	cut off		from this place
		every remnant of the Baal,	
		and the name of the idolatrous priests	
			with the priests,
		those who bow down	on the roofs
			to the host of heaven,
		those who bow down	
		and swear	to YHWH
		but also swear	by Milcom,
		those who turn back	from following YHWH,
		who have not sought YHWH	
		nor inquired of him.	

As the prophet constructs it, the pressure of YHWH's wrath smolders inside a tight artistic structure of three lists of six elements each. Most obviously we note that the phrase *from the face of the earth, says YHWH* frames the first section of the poem. By that phrase the poet might intend that the hearers reflect on the earliest account of the flood story, in which *the face of the earth*, appearing seven times, becomes an identifying echo of the old story.[47] The audience is invited to ask: Has YHWH's anger again risen to earth-destroying levels? Was that reassuring covenant of the old story too idealistic? Within this frame six poetic lines identify the objects of YHWH's destruction:

- *everything*
- *humans and animals*
- *the birds of the air*
- *and the fish of the sea*

47. Almost all commentators observe the echoes of the creation and flood stories. See, for example, Ball, *Rhetorical Study of Zephaniah*, 46–48; Berlin, *Zephaniah*, 81.

- *and the stumbling-blocks with the wicked*
- *humanity.*

Almost all commentators have recognized that the central objects—humans, animals, birds, and fish—appear in reverse order from the creation story in Genesis 1 and likely from even earlier tradition. Allusion to the flood story and reversal of the traditional order of created things poetically enhance the threat of that first stark announcement of doom: *I will utterly sweep away everything*. Although scholars frequently emend the difficult fifth object, *the stumbling-blocks with the wicked*, we could adopt Adele Berlin's prudent conclusion that relates the object to others in the list and obviates the necessity for emendation:

> On the one hand, Zephaniah is describing a reversal of creation; on the other hand, as becomes clear in the following verses, he is describing the destruction of idolatry. He can achieve this double message because the elements of creation (animals, birds, fish) may also be the elements of idolatry. The "stumbling blocks" can be understood as referring to the replicas. . . . The "stumbling blocks" are, then, not an additional item slated for destruction, but an explanation of the previous items.[48]

If we adopt this conclusion, the reference to stumbling-blocks refers to the idol images of the things of creation and makes a fine transition between this set of six lines about the wiping out of all creation and the next set of six objects, all referring to YHWH cutting off idolaters in Jerusalem.

The prophet's focus then moves down the cosmic slide from YHWH's broad vision of the face of the earth to Judah, to the streets of Jerusalem, and finally to *this place*, most likely the temple. Here YHWH directs divine wrath against idolaters, variously identified in a list of six objects, each introduced either by the Hebrew object marker ʾ*et-(*אֶת־*)* or the relative pronoun ʾ*ašer (*אֲשֶׁר*)*[49]

- *every remnant of the Baal*
- *and the name of the idolatrous priests with the priests*
- *those who bow down on the roofs to the host of heaven*
- *those who bow down and swear to YHWH but also swear by Milcom*

---

48. Berlin, *Zephaniah*, 73–74.

49. Ball, *Rhetorical Study of Zephaniah*, 53–61. Ball offers a very insightful discussion of various possibilities for understanding the relationship among the objects. My chart adopts his understanding and charting of the structure of the lines on p. 61.

- *those who turn back from following YHWH*
- *[those] who have not sought YHWH nor inquired of him.*

Many scholars have recognized that this list of objects correlates with the depiction of idolatry in Jerusalem presented as the challenge to the reign of Josiah in 2 Kings 23 (Baal, idolatrous priests, astral deities, and the Ammonite god Milcom).[50] Whether that correspondence is from literary design or historical reality, the important point for the present study is that Zephaniah addresses a very concrete issue of a particular time—religious syncretism in Jerusalem—and lends it a cosmic focus. He achieves that connection between the cosmic and the historical through the force of poetic parallelism.

A third list of six elements appears in the verbal column of the chart with parallels threatening YHWH's wrathful actions: *utterly sweep away,*[51] *sweep away, sweep away, cut off, stretch out [my hand], cut off.* Particularly notable is the way the parallel verbs spill out of the confines of the framework created by the repetition of *from the face of the earth, says YHWH.* Often such verbal frames serve as stable markers of poetic units, but here the expression of YHWH's threats spills outside of the frame with the verbal parallels and repetition of *I will cut off* both inside and outside the frame. This elaborate network of parallels throughout Zephaniah 1:2–6—six lines of objects within the frame, six more objects introduced with the direct object marker or relative pronoun, and six dynamic verbs threatening YHWH's destructive action—comes to an abrupt halt in the stark pronouncement:

> Hush before Adonai YHWH,
> for the Day of YHWH is near! (Zeph 1:7)

These two non-parallel lines exemplify a frequent stylistic feature of prophetic poetry: tense, impassioned lists often "uncoil" in lone lines or two or three lines without parallels. In this case the lines are an emphatic announcement of the theme of the entire poem, the imminent arrival of the Day of YHWH.

---

50. There are a number of possibilities for translation of MT *Malkām*: repointing to read as a reference to the Ammonite god Milcom; reading with the MT as "their king/King," either a reference to the human king or a title of Baal; or understanding the term as a reference to a type of human sacrifice or epithet for a god associated with such a sacrifice. See the discussions in Berlin, *Zephaniah*, 76–77; Ball, *Rhetorical Study of Zephaniah*, 32–33; Sweeney, *Zephaniah: A Commentary,* 70–71. Berlin and Ball choose the third option, and Sweeney opts for the second as a reference to the human king. I am tentatively choosing the first option as a fine parallel to the personal name of YHWH.

51. This translation from the NRSV captures the meaning of the words and picks up the fine onomatopoeia of the Hebrew *'āsōph 'āsēph* but obscures the textual peculiarity of an infinitive absolute followed by a finite verb from a different root and the fact that neither root by itself means "sweep away." See the discussion in Berlin, *Zephaniah*, 72.

The prophetic poet has not finished with impassioned lists in Zephaniah 1. After another specification of five objects of YHWH's impending visitation in verses 8 and 9, the emotional pitch rises to a raging climax in the description of the Day of YHWH against idolaters, the violent, and the complacent in Jerusalem in the passage I cited at the beginning of this chapter:

That day is   a day of wrath,

                a day of distress and anguish,

                a day of ruin and devastation,

                a day of darkness and gloom

                a day of clouds and thick darkness,

                a day of trumpet blast and battle cry

                                    against the fortified cities,

                                    against the lofty battlements.

In the six anaphoric lines beginning *a day of* and using the visual and auditory imagery of a storm and war, the prophet passionately enacts the horror of YHWH's coming wrath.

While extensive lists of parallels are not unique to prophetic rhetoric, they are characteristic of it and contribute to the luminosity and explosiveness of the poems (Heschel's description again). Interpreters who view the bicolon and tricolon as the essential building blocks of prophetic poetry might miss the extent of meaningful associations among lines and the raging fire of the prophetic voice.

Relationships *among* Lines: Intricate Sprawling Structures

Another feature of prophetic parallelism which argues against the bicolon and tricolon as the basis of prophetic poetry is complex, sprawling networks of lines that spill out of frameworks and develop tentacular extensions to specify and qualify. In the terminology of linguists, we would probably label this *hypotaxis*, "which involves complex subordinating structures where interclause relations are explicitly indicated."[52] Although such structures might indeed suggest that a poem is remote from its roots in oral tradition,

---

52. Dobbs-Allsopp, *On Biblical Poetry*, 131. It should be noted that Dobbs-Allsopp observes that biblical poetry, with roots on oral culture, "favor parataxis" (132), while hypotaxis "is in large measure a product of writing" (134).

I would argue that not all biblical poetry is terse or paratactic; and prophetic poetry frequently includes lines with relationships extending beyond simple links between two or three discrete units. Yet this lack of terseness does not necessarily signal prose,[53] and recognition of complex poetic parallels contributes depth and richness to our reading. We might return to the analogy with New Zealand roads from the introductory chapter: "Prophetic Poetry Is Different." Because this complexity is such a pervasive feature of prophetic poetry, we will turn to several examples.

First we can return to the network of lines through which Amos conveys YHWH's wrathful message that Israel cannot escape the day of reckoning (9:2–4):

Though they dig	into Sheol,		
from there	*my hand*	*will take*	*them;*
though they climb	to heaven,		
from there	*I*	*will topple*	*them;*
though they withdraw	to the top of Carmel,		
from there	*I*	*will search out and take*	*them;*
though they hide	from my sight at the floor of the sea,		
from there	*I*	*will command*	*the sea serpent,*
	and it	*will bite*	*them;*
though they go	into captivity before their enemies,		
from there	*I*	*will command*	*the sword,*
	and it	*will slay*	*them.*

This is a less complex case of "linear sprawl" than others we will examine, since the anaphoric *though* and *from there* give the lines unmistakable binary or ternary structure and keep them locked together as a unit. In fact, we can identify a rather conventional pattern of alternating parallel lines: ABA'B'

---

53. Committed to the view that poetry is always terse, Freedman developed statistical criteria for distinguishing between prose and poetry on the basis of frequency of the Hebrew definite article *h-*, relative pronoun *ʾašer*, and definite article marker *ʾet*. See "Pottery, Poetry, and Prophecy," 6–8; and Freedman and Andersen, *Hosea: A New Translation*, 61–64. By such criteria, passages like Zephaniah 1, with an abundance of these Hebrew particles would be prose. I am rejecting Freedman's statistical approach to distinguish between prose and poetry. The kind of terseness Freedman observes characterizes the earliest Hebrew poetry and liturgical poetry quite well but doesn't necessarily fit later prophetic texts. That need not mean prophetic texts are *not poetic*, but can just as well mean they are a *different kind* of poetry or that they have become remote from their oral roots.

A″B″A‴B‴CA⁗B⁗C′. What is unconventional is the extension of the pattern through five sets of lines, the lengthening of the parallel prepositional phrases identifying the hiding places (*into Sheol, to heaven, to the top of Carmel, from my sight at the bottom of the sea, into captivity in front of their enemies*), and the additional set of parallel clauses in the final lines (*and it will bite them, and it will slay them*). One who reads the lines aloud falls into a rhythm established by pronouncing only a few words (two or three words in Hebrew) for each line introduced by *though* and *from there*; but then the reader must quickly fit the longer runs of prepositional phrases (*to the top of Carmel, from my sight at the bottom of the sea, into captivity before their enemies*) and additional clauses into the confines of the established rhythm. The effect is a rush of words bursting from the bonds of the structure, well suited to expressing YHWH's furious insistence that there is absolutely no impunity for Israel. YHWH commands all the escape routes, either directly or through YHWH's emissaries the serpent and sword.

Other cases of complex, sprawling lines are not so clearly structured, but attempts to chart the parallels uncover meaningful relationships that enhance understanding and appreciation of the poetry. Criticizing Edom, here called Esau, for pride and treachery, Obadiah 5–6 conveys YHWH's message of judgment in two analogies. Initially the lines seem disorganized, but a chart of the parallels uncovers the intricate relationship among them:

If thieves	came to you,		
if assailants of the night—			
		How you	have been cut off!—
			would they not steal [only] enough for themselves?
If grape gatherers	came to you,		
			would they not spare gleanings?
		How Esau	has been exposed,
		his hidden treasures	have been sought out!

Repetition of words at the beginning of clauses (*if, how, would they not*) and the verb phrase *came to you* help the reader identify the parallels in this eight-line unit. Those who argue that Hebrew poetry is always terse and consists almost exclusively of bicola and tricola would be likely to label these lines prose rather than poetry, rearrange the lines, or conclude that a redactor or the accident of transmission has scrambled them.[54] However, charting the parallels helps us recognize the careful poetic structure. We can clearly identify the two parallel analogies: thieves steal only as much as their arms can carry, leaving many goods behind; grape gatherers leave behind a few clusters for the gleaners. In contrast, Esau/Edom will be absolutely "clean picked" of all its wealth. The sense of disorder is created mainly by the disruption of the independent and dependent clauses about thieves with the exclamation, *How you have been cut off!* The reader who does not recognize the unit as consisting of all eight lines might consider this exclamation to be without parallel. However, charting the lines together reveals a triad of well-matched exclamations:

How	you	have been cut off!
How	Esau	has been exposed,
	his hidden treasures	have been sought out!

The parallel subjects of the exclamations move toward greater specificity, first reminding the reader that the addressee is Esau/Edom and then specifying the country's protected treasures as marked for destruction. If we read the verb tense (Hebrew perfect) from the prophetic perspective in which divine judgments are already accomplished facts once they are pronounced,[55] the parallel passive verbs—*have been cut off, have been exposed, have been sought out* (all *niphal* in Hebrew)—suggest that Edom will assuredly be robbed not only of treasures but also of control over its own fate. The separation of the first exclamation, *How you have been cut off!* from its parallels and its disruptive placement seem stylistically meaningful for several reasons. A line exclaiming the cutting off of Edom fittingly cuts off a complete sentence, and the placement of the exclamation in the midst of the lines expressing the analogies solidifies the connection between the figurative scenes featuring thieves and grape harvesters and the real subject of the lines, Edom's total ruin. Furthermore the abruptness of that first exclamation conveys impatient excitement over the impending ruin of Edom. It is as if the vision of Edom's destruction is progressing swiftly right in front

---

54. For example, Barton offers this conclusion about the first exclamation, *How you have been cut off!*: "But in any case the line falls outside the structure of the oracle and is probably a comment on it rather than part of it: a scribal interpolation, reflecting on Obadiah's words, perhaps after Edom had, in fact, been destroyed" (*Joel and Obadiah*, 141).

55. Barton, *Joel and Obadiah*, 141.

of the reader or listener, and the poet's rush to tell of it disrupts the logical unfolding of the analogies.

If we recognize all seven lines of Zephaniah 3:6 as a unit of parallels (a septacolon!), we can follow the poet's strategy of depicting YHWH's judgment of the haughty nations:

I have cut off   nations.

                    Desolated   are their battlements.

I have devastated   their streets,

                                          with no passer-by.

                    Wasted   are their cities,

                                          with no human,

                                          without inhabitant.

While the changes in construction of the lines are easier to follow in Hebrew because of sounds and verb forms, they are observable in translation as well. In the first columns of subjects, verbs, and objects above, YHWH as speaker is the subject of lines with dynamic active verbs, *have cut off, have devastated* (assonant *hiphil* verbs הִכְרַתִּי *hikrattî* and הֶחֱרַבְתִּי *heḥĕrabtî*). The middle columns chart a second set of subjects and verbs. Now the nations' battlements and cities, semantically related to the ruined nations and streets which were objects of YHWH's destruction in the first columns, become subjects; but the new subjects govern passive verbs (*desolated, wasted*; the rhyming *niphal* verbs נָשַׁמּוּ, *nāšammû,* and נִצְדוּ, *niṣdû* in Hebrew). They are acted upon, incapable of defense against the powerful hand of YHWH. Finally, the last column displays the parallel prepositional phrases expressing no actions but only negative conditions: *with no passer-by, with no human, without inhabitant.* Reading the lines horizontally, that is, sequentially as they appear in the text, might leave the impression of disconnected statements. But that horizontal reading misses the skilled interweaving of active, passive, and nominal lines and the dramatic shift from YHWH's furious activity of cutting off and devastating haughty nations to the their hopeless condition stated and reinforced in the final two lines. Vertical reading and recognition of the seven-line unit allow us to appreciate the masterful strategy the prophetic poet employs to convey the finality of YHWH's judgment.

Another example of sprawling lines appears in the depiction of the advancing Chaldean army in Habakkuk 1:6, where the poet stretches out the portrait by connecting the first three lines to one another with one or two parallel links:

> For look! I am rousing   the Chaldeans,
>
>   the nation   fierce
>
>   and hurried,
>
>   marching
>   over the breadth of the land
>
>   to seize dwellings not his.

In the second line the poet specifies the object *Chaldeans* with the characterization of the nation as *fierce*. Then he further qualifies what it means to be fierce with two participles, *hurried* and *marching over the breadth of the land*. Hebrew readers will appreciate the connection in sound between *fierce* (*hammar* הַמַּר) and *hurried* (*hannimhār* הַנִּמְהָר). Readers who wonder with Habakkuk why YHWH would rouse such a terrifying and acquisitive foe, who *seizes dwellings not his* (לֹא־לוֹ) find a clue in the recurrence of the last phrase later in the book, where the prophet delivers a woe oracle against *the one who multiplies what is not his* (לֹא־לוֹ in Hab 2:6), suggesting that the terrifying foe, initially an instrument of YHWH, has exceeded his mission. Perhaps that excess is hinted in the unparalleled final phrase, which stretches outside the bounds of the careful network of parallels.

Poems expressing exuberance and lavish promises also exemplify some of the same expansive strategies as poems of wrath, since both are efforts to convey emotional extremes. The poetry in Joel 2:28–31 (Heb. 3:1–4), includes sprawling development of clauses and parallels spilling out of a verbal framework. Its theme is the positive counterpart to the dark Day of YHWH in Zephaniah and elsewhere in Joel. "That day," a dramatic transformation of the cosmos, appears as promise—but not without terror.

> *It shall happen afterwards*
>   I will pour out   my spirit   on all flesh.
>
>   Your sons
>   and your daughters
>   will prophesy.

                                            Your old men
                                                will dream dreams.

                                            Your young men
                                                will see visions.

                                        Even on your
                                            servants

                                        and on your
                                            maidser-
                                            vants

in those days
    I will pour out   my spirit.

    I will give   portents   in the heavens

                                                    and on earth:

                          blood

                          and fire

                          and columns
                                of smoke.

The sun   will turn   to darkness

and the moon   to blood

before the coming of the Day of YHWH,

great and terrible.

The lines sprawl outward as the prophetic poet describes how the pouring of YHWH's spirit, the dramatic power and inspiration from God, will be manifest: young and old and men and women will prophesy, dream, and have visions. The grammatical parallels, specifying that *all flesh* includes even the male and female slaves, also convey the universality of the outpouring of the spirit; and the additional prepositional modifiers include the whole cosmos—heaven and earth—in the promised spiritual transformation. Appropriate to the message about the outpouring of spirit, grammatical parallels spill out of the frame created by repetition of the clause *I will pour out my spirit*. YHWH promises other gifts besides spirit: portents, specified as blood, fire, and columns of smoke. While these portents are semantically linked to the sun turning to darkness and the moon to blood in the next lines, the grammatical parallels connect the portents with YHWH's spirit and recall the Exodus story, where YHWH poured out the divine spirit on all whom YHWH willed (Numbers 11), showed portents like water turning to blood, appeared at Sinai in smoke and fire, and led the people with a pillar of fire.[56] The new manifestation of YHWH's presence on *the great and awesome Day of YHWH* is the old story writ so large as to encompass a transformation of the cosmos. By linking the gift of the spirit with the parallel objects—*portents, blood, fire, and columns of smoke*—the poet not only echoes the old story but also suggests that the outpouring of the spirit on that day will be as awesome and terrifying as it will be beneficent. Although one could divide this passage into a series of connected bicola and tricola, such a view would miss the grandeur of the poet's vision, sliding from the earthly to the cosmic and connecting the past and future through an intricate network of parallels spanning all lines of the text.

Relationship among Lines which are *Usually* Adjacent

The proposed definition of parallelism suggests that the literary device operates among lines that are *usually* adjacent. *Usually* introduces another note of qualification—or, I would say, openness—to the definition. Certainly contiguity is important to our perception of a parallel relationship among lines, but occasionally we can recognize parallelism among non-contiguous lines if other literary devices (e.g., sound play, repetition, refrains) work together to pull the lines into association with one another.[57] This is most obvious when a refrain divides the text into parallel units, as in Amos 4:6–11. The refrain, *Yet you did not return to me, says YHWH* (vv. 6, 8, 9, 10, 11), divides the text and encourages readers to recognize parallels among the lines which open each section, as well as the repeated refrain at the end:

I myself	gave	to you	cleanness of teeth	in all your cities,
			and lack of bread	in all your places....
I myself	withheld	from you	the rain....	
I	struck		you	with blight and mildew;
I	devastated		your gardens	
			and your vineyards....	

---

56. Barton, *Joel and Amos*, 95–97; Henshaw, Notes on Joel, in *HarperCollins Study Bible*, 1213.

57. Couey, *Reading the Poetry of First Isaiah*, 117–21.

I	sent	among you	pestilence	in the manner of Egypt;
I	killed		your young men	with the sword....
I	overturned	among you		like Elohim's overturning of Sodom and Gomorrah.

The parallels hold together the long recitation of YHWH's afflictions through famine, drought, pestilence, and sword; remind the Israelites of the stories of the Egyptian plagues; and express YHWH's frustration in the kinds of angry reactions with which YHWH confronted the hard-hearted Pharaoh. YHWH's ferocity is particularly notable to the reader who surveys the verbal column, including *withheld, struck, devastated,*[58] *killed,* and *overturned.*

Similarly, the opening *woe*, the Hebrew *hôy* from expressions of grievous distress or mourning, and the series of participles in the oracles in Habakkuk 2 associate these warnings:

Woe to the one	who multiplies	what is not his ...		
	who piles	a weight of debt	over himself....	
Woe to the one	who gains	evil gain	for his house....	
Woe to the one	who builds	a city	with bloodshed,	
	establishes	a town	with injustice....	
Woe to the one	who intoxicates	his neighbor....		
Woe to the one	who says		to the wood,	"Wake up!"
				"Rouse yourself!"
			to silent stone.	

Recognition of the parallels in these woe oracles helps the reader to identify the group called "the wicked" in Habakkuk, a matter of contention among interpreters.[59] In some contexts "the wicked" seem to be the violent and ruthless within Israel. This is perhaps the connotation at the

---

58. In the line *I devastated your gardens and your vineyards* (Amos 4:9), I am reading החרבתי for MT הרבות. See Jeremias, *Book of Amos*, 66. Jeremias translates, *I caused ... to wither.* See also Wolff, *Joel and Amos*, 210. Wolff translates, *I scorched.* Both credit Julius Wellhausen with the suggestion of scribal error in the MT and the proposed correction.

59. For a survey of views, see Sweeney, *Twelve Prophets*, 2:455–6.

beginning of Habakkuk, where the prophet complains that Torah has grown numb because *the wicked surrounds the righteous* (1:4). Elsewhere it seems that Habakkuk's complaint is about the brutal Chaldean army. The introductions to the *woe* oracles above identify the wicked by their actions "inconsistent with Yahweh's justice"[60] rather than their national identity—acquisitiveness, theft, bloodshed, violence, and idolatry. Anyone who does these deeds—internal foes or foreign invaders—is "the wicked," under threat from these prophetic oracles.

The examples I have offered in this chapter are, of course, only excerpts from prophetic books to illustrate my understanding of parallelism and vertical reading. However, understanding of a poem requires an analysis of lines in context. We turn now to the analysis of Joel 2 to see how these ideas might enrich the reading of a whole poem. Mapping out a vertical reading through diagrams of parallels, we can observe how the prophetic poet moves up and down the cosmic slide to connect a locust plague in Judah to the *great and terrible* Day of YHWH and communal lamentation to divine repentance.

---

60. Mathews, *Performing Habakkuk*, 137.

3

The Day of the Lord/Locust

Moving Up and Down the Cosmic Slide in Joel 2

SET IN HOLLYWOOD IN the midst of America's Great Depression, Nathanael West's novel *The Day of the Locust* (1933) paints a horrifying picture of Midwesterners swarming to the movie capital in pursuit of utopian dreams, only to meet with frustration and then turn to mob violence. West borrows imagery from the scene of the eighth plague of Exodus 10, the depiction of a locust infestation in Joel 1–2, and the vision of demonic locusts in Revelation 9 to portray the horde coming to Hollywood from the east, devouring the land of dreams in boredom and rage. In the final chapter a theater premier turns into a riot, with imagery of a flood and demonic swarm transforming the event into a vision of apocalyptic catastrophe:

> At the sight of their [movie star] heroes and heroines, the crowd would turn demonic. Some little gesture, either too pleasing or too offensive, would start it moving and then nothing but machine guns would stop it. Individually the purpose of its members might simply be to get a souvenir, but collectively it would grab and rend. . . . Until they reached the line [of the mob], they looked diffident, almost furtive, but the moment they had become part of it, they turned arrogant and pugnacious. It was a mistake to think them harmless curiosity seekers. They were savage and bitter, especially the middle-aged and the old, and had been made so by boredom and disappointment. . . . [The main character Tod was] sent to his knees by a blow in the back of the head that spun him sideways. The crowd in front of the theatre had charged. He was surrounded by churning legs and feet. He pulled himself erect by grabbing a man's coat, then let himself be carried along backwards in a long, curving swoop. . . . There was another dizzy rush. Tod closed his eyes and fought

to keep upright. He was jostled about in a hacking cross surf of shoulders and backs, carried rapidly in one direction and then in the opposite.[1]

To lend weight to his creative critique of the American dream and its pursuers, West formulates his title, *The Day of the Locust*. Taking advantage of alliteration between LORD and *Locust*, he combines the biblical depiction of a literal locust plague from Joel and Exodus and demonic locusts from Revelation with the prophetic phrase *Day of the* LORD, which had become a reference to a final Day of Judgment in Jewish and Christian tradition. Although West's title and hyperbolic language are ultimately ironic, his creative maneuver is the strategy of the prophetic poets: focusing on a particular earthly scene (here an imagined riot in Hollywood) and elevating its significance through cosmic imagery. In West's novel this and other apocalyptically rendered scenes ultimately collapse into insignificance to express his grim view of the triviality and meaninglessness of the American dream.[2] The effectiveness of his irony, however, depends on his readers' familiarity with the opposite perspective of the biblical prophets, which slides between the mundane and cosmic, suggesting that human experience is charged with significance.

West's title *The Day of the Locust* inadvertently captures the book of Joel's perspective that an actual infestation of locusts represents a Day of the Lord (=Day of YHWH; Hebrew *Yôm YHWH*). For West a riot in Hollywood is the mundane event he describes, and the locusts and reference to Day of the Lord are biblical allusions rendering (ironic) transcendent significance to the scene; while for Joel the locust plague is the concrete reality, and the Day of the Lord imagery conveys the cosmic significance of the event. I understand *the Day of YHWH* to be a prophet's designation for a major transforming event in Israel's life as a result of a dramatic manifestation of YHWH, not the singular Judgment Day of later Jewish and Christian tradition.[3] Support-

---

1. West, *Day of the Locust*, 176, 177, 181.

2. We can detect the irony of the mob scene when it collapses into the protagonist's mad laughter and the wail of an ambulance siren. West employs the same strategy in other apocalyptic scenes in the novel to convey his perspective on the essential triviality and even meaninglessness of the American dream: the opening "apocalyptic battle" disintegrates as a ridiculously dressed "little fat man" cuts the scene (59); the set of the Battle of Waterloo literally collapses on the actors (130–35); and the swell and intensity of Bach's music inviting Christ to come is silenced at the signal of an officious woman assuming command at a funeral (128–29).

3. There have been numerous studies of the phrase *Yôm YHWH* in biblical literature, many of them speculating about the origins of the phrase. For very fine surveys of the scholarly literature on the subject, one can consult Crenshaw, *Joel*, 47–50; and Simkins, "Day of Yahweh and the History of Creation," in *Yahweh's Activity in History*

ing Ronald Simkins's thesis on "the identification of the natural catastrophe [of the locust plague] with the day of Yahweh" in his book *Yahweh's Activity in History and Nature in the Book of Joel*,[4] I will argue that a vertical reading of the parallels in Joel 2 suggests that the Day of YHWH is not a reference to the distant future in this context—certainly not an eschatological or apocalyptic future; but rather it refers to the transcendent meaning of a specific experience of the writer's present. As the Joel poet brings a devastating locust plague "into divine focus,"[5] his language masterfully shifts perspective up and down the cosmic slide from description of the concrete reality of locusts devouring the grain, vines, and fruit trees of Judah to a vision of the transcendent realm of YHWH. The Day of YHWH, then, refers to the present and the Presence which give meaning to human experience. From the prophetic perspective of the book of Joel, Judah is not just experiencing an insect plague but the Day of the Lord/Locust.

The Day of Joel

Although the book of Joel is grounded in a concrete experience of ecological disaster, there is little agreement among scholars about the specific historical background or unity of the text. The editor's superscription offers only: *The word of YHWH was to Joel ben Pethuel* (1:1). Proposed dates for the original context of the prophetic poems range from the ninth to the second centuries

---

and Nature, 243–73. See also Everson's short article, "Days of Yahweh," 329–37; and a critique of Everson and others by Hoffmann, "Day of the Lord as a Concept," 37–50. Even though Everson's study expands the data to phrases related to *Yôm YHWH* rather than confining the evidence to the exact expression itself, his conclusion has merit in demonstrating that the concept of the Day of YHWH is not always a reference to a future, singular event: "The writers look back on different historical events. In striking contrast to the thesis that the Day of Yahweh is always set forth as a singular event in the future, these texts demonstrate that it is not only appropriate but extremely helpful to speak of a sequence of historical days of Yahweh when speaking of the prophetic interpretation of history. . . . Events such as war, earthquakes or plagues, which mark the eras or turning points in the life of the nation, are the kind of events which can be described as days of Yahweh. They are events which have the potential for turning history in various directions" ("Days of Yahweh," 331, 337). More recently, Linville also adopts this conclusion: "In general, however, it [Day of Yahweh] refers to any of numerous historical and future days associated with dramatic acts of God" ("Day of Yahweh and the Mourning of the Priests," 106.) I will argue that an analysis of the parallelism in Joel 2 offers additional insight for our understanding of the prophetic use of *Yôm YHWH*; in my view the focus of the expression is not so much on the past or on the future, the choices most scholars consider, but rather on the present.

4. Simkins, *Yahweh's Activity in History and Nature*, 97.
5. Heschel, *Prophets*, 29.

BCE, with the arguments for the fifth or late sixth century probably being the most persuasive.[6] While some scholars view the book as a unified whole essentially originating in the speeches of one prophet, others consider it an anthology of loosely connected poems from different periods.[7]

For purposes of this poetic analysis of Joel 2, it is important only to offer a couple comments on the position I am adopting on historical and literary background. First, as stated above, the book of Joel (at least chapters 1 and 2) is grounded in a real ecological disaster of unrecoverable date, a devastating locust plague and drought which follows afterward in Judah. That assertion, simple as it sounds, argues against two alternate literary conclusions which scholars sometimes propose: that Joel 2 describes an invasion of a foreign army using *imagery* of a locust plague, rather than depicting a locust plague using imagery of an army;[8] and that the chapter, although perhaps inspired by an ecological crisis, is an apocalyptic vision of "the invasion of a massive otherworldly force."[9] The vertical reading of Joel 2 which I offer will argue against both of these proposals and suggest, consistent with the previous chapter on parallelism, that the poem of Joel 2 clearly exhibits the typically prophetic "semantic skid from the historical to the cosmic"[10] as the prophet envisions a real locust plague and drought from a transcendent view. There is no bloodshed, as we would expect in the case of an invasion of an army; primary victims are vines, fields, and trees; humans and animals suffer not from the sword but from lack of food for sustenance and offerings; the invaders are described in similes comparing them to *the appearance of horses, the sound of chariots, a mighty people arranged for battle* (2:4-5); and the parallels gradually but explicitly uncover the identity of the invaders with the different kinds of locusts introduced in the first chapter of Joel (1:4;

---

6. See surveys of scholars' proposals for the historical context in Crenshaw, *Joel*, 21-29; and Barton, *Joel and Obadiah*, 14-18. Probably the most thorough examination of terminology in Joel, Ahlström's *Joel and the Temple Cult*, 111-29, concludes that 515-500 BCE is the most defensible context for the book of Joel.

7. Crenshaw, *Joel*, 29-34, summarizes the views clearly.

8. For example, in *Art of Biblical Poetry*, 49, Alter adopts the view that the description of the invaders "like horses . . . like warriors" are "in fact designations of an army rhetorically masquerading as similes." His later translation and commentary in *Hebrew Bible*, however, recognizes the locusts as the target metaphorically represented as an army (1245). Another argument for the invaders as a foreign army envisioned with locust imagery appears in Andiñach, "Locusts in the Message of Joel," 433-41.

9. Cook, *Prophecy & Apocalypticism*, 175. Wolff also argues that the real locust plague of Joel 1 has shifted to a "harbinger" of the great eschatological day of judgment in Joel 2: ". . . these locustlike apocalyptic creatures (that are, however, never designated as locusts) are announced as the apocalyptic enemy army" (*Joel and Amos*, 42).

10. Alter, *Art of Biblical Poetry*, 192.

2:25). Furthermore, the hyperbolic language does not point to an apocalyptic collapse but communicates the prophet's view that the ecological disaster is charged with significance, since this insect horde is under the command of General YHWH. That is a troubling theological view indeed, but not one which pushes the prophet to apocalyptic visions. As the language of the Joel poems moves up and down the cosmic slide from concrete to cosmic, the prophet is dealing with an ecological and theological crisis in his own present, difficult though it is to supply a date for that day.

Considering the severity of ecological devastation caused by a locust plague, we could conclude that the slide from the concrete to the cosmic is not so steep. In his chapter "A Great Scourge upon the Land," Simkins assembles reports of locust infestations in Africa and Asia from the late eighteenth to the early twentieth centuries CE.[11] Among them is J. D. Whiting's account of an infestation of locust hoppers in the area of Jerusalem in 1915:

> Countless numbers of the young locusts poured into the broad, walled road leading into the city [of Jerusalem] from the west.... For three or four days an incessant and unending stream filled the road from side to side, like numberless troops marching on parade.... Up and up the city walls and the castle they climbed to their heights.... After a few days' effort, however, they reversed their course, and for several days streams of them made for the opposite direction, but only far enough to escape the barrier which the city afforded; and, this once attained, they swung around into the very direction heretofore pursued....
>
> Disastrous as they were in the country, equally obnoxious they became about the homes, crawling up thick upon the walls and, squeezing in through cracks of closed doors and windows, entering the very dwelling rooms. When unable to find entrance they often scaled the walls to the roofs, and then they got into the houses by throwing themselves into the open courts, such as most Oriental houses are built around.... About our houses they became so thick that one could not help crushing them with every step.[12]

Acknowledging, as Simkins does, that Whiting's account might have been influenced by the writer's familiarity with the book of Joel, the resemblance to the poetic description of the locust plague in 2:4–10 nevertheless testifies to the disastrous ecological effects of such an infestation and suggests that the prophet also was describing a concrete event in Jerusalem

---

11. Simkins, *Yahweh's Activity in History and Nature*, 121–69.

12. Whiting, "Jerusalem's Locust Plague," 525–6, 533; quoted in Simkins, *Yahweh's Activity in History and Nature*, 165.

in his own day. The following modern statistics on the desert locust from *The National Geographic* Web site further help us imagine the devastation caused by a swarm of locusts:

> A desert locust swarm can be 460 square miles in size and pack between 40 and 80 million locusts into less than half a square mile. Each locust can eat its weight in plants each day, so a swarm of such size would eat 423 million pounds of plants every day.[13]

According to the ancient world view, in which spiritual, social, and natural worlds are intricately connected, an ecological disaster of this magnitude presents an equally urgent theological crisis. The prophet's challenge is to address these questions: What is YHWH's role in the locust invasion? How should the community respond to restore harmony among the interwoven spiritual, social, and natural realms?

A second important observation about the day of Joel is that the book presupposes a functioning temple in Jerusalem for worship of YHWH, probably the second temple built around 515 BCE in the era of Persian control over Judah and its neighbors. For the prophet the appropriate response to the devastating locust plague and drought is communal assembly before the altar in Jerusalem with weeping and fasting under priestly leadership (2:12–17). Although we know nothing of the prophet Joel, the emphasis on the efficacy of communal rites and the ritual directions to both people and priests suggest that the writer of the book presents Joel as a cultic prophet or priest himself as well as a prophet.[14] In the following discussion of Joel 2, we shall see the aptness of James Linville's assessment that "the text affirms the status of the priesthood in the writer's society by reinforcing the view that they are essential players in the divine/natural/human economy of the cosmos."[15] Though we can say little about the day of Joel or the person called Joel, we can conclude that a locust plague and following drought, the temple in Jerusalem, and an emphasis on the importance of priestly leadership are part of the context of the poem in Joel 2.

---

13. "Locusts," accessed May 17, 2017, http://www.nationalgeographic.com/animals/invertibrates/group/locusts/.

14. This argues *against* Wolff and others, who identify an antitheocratic bias in Joel (*Joel and Amos*, 12, 49, 52–53), and *with* Cook (*Prophecy & Apocalypticism*, 167–209), Linville ("Day of Yahweh and the Mourning of the Priests," 98–114), and Ahlström (*Joel and the Temple Cult*), who point to the emphasis on the importance of the cult and its priestly leaders in the book of Joel.

15. Linville, "Day of Yahweh and the Mourning of the Priests," 99.

The Contours of the Poem

The book of Joel might be an anthology, but at least the first two chapters in the Hebrew Bible (1:2—2:27 in English) are likely to originate from one prophetic poet. Although a locust plague features in both Joel 1 and 2, scholars argue about the relationship between the chapters, in terms of subject, sequence, and perspective. It is clear that an infestation has already occurred from the perspective of Joel 1, which specifically identifies the voracious locusts and calls on various groups—elders and inhabitants of the land, wine drinkers, plowmen and vinedressers, and priests—to lament the devastation of fields, trees, vineyards, and ritual offerings. Chapter 2, however, begins with a warning of an *imminent* Day of YHWH, expected to be a day of gloom and disaster from initially unspecified invaders. Commentators therefore puzzle over the chronological sequence of the chapters. Are the chapters out of order? Does Joel 1 describe a locust plague and drought that has already occurred and Joel 2 revert back to an earlier moment when the plague was anticipated? Are there two different infestations—the one described as past in Joel 1 and the next one anticipated in Joel 2? The perspective also shifts enough for some commentators to argue that Joel 1 is about a real locust plague and drought, while Joel 2 views that recent catastrophe as a harbinger of a great apocalyptic event, an eschatological Day of YHWH.

Against those who see a past event as the subject of Joel 1 and a future event in Joel 2—a second infestation of locusts, an impending invasion of foreign armies, or an apocalyptic cataclysm—we might alternatively argue that both chapters, addressing the same locust plague, shift between the earthly and the cosmic. Among the descriptions of ruined fields and vines and lamenting priests and cattle, Joel 1 also includes the exclamatory warning of doom, similar to the rhetoric of Joel 2:

> Alas for the day!
> For the Day of YHWH approaches
> like ruin from Shaddai. (1:15)

On the other hand, Joel 2, which begins with a similar warning of the approach of the Day of YHWH, also returns to earth with a vivid description of the effects, appearance, movement, and sound of the invading locust army in verses 4–10. What is past and what is future? Although that is always difficult to determine in prophetic texts, my view remains with the understanding stated above that the language of the approaching Day of YHWH conveys the cosmic perspective on the concrete, earthly experience of a locust plague and drought. Rather than shifting confusingly between past and future, the prophet is grounded in the *present*[16] as his language moves up and down the cosmic slide between the concrete, earthly event and the transcendent vision of that event. In this view, Joel 1 and 2 are about the same experience. However, Joel 1 generally stays earth-bound, with a brief slide to the cosmic in verse 15; while Joel 2 moves more fluidly up and down the cosmic slide in a heightened effort to present the disaster as the Day of the Lord/Locust. Although it would be reasonable to analyze both chapters together as a unit, readers who view Joel 2 as a separate poem on the same experience as in chapter 1 benefit from an appreciation of the fluidity of the movement between the concrete to the cosmic, perception of a coherent tripartite structure of the chapter, and recognition of a strategy of withholding the identity of the invaders to enhance the dramatic conclusion.

As many commentators recognize, Joel 2:1-27 divides naturally into three sections or stanzas on the basis of major shifts in content. Each stanza builds upon the content of the previous unit: verses 1-11 describe an invasion of a mysterious horde; verses 12-17 prescribe the proper communal response to the invasion; and verses 18-27 convey YHWH's gracious response to the afflicted, mourning community. Formal literary devices also delineate the sections. Robert Alter observes the way the end mirrors the beginning in Joel 2:1-11, creating an effective frame around that section of the poem. The unit begins and ends with a declaration of the Day of YHWH (vv. 1, 11); the blast of the horn in verse 1 finds an echo in the booming voice of YHWH in verse 11; the inhabitants of the land quake (רגז–v. 1), as does the whole earth (v. 10); the initial darkness spreading over the mountains

---

16. Simkins offers a very thoughtful excursus on the difference between perceptions of time in ancient Israel and in the modern West. He describes the former as present orientation, in contrast to future orientation of the modern West: "In a present oriented society, a person's present activity seeks to achieve proximate goals. The present is experienced time. It is the duration of everyday experiences; it is not simply a moment. It includes all forthcoming and recent events. . . . In understanding present orientation, a distinction needs to be made between the forthcoming and the future. The forthcoming is the horizon of the perceived present; it forms an organic unity with the actual present. It is a time of potentialities which are directly perceived as a part of the present. The forthcoming is tied to the present within the unity of a single context of meaning. The future, on the other hand . . . is the world of the imagination, unbound by the experiences of the present. The future is the realm of God who determines the possibilities; human actions are ineffectual in altering its outcome" (*Yahweh's Activity in History and Nature*, 263). My view of the orientation of prophetic poetry shares much with that of Simkins but differs in two respects. He maintains the linear model of a time line to envision the distinction between past, present, and future; while my view employs a vertical model (present earthly experience linked to the cosmic, mythic realm). Also he calls the future the realm of God, while in my view the realm of God in prophetic texts is timeless, or maybe more accurately, encompassing all time; a prophet seeks to link present experience of humans to the mythic realm, in which all time is the present.

of Jerusalem (v. 2) presages the darkened sun, moon, and stars (v. 10); and the *vast and mighty* horde descending over the city (v. 2) becomes YHWH's *vast* and *mighty* army (v. 11).[17] Similarly the second section begins with a command for communal weeping (v. 12) and ends with instructions for the priests to weep (v. 17). The final stanza begins and ends with YHWH's promise of *satiety* (vv. 19, 26). Through vertical reading of the parallels, we can now examine the dynamics of each stanza of the poem as it progresses with dramatic movement and startling revelations.

The Invasion (Joel 2:1–11)

Scene 1: Announcement of the Approaching Invaders (Joel 2:1–3)

With the blast of a ram's horn (*šôfār*), a dramatic scene unfolds cinematically:

¹Blow the *šôfār* in Zion,
and shout on my holy mountain.

Let all the inhabitants of the land quake!

For the Day of YHWH approaches;
for (it is) near—
²a day of darkness and gloom,
a day of cloud and thick cover.

---

17. Alter, *Art of Biblical Poetry*, 48.

Like blackness[18] spread over the mountains

is a people vast and mighty.

Something like it	has not been	from of old;
something after it	will not be again	for generations to come.

³Before it	a fire	devours,
and after it	a flame	sets ablaze.

Like	the Garden of Eden		is the land	before it,
				and after it

a desolate wilderness.

There is absolutely no escape from it!

Beginning in the heights of the divine realm, Joel 2 represents YHWH's voice commanding a blast of the *šôfār* in Zion, the temple mount, home of YHWH. Initially the dramatic summons is ambiguous. Does YHWH summon to war or worship, both occasions involving the blast of the horn and the ritual shout? If the context is war, is YHWH calling the Jerusalemites to defend themselves and YHWH's temple from invaders, or is YHWH summoning the invaders to come to Jerusalem? Only gradually and evocatively does the scene unfold.

---

18. Reading שְׁחֹר (*blackness*) with BHS notes and several commentators, instead of the MT שַׁחַר (*dawn*), although the LXX and other versions read with the MT. Coggins tries to derive some sense from the MT: "This [change to שְׁחֹר] might be right, but it is unusual to speak of *blackness spread upon the mountains*; that is the usual way of speaking of dawn. Since both the Hebrew and the ancient versional evidence are unanimously in favor of 'dawn' as the correct reading, perhaps the sense here is that even the dawn, normally a time of renewed hope, will prove to be a 'false dawn', for it will reveal the great and powerful army, somewhat in the manner described in narrative form in Judg. 9.34–41" (*Joel and Amos*, 39). Alter, *Hebrew Bible*, also translates as *dawn*, and recognizes the image as a "poetic paradox" (1244). Simkins chooses the reading *blackness*, relating it to the realistic coloration of hopper bands of locusts (*Yahweh's Activity in History and Nature*, 155–56). While either is possible, the connection to the looming dark clouds in the previous lines might favor *blackness*, a reading which requires only a repointing of the MT.

The following poetic line, emphatically standing without parallels—*Let all the inhabitants of the land quake!*—could imply either a divine or human speaker. Typically prophetic texts shift suddenly and often imperceptibly between YHWH's voice and the prophet's because the prophets present themselves as conveying messages from YHWH, even as they shape the words according to their own poetic design. The strategy of directing or reporting the observers' terrified response to the unfolding catastrophe in this line and in the next section of the poem (vv. 6, 10) guides the audience to appropriately tense emotional involvement. Perhaps we might think of such directives as functionally equivalent to modern film music guiding the audience's response. Here the inhabitants of the land are directed to *quake* (רגז), a term often associated with terrified response to a theophany (e.g., 2 Sam 22:8=Ps 18:8; Ps 77:17, 19; Hab 3:7, 16) and therefore appropriate for a Day of YHWH.

The prophetic voice now takes over the poem to describe the Day of YHWH descending as a thick cloud over the mountains:

For	the Day of YHWH	approaches;
for		(it is) near—

²a day of darkness and gloom,

a day of cloud and thick cover.

Charting the parallels grammatically, one notices not only the repetition of *day of* but also the correspondence among the prepositional objects: *YHWH/ darkness and gloom/ cloud and thick cover*. Unmistakably the poet recognizes the presence of YHWH as ominous for the people of Judah. The metaphor of a descending dark cloud, initially characterizing the disposition of YHWH, then takes independent shape in *blackness spread over the mountains* as the prophetic poet's vision skillfully focuses downward from the realm of YHWH to the heights of the land. Gradually the darkness reveals itself as an invading horde, *a people vast and mighty*.

Although the original audience could recognize the aptness of this poetic description to their sighting of a swarm of locusts darkening the sky, the prophetic voice suspends further identification of the invaders for characterization of their attack as utterly unprecedented and thoroughly devastating. Three bicola connect parallel lines with a *before/after* hinge. In the first set, *before* (the concept but not the word in this case) and *after* have temporal connotations, as the lines depict these invaders as utterly unique, without precedent or antecedent:

Something like it	has not been	from of old;
something after it	will not be again	for generations to come.

The next bicolon shifts the meaning of *before* and *after* from temporal to spatial[19] in lines using the same words and images of fire to assess the destructiveness of the locusts as in Joel 1:19:

³Before it	a fire	devours,
and after it	a flame	sets ablaze.

Here *before* and *after* do not imply a contrast but form a merismus, suggesting that the metaphorical fire accompanies the invaders all around. A clear example of intensification through parallels, the subjects and verbs are semantic pairs, with the second term being the more colorful of the pair in each case: *fire / flame, devours / sets ablaze*. While the image of fire connotes the thorough devastation of the invading horde, James Crenshaw observes that the metaphorical fire also hints of the invasion as a manifestation of the appearance of YHWH: "Ancient theophanic imagery animates this account of YHWH's army being preceded by fire (cf. Pss 50:3; 97:3)."[20] In the third bicolon the *before/after* pairing expresses both a spatial and a temporal contrast:

Like	the Garden of Eden	is the land before it,
		and after it
	a desolate wilderness.	

The land in front of the invaders and before their attack is as fecund and lush as the mythical Garden of Eden, but the land behind their advance and in the wake of their attack is as barren as a desert. A couple of poetic strategies enhance the "punch" of this bicolon. First, these lines along with the previous pair provide an effective example of foregrounding. The previous bicolon, with semantically matching parallel terms *fire / flame* and *devours / sets ablaze* establishes an expectation of similarity as the basis of the relationship between the components; but here the parallel terms *Garden of Eden* and *a desolate wilderness* are in starkest contrast with one another.[21]

19. Crenshaw, *Joel*, 120.
20. Crenshaw, *Joel*, 120.
21. Alter, *Art of Biblical Poetry*, 48–49.

Also, this bicolon reverses the word order of the parallel terms within their respective lines so that the opposite images of the Garden of Eden and the desolate wilderness frame the lines, enhancing the contrast and emphasizing *a desolate wilderness* as a grim climax.

The tight parallels "unwind" in the exclamatory lone line closing the first scene of this stanza of the poem: *There is absolutely no escape from it!* (2:3). The exclamatory nature and the singularity of the line echo the emphatic character of the lone line at the beginning of the poem—*Let all the inhabitants of the land quake!*—which followed the opening bicolon of clear parallels and removed the ambiguity about whether the blasting horn and shout signaled worship or war. The closing exclamation serves both as a forceful conclusion to the first scene and an apt introduction to the next section on the relentless momentum of the invaders, from whom there is no escape.

Scene 2: Description of the Invaders and Reactions to Them (Joel 2:4–10)

An interpreter who charts the parallels in the next scene of the poem can appreciate its stunning imagery and intricate artistic structure. Two sets of parallel lines alternate in this section: 1) lines beginning with *like* (Hebrew כ) or various locative prepositions (Hebrew ב) and consisting of similes and metaphors depicting the appearance, sound, and energetic movement of the invaders; and 2) lines introduced by *before it* (Hebrew מפניו or לפניו) and describing reactions to the invasion (vv. 6 and 10, in italics in the chart below). Those who regard the bicolon and tricolon as the basis of all Hebrew poetry will appreciate the regularity of the opening scene above but will miss the dynamism of the poetic lines in this new scene, with parallels extending well beyond two or three lines.

Examining the first column of prepositional modifiers in the chart below, we notice the impressive build-up of parallel phrases describing the invaders, which begins with five similes vividly depicting their appearance (*like the appearance of horses, like a mighty people arranged for battle*), sound (*like the sound of chariots upon the tops of the mountains, like the sound of a flame of fire devouring the stubble*), and movement (*like steeds*). Like the leaping invaders, the description itself "leaps over" a bicolon depicting the reaction of people to the invasion (2:6) and continues with two more similes to characterize the movement of the horde: *like warriors, like men of battle*. Through the language of simile, the poet reveals that the invaders are not *actually* an advancing army, but they *are compared to* an army. Recalling

Whiting's description of the 1915 locust infestation of Jerusalem, we can recognize the unnamed invaders as a locust horde, with elongated heads like horses,[22] mandibles chewing the vegetation with the sound of crackling fire, and fantastic advance row-on-row like a well-trained army.

⁴Like the appearance of horses
   is its appearance,

and like steeds   thus   they   charge.

⁵Like the sound of chariots
   upon the tops of the mountains   they   leap,

like the sound of a flame of fire devouring
   the stubble,

like a mighty people arranged for battle.

⁶*Before it*   *peoples*   *writhe;*
           all faces   *gather*   *luster.*
                               [=grow pale]

⁷Like warriors   they   charge.

Like men of battle   they   climb a wall.

                               Each in his
                                   own way   they   march.

                                                  They   do not bend
                                                                        their paths.

                               ⁸Each   his brother

                                                  they   do not crowd.

                               Each in his
                               own track   they   march.

Through the weapon   they   fall;

                                                   they   do not stop.

⁹Into the city   they   rush.

Over the wall   they   charge.

---

22. Revelation 9:7 literalizes this simile comparing locusts to horses in its vision of the demonic locusts from the bottomless pit. Comparison between locusts and horses appears in several ancient literary accounts surveyed by Simkins in *Yahweh's Activity in History and Nature,* 101, 162–64.

Into the houses	they	climb.
Through the windows	they	enter
like a thief.		

¹⁰Before it	earth	quakes;	
	heavens	tremble;	
	sun and moon	darken,	
	and stars	collect	their brightness.

After the series of similes, the following prepositional modifiers (all beginning with the same Hebrew preposition ב)—*through the weapon*,[23] *into the city, over the wall, into the houses, through the windows*—construct a narrative sequence of the advance of the locust army. Through the poem's detail we watch the swarm of tiny insects hyperbolically slip through defensive weapons, advance into Jerusalem, scale the wall, and sneak into every house through the windows. The poet concludes the entire narrative of their advance with a return to a simile, *like a thief.* No one escapes as the invaders advance into everyone's living space.

Likewise the parallel verbs do not conclude with *charge* and *leap* from the opening lines but jump across the interruption on people's reactions and continue with twelve more active, dynamic verbs of movement: *charge, climb, march, do not bend,*[24] *do not crowd,*[25] *march, fall, do not stop, rush, charge, climb, enter.*[26] Reading through the column of verbs, we receive a vivid

---

23. Translation here is also uncertain. A plausible understanding is that the locust "army" slips through weapons. Of course no one would venture to attack locusts with spears or swords, but this is poetry; and the point, apparently, is that this group of invaders is unstoppable. There is no defense against them.

24. The usual meaning of the root of this verb עבט, "to pledge," is nonsensical here. The LXX has "they do not bend aside," giving plausible sense. For a full discussion of the options, see Simkins, *Yahweh's Activity in History and Nature,* 157; or Crenshaw, *Joel,* 123.

25. The meaning of the Hebrew verb, appearing only twice in the MT, is somewhat uncertain, but my reading follows the usual suggestion. My translation, *Each his brother they do not crowd,* is, of course, a bit awkward in word order and is also ungrammatical. (*Each does not crowd his brother* would be better.) However, I want to preserve the plural verb in the MT for the parallelism with the other verbs, and the chart requires the odd word order.

26. Many of the verbs include the enhanced poetic spelling, the *energic nûn,* in

portrait of energetic, unstoppable action. Robert Alter's eloquent description of the sequence and repetitions in the impressive list of parallel verbs shows appreciation of the rhythmic progression of the lines:

> The poet here is less interested in an illusion of seamless temporal progression than in a steady, solemn advance—spatially, from the distant mountains up to and over the walls of the city and into the houses—marked by a mounting drumbeat, and for this the model of incremental repetition is particularly apt: they run, they dance, they run, they scale a wall, they go; indeed, they go, they swarm, they run, they scale, they come in at the windows like thieves. A narrative tempo like this brings us close to the mesmerizing rhythms of the Song of Deborah. . . .[27]

As we note from the chart above, even the adverbial *thus* has parallels in modifying phrases from the resumed description of the invaders: *each in his own way, each in his own track*; thus they move as a disciplined, efficient force. Terrifying and destructive though these invaders are, the poet stands in awe of their order and efficiency. We are reminded of their inclusion in the list of four things which are *small, yet . . . exceedingly wise* in Proverbs: *The locusts have no king, / yet all of them march in rank* (Prov 30:24, 27 NRSV).

The Joel poet signals his listeners or readers to associate the two sections on reactions to the advancing army (vv. 6 and 10, in italics in the chart above) not only through the semantically related content but also with the opening phrase *before it* (מפניו in verse 6 and לפניו in verse 10) and with the grammatical parallels, which we can observe clearly if we chart the lines together:

Before it	peoples	writhe;	
	all faces	gather	luster [=grow pale].
Before it	earth	quakes;	
	heavens	tremble;	
	sun and moon	darken,	
	and stars	collect	their brightness.

Hebrew. This unusual form helps connect the verbal parallels.

27. Alter, *Art of Biblical Poetry*, 49–50.

As a reading through the column of subjects shows, the depiction of reactions to the invaders moves from the earthly world up the cosmic slide to the heavenly bodies. Of course the description displays greater hyperbole in the second set, as the earth quakes; the heavens tremble; and the sun, moon, and stars suddenly put out their lights. At this point some biblical commentators insist that the poet has lost sight of the locusts and moved on to apocalyptic vision:

> [There is a] clear movement in the direction of theophanic description, phenomena that locusts cannot generate even in one's wildest imagination. To be sure, locusts can temporarily obscure the sun for onlookers below, and the rolling motion of these insects on the ground simulates a mild tremor, but the extent of cosmic manifestation in vv 10–11 implies something far more terrifying than such phenomena as these. If locusts remain in Joel's thoughts at all here, they have been transformed into an apocalyptic army in the fullest sense.[28]

However, one could also argue that the poet's imagination *is* wild, and depiction of the exaggerated reaction of the cosmos does not mean the prophetic poet has left the concrete experience of a locust plague to enter an eschatological or apocalyptic realm. I concur with Simkins's judgment: "On the contrary, everything else in this unit points to the invasion of an actual locust plague. The cosmological phenomena, however, do indicate that this locust plague is no ordinary infestation; that is, it has cosmological, or better, cosmogonic significance."[29] This hyperbolic description is simply a prophetic poet's strategy for shifting the focus from the mundane to the cosmic, i.e., moving up the cosmic slide to invest the locust plague with significance. From the prophet's transcendent view the whole cosmos responds personally and extremely to the locust plague in Judah, as we see particularly from the verbs *writhe* (usually applied to women in childbirth in biblical texts), *quake, tremble, and darken.*

Charting these lines together also provides a clue to the interpretation of the enigmatic Hebrew word פָּארוּר in the phrase translated *gather luster* above (v. 6). Since the term appears only here and in an identical expression in Nahum 2:10 in the Hebrew Bible, the meaning of the word is uncertain. It is plausibly related to the verb פאר, meaning *to beautify, to glorify,* but what would it mean for human faces to *gather beauty/glory*? Parallelism provides a suggestion. Only two of the verbs in the chart above, *gather* and *collect,* have objects; and they are a standard pair, appearing together often, even later in

---

28. Crenshaw, *Joel,* 125–26.
29. Simkins, *Yahweh's Activity in History and Nature,* 167.

the chapter (v. 16). The objects of these verbs also line up in the grammatical parallelism between verses 6 and 10. The meaning of the second object, *brightness*, is not problematic; and the final line presents a vivid image of stars sucking in their brightness in terror before the advancing locust army. If the parallel verb phrase *gather* פָּאר֥וּ is semantically related to *collect their brightness*, then we might conclude that the former line refers to faces suddenly gathering in their color or natural glow. As the stars suddenly suck in their light, so human faces drain of all color in terror before the advancing locust horde. The first reactions, people writhing and faces growing pale, are not too hyperbolic, since the terrifying approach of a huge cloud of locusts must surely have prompted such physical reactions. The parallel trembling and darkening of heavenly bodies are not only descriptive of the blackening of the sky from the locust swarm, but they also express the prophetic poet's perception that this is not just a locust plague but the Day of the Lord/Locust. The final lines of the stanza tell us why.

Scene 3: Identity of the Foe—Invaders as YHWH's Army (Joel 2:11)

Now that the Joel poet has guided his audience up the cosmic slide to the heavenly realm, he can offer his shocking revelation of YHWH's involvement in the earthly crisis:

YHWH utters his voice

before his army.

Truly	very vast	is his camp!
Truly	mighty	are those who obey his command!
Truly	great	is the Day of YHWH
	and very terrifying!	

Who can endure it?

Here is a surprise (perhaps less for the ancient audience than for the modern reader): the terrifying army invading the land of Judah belongs to Commander YHWH; it is *his army*. Returning now to the first line of the poem, we even wonder if the initial command to blow the *šôfār* in Zion might not have been a summons to the invaders. So jarring is this interpretation of the lines for the modern reader that Simkins, one of the most astute commentators on Joel 2, regards this army as a different force than the locust troops of the previous verses; it is, in his view, YHWH's heavenly hosts coming *to rescue* the distressed Judeans from the locust invaders, whose march against Zion has "assaulted Yahweh and challenged his kingship."[30] Simkins defends this view by reference to the conflict myth in biblical passages, in which YHWH comes to the rescue of YHWH's people; by the observation that the locusts are attacking YHWH's own land, vines, and figs; and by the depiction of YHWH's defeat of the locusts at the end of the poem.[31] Against those arguments, we might point out that the locust army is the most natural referent here, since the connection with the previous description of the invading force is perfectly smooth. Furthermore, as we shall see, the poet explicitly portrays YHWH as identifying the various types of locusts from Joel 1:4 with *my great army, which I sent against you [i.e., people of Jerusalem]* (Joel 2:25). If there is a conflict myth here, it is closer to the modified version in which YHWH sends the invading force against YHWH's own people, as in Isaiah's poem about an attack on Jerusalem/Ariel (Isa 29:1–8) or Ezekiel's narratives about the mythic Gog, whom YHWH summons against the restored Israel (Ezek 38–39).

After announcing that this is YHWH's own army in the lines above, the prophet clarifies the relationship in three nominal lines introduced by *truly* (Hebrew כִּי, interpreted here as asseverative or intensive). The parallel subjects are particularly significant, as they gradually disclose more about the relationship and move up the cosmic slide from the earthly "encampment" to the Day of YHWH. We learn that the vast camp is not only efficient and disciplined, as the description of the invaders in the previous scene revealed, but it is also obedient to Commander YHWH, acting on divine orders. Moreover, this invasion is a Day of YHWH, a manifestation of YHWH in an earth-transforming event. The parallel adjectives set the ominous tone: *very vast, mighty, great, very terrifying*. Similar to the first scene, this section concludes effectively in a non-parallel line, the question, *Who can endure it?* Setting those concluding lines together, we can appreciate the semantic connection between them and the tone of doom in the climax of both these scenes of the first stanza:

> There is absolutely no escape from it! (2:3)
> Who can endure it? (2:11)

---

30. Simkins, *Yahweh's Activity in History and Nature*, 167.
31. Simkins, *Yahweh's Activity in History and Nature*, 167, 245–73.

What is missing is the question *we* might ask: *Why* has YHWH commanded a locust attack on YHWH's own people? For now, we might simply observe that this is *not* the question of the prophet in this enigmatic poem.

Communal Response: Public Lamentation Confronting Public Shame (Joel 2:12–17)

The focus now shifts from description of the invading horde to prescription of the appropriate response to the disaster. Stanza 1 concluded with the question, *Who can endure it?* On the one hand, the question is rhetorical, with the implied answer, "No one." No one can escape these invaders, whose destructive march through the fields and vineyards of Judah and into the very windows of the houses of Jerusalem is irresistible. On the other hand, there is a way to prevail in the midst of the disaster. This next stanza prescribes a specific response which will enable the community to endure despite the devastation.

As in the first stanza, this new section begins with a command from YHWH and then suddenly shifts to the prophetic voice to supply a motive for the command. The smooth "hand-off" from YHWH as speaker to the prophetic voice is apparent in the parallel between *turn to me* and *turn to YHWH your God,* clearly visible in the chart below. The same mystifying God whom the prophet has just identified as the Commander of the invading forces now instructs the community in the appropriate ritual response; the prophet himself must supply motive and perspective:

¹²But even now—saying of YHWH—

Turn	to me	with all your heart,
		with fasting
		and with weeping
		and with wailing.
¹³Rend		your hearts
		and not [only] your garments;
and turn	to YHWH your God.	

Rather than demanding repentance or acknowledgment of some communal guilt, YHWH calls for lamentation through cultic acts performed with sincerity: fasting, ritual mourning, and rending of garments.[32] In light of the other ritual prescriptions here, I do not read a contrast in the line, *Rend your hearts and not your garments*. Therefore my translation adds the brackets, *and not [only] your garments*, to discourage reading of an anti-cultic bias here. If the community can fast and mourn together *with all [their] heart*, they can also *rend [their] hearts* along with their garments. All are sanctioned cultic actions of ritual mourning, and there is no critique of cultic action in favor of inner remorse here.[33] As Gary Anderson observes in his study, *A Time to Mourn, A Time to Dance: The Expression of Grief and Joy in Israelite Religion*, "The emotional experiences of grief and joy [in Ancient Israel] were inseparable from their behavioral components. . . . [R]itual activity can create a certain sentiment just as much as it can follow from one."[34] Linville even more specifically suggests how the particular ritual behaviors of fasting and weeping are appropriate to this situation of ecological disaster:

> God used to give food, but now in Joel the deity gives starvation. Yet, the recommended ritual fast and lamentation assimilates even this suffering to the exchange system which grounds creation, tenaciously rejecting defeatism. Thus, the hunger and grief is symbolically returned to its source in ritual time and place on behalf of the people, and, presumably nature itself. . . . [T]his sanctification [of fasting] symbolically transforms the hunger: it is not destruction from, but communion with the numinous 'Other.' So, too, the lamentation. . . . In Joel, the ritual weeping is part of the communalization of private grief. . . .[35]

In Joel 2, YHWH commands appropriate cultic actions—fasting for those whose crops have been devastated in plague and drought, rending of garments for those whose lives and hearts have been rent asunder by disaster,

---

32. This is in agreement with the argument by Barker, "One Good 'Turn' Deserves Another?" 115–31. Defending his view that Joel 2:12–17 should be read as a call to lamentation rather than repentance, Barker notes that the only other occurrence of the three words *fasting, weeping, and wailing* together is in Esther 4:3, where the innocent Jews lament after learning of Haman's decree (122).

33. In his study of ritual joy and mourning in Ancient Israel, Anderson identifies these behavioral components of communal mourning: fasting, sexual continence, lamentation, putting dust or ashes on the head, wearing sackcloth or torn clothes (*Time to Mourn*, 49). For the argument against an anti-cultic bias here, see also Barker, "One Good 'Turn' Deserves Another," 122.

34. Anderson, *Time to Mourn*, 2, 4.

35. Linville, "Day of Yahweh and the Mourning of the Priests," 107.

and communal lamentation for those who grieve—but YHWH does not demand communal repentance or confession.

That notoriously troublesome little word šûb (שׁוּב), *turn* or *return*,[36] which *sometimes* but not always refers to repentance from sin, combined with the disturbing revelation that YHWH has *sent* the locust horde, has inspired a veritable Joban debate among biblical scholars as they search for the sin for which the Judeans are being punished in Joel 2. In a very perceptive chapter, "Who Knows What YHWH Will Do? The Character of God in the Book of Joel," Crenshaw "entertain[s] the possibility that modern scholars have joined the ranks of Job's friends in being too quick to associate calamity with guilt in the book of Joel."[37] If YHWH commands a swarm of locusts to decimate the fields and vines of Judah and then calls on the community to repent—so the argument goes—then certainly this locust plague must be divine punishment for some transgression of the Judeans. Maybe we can hear the Joban friends in these modern voices:

> As used by the Deuteronomistic historian, . . . the verb [šûb] meant precisely listening to the voice of Yahweh as it had received expression in the Mosaic word of Deuteronomy. In similar fashion Joel recalls indirectly the prophetic word spoken in earlier times. The cultic community of Jerusalem, which is perhaps already beginning to pride itself on its fulfilling of the Torah, is to search forth anew toward the God who does not allow the prophetic word to become void of meaning.[38]

> Joel has seen the main reason for the disaster of the people as the abandoning of Yahweh. Instead of worshipping Yahweh in his temple, other gods have been worshipped.[39]

> [T]he people of Judah had been put to shame by their non-Yahwistic neighbors because of Yahweh's failure to protect them from the devastating locust plague. In response to this shame, the people had disassociated themselves from Yahweh, perhaps withholding the daily sacrifices from the food which remained to them. . . . Joel's reference to the fact that the grain offering

---

36. The Hebrew word שׁוּב can mean either *turn* or *return*. Most translators choose the latter, but that seems to imply some sin from which the Judeans must turn. Joel 2, however, does not identify any sins of the Judean audience; therefore, the former translation seems preferable and is certainly less tendentious.

37. Crenshaw, "Who Knows What YHWH Will Do?" 147. Similarly, see Barker, "One Good 'Turn' Deserves Another?," 117–25; and Simkins, *Yahweh's Activity in History and Nature*, 172.

38. Wolff, *Joel and Amos*, 49.

39. Ahlström, *Joel and the Temple Cult*, 75.

and wine libation were withheld from the temple (1.13) suggests that the people were saving what little food they had left for themselves. Yahweh's inactivity on their behalf had brought shame on them, and thus they were unwilling to offer their meager supplies to Yahweh.[40]

However, the book of Joel offers no indictment of the people of Judah. If they could respond to modern biblical scholars, they might take up the refutation of Job himself:

> Teach me, and I will be silent;
>
> make me understand how I have gone wrong.
>
> How forceful are honest words!
>
> But your reproof, what does it reprove? (Job 6:24–25 NRSV)

Scholars must fill in the blanks or read between the lines to supply the transgressions of Judah in Joel; the text itself includes no reproof but simply calls Judah to turn to YHWH in appropriate communal worship. The prophetic voice calls them to lament, not to repent.

However, the prophet suggests that *YHWH* might repent. The next lines begin as a continuation of those above by stating a motive for turning to YHWH (2:13c–14):

[13]For he is gracious

and merciful,

slow to anger

and great in *ḥesed*.

                And he repents of disaster.

Who knows?   He might turn

and repent

and leave behind him a blessing,

a grain offering

and drink offering for YHWH your God.

---

40. Simkins, *Yahweh's Activity in History and Nature*, 184, 189. This is a rather strange argument from Simkins, who otherwise argues that Joel recognizes no sin of the Judeans and does not call them to repent (171–2).

Despite the previous identification of YHWH as the Commander of the invading forces, the prophet urges the community to turn now to YHWH, the gracious and compassionate deity, full of patience and *ḥesed* (covenant faithfulness). The Joel poet characterizes YHWH in terms of a formulaic list of attributes appearing with slight variations in nine other passages in the Hebrew Bible.[41] The closest in wording to Joel 2:13 is Jonah 4:2, the only other list which adds that YHWH characteristically *repents of disaster* (נִחָם עַל־הָרָעָה). In that text the recalcitrant prophet ironically complains about these attributes of YHWH when YHWH repents of the disaster intended for the Ninevites. In Jonah and in other passages the verb נחם, which I have translated *repent*, refers to a change of mind or direction (e.g., YHWH repents of creating humans in Genesis 6:6–7; YHWH repents from the threat of sending locusts and fire in Amos's visions in Chapter 7; or the people of Jerusalem do not repent of their wickedness in Jeremiah 8:6). Both the Ninevites in Jonah and the prophet in Joel also acknowledge the mystery and freedom of YHWH with that wonderfully evocative little question, *Who knows?* (Jon 3:9; Joel 2:14). Since the qualities of the enigmatic YHWH simply cannot be captured adequately in a traditional formula, the Joel poet retreats from the confident, *He repents of disaster* to *Who knows? He might turn and repent*. The chart of parallels above indicates that the assertion *He repents of disaster,* with its active verb, is more closely linked to the following lines translated with modal verbs, *might turn and [might] repent and [might] leave,* than to the list of attributes of YHWH (*gracious, merciful, slow to anger, great in ḥesed*). Along with the question *Who knows?* the parallelism also suggests a distance between traditional formulations about YHWH's attributes and uncertainty about YHWH's actions. Having acknowledged YHWH's freedom, the prophet rather subtly and delicately includes a suggestion that it might be in YHWH's best interest to repent of the disaster. The parallel between *blessing / grain offering / drink offering for YHWH your God* implies that the blessing of revived fields and vineyards also benefits YHWH, since Judah's communion with the deity through offerings of grain and wine at the temple depends upon the restoration of the land.[42]

In a repetition of the opening command of the poem, the prophet now calls the people of Jerusalem to communal lamentation. While YHWH's ambiguous summons in Joel 2:1 was disclosed as a call to war, here the *šôfār* summons the community to worship:

41. Most commentators cite the passages. They are printed out helpfully in Crenshaw, *Joel*, 136. The passages are Exodus 34:6–7; Numbers 14:18; Psalm 86:15; Psalm 103:8; Psalm 145:8; Nahum 1:3; Jonah 4:2; Nehemiah 9:17, 31.

42. This is also one of the observations which Barker offers in his chapter, as suggested by his title "One Good 'Turn' Deserves Another?"

¹⁵Blow	the *šôfār*		in Zion.
Sanctify	a fast.		
Call	an assembly.		
¹⁶Gather	the people.		
Sanctify	the congregation.		
Assemble	the aged.		
Gather	the children,		
	even those who suck the breast.		

Let the bridegroom   exit   his chamber,
and the bride   her canopy.

In the verbal column of the first set above are seven insistent imperatives, with the repetition of *sanctify* and *gather* establishing a rhythmic ABCADC pattern after the initial command to blow. Following that first summons, the commands have the form of truncated lines consisting only of an imperative verb and single object (two words in Hebrew, as compared to the more usual three-word poetic lines), creating the effect of staccato blasts of the horn.[43] Unlike calls to war, which allow exceptions for participation due to age, gender, and circumstance (e.g., Deut 20:1–9; 24:5), here everyone must assemble at the altar—from elders to newborns, male and female. The situation is so urgent that even the bride and groom are to interrupt their celebrations to consecrate themselves with fasting, mourning, and presumably abstinence (implied in the command to "sanctify").[44]

The prophetic, perhaps also priestly, voice then instructs the priests in their ritual weeping and the words of their petition to YHWH at the communal assembly (2:17):

Between the vestibule and the altar
                             let   the priests   weep—
                                   the ministers of YHWH—   and say:

---

43. Crenshaw, *Joel*, 139.
44. Crenshaw, *Joel*, 140.

> "Have pity, O YHWH, upon your people;
> do not make your heritage
> into a reproach,
> into a byword among the nations.
>
> Why should they say among the peoples:
> 'Where is their God?'"

Who knows what YHWH will do? But enduring the disaster depends on priests calling the community to the area of sacrifice between the vestibule and altar of the temple[45] for lamentation and saying the right words. The *right* words are carefully conceived. In the first lines of the petition, there is a meaningful tension between semantically and syntactically corresponding terms, as I pointed out earlier in the introductory chapter. *Your people*, semantically related to the more specific and intense designation *your heritage*, is syntactically matched with the other objects of prepositions, *a reproach* and *a byword*.[46] The poetic structure expresses the complaint implied in the priests' petition: the people, who should be YHWH's precious heritage, are instead an object of ridicule and scorn among their neighbors, as they become an exemplar of a nation abandoned by its god. Thus the petition builds the case that YHWH has a stake in repenting of the disaster.

The final two lines of the petition, in an expression familiar from the Psalms (e.g., 42:4, 11; 79:10; 115:2), take the form of a question within a question:

> Why should they say among the peoples:
> "Where is their God?"

The questions recall the previous interrogatives: *Who can endure it?* (2:11) and *Who knows?* (2:14). All four are significant and subtle; none is entirely rhetorical. *Who can endure it?* leads to a new poetic stanza on the way the

---

45. Sweeney, *Twelve Prophets*, 1: 168.

46. This translation follows a proposed emendation of the MT, which has לִמְשָׁל־בָּם גּוֹיִם, *nations to rule over them*. This reading from the MT has many defenders, among them Ahlström, *Joel and the Temple Cult of Jerusalem*, 20–21, who argues that the nations here are the locusts; and Wolff, *Joel and Amos*, 52, who uses this line as additional defense of his argument that the threat in Joel has shifted from locusts to foreign nations. My reading of the text omits the final *mêm* in בָּם and is influenced by Psalm 44:15 (תְּשִׂימֵנוּ מָשָׁל בַּגּוֹיִם, *you have set me as a byword among the nations*) and Jeremiah 24:9, where YHWH threatens to make Zedekiah and the officials of Jerusalem *a reproach, a byword, a taunt* (לְחֶרְפָּה וּלְמָשָׁל לִשְׁנִינָה). See Barton, *Joel and Obadiah*, 82–83.

community can endure the disaster. *Who knows?* acknowledges the freedom of YHWH and dismisses any narrowly moralistic interpretation of disaster as punishment for sin and the assumption that YHWH will act according to prescribed formulas about the divine character. The peoples' mocking question, *Where is their God?* is a query that even the Joel poet and the Judean community must find compelling. It also relates to the thematic development of the entire prophetic poem. In Hebrew the vocalization of the question, *'ayyeh 'Elôhêhem, Where is their God?* plays upon the words of the expression repeated five times in Joel 2: *Yahweh 'Elôhêkem, YHWH your God* or *YHWH (is) your God* (2:13, 14, 23, 26, 27). The dynamic of the poem as a whole rests upon the question of YHWH's presence and what that presence means for the Judean community in the light of the locust disaster. The petition ends with a question for YHWH: *Why should they say . . . ?* a challenge to YHWH to supply evidence of YHWH's gracious presence among the people of Judah as a witness to the nations.

YHWH's Response: Presence in Bane and Blessing (Joel 2:18-27)

Moved by the communal lamentation and the priestly petition, YHWH does repent, turning from assailant to defender. The poet again shifts between divine oracle and prophetic voice, now to depict YHWH's salvific response in a concluding stanza. Although many commentators consider this section of the poem, Joel 2:18-27, to be a later addition or a separate poem in the Joel anthology, the connections to the previous stanzas seem organic. First, the stanza responds directly to the complaint about the destructive horde devastating the land and the petition that Israel not be an object of reproach among the nations. It also explicitly discloses the identity of the invaders, suspended in the previous sections. Furthermore, it continues the development of the theme, *YHWH 'Elôhêkem, YHWH (is) your God* (vv. 23, 26, 27) in response to the nations' mockery, *'ayyeh 'Elôhêhem, Where is their God?*

From the perspective of a time somewhat later than the priestly petition in 2:12-17, the prophetic voice describes YHWH's gracious response:

¹⁸Then YHWH	became zealous	for his land
	and had compassion	for his people.
¹⁹And YHWH	responded	
	and said	to his people:

> See, I am sending to you
>
>> the grain
>>
>> and the new wine
>>
>> and the fresh oil;
>>
>>> and you will be satiated with it.
>
> And I will no longer make you
>
> a reproach among the nations.

The opening parallels specify that YHWH's zeal here refers to compassion and responsiveness both to the devastated land and to YHWH's people. YHWH is sending *the grain and the new wine and the fresh oil*, the traditional list of the products of the land, previously devoured by the invading horde (Joel 1:10). The Judeans will not only have enough to subsist, but they will be satiated with the gifts of YHWH. In direct response to the priestly petition, *Do not make your heritage into a reproach* (2:17), YHWH now resolves, *I will no longer make you / a reproach among the nations* (2:19).

Not only will YHWH restore the fertility of the land, but YHWH also promises to conquer the invaders:

> [20]The "Northerner" I will distance   from you
>
>   and banish   to a land dry
>   and desolate,
>
>   with his front
>   to the eastern sea
>
>   and his back
>   to the western sea.
>
> His stench   will ascend;
>
> his foul odor   will rise,
>
> for he has magnified himself to act.

Resuming the imagery of the locusts as an invading army, the poet calls them *the Northerner*. The fact that actual locust infestations usually came to

Israel from the east and south is no argument against the locusts as a referent here. Associated with the mythological home of the Canaanite god Baal and with the great armies of Assyria and Babylon to the northeast, "the North" was a symbolic designation to characterize threats "as dangerous as the chaos power itself."[47] The prophet Jeremiah particularly develops the motif of the enemy from the North (e.g., 1:14–16; 4:5–31; 6:1–8), and Ezekiel's mythic Gog attacks restored Israel with a hostile host from the far North (Ezek. 38–39). As Simkins concludes, ". . . it does not matter from which direction the locusts invaded the land, for הצפוני [Northerner] refers to the significance of the locust plague, not to its geographical origin."[48]

The initial column of parallel prepositional phrases designating the place of banishment for the Northerner, *from you* and *to a land dry and desolate*, expresses the reversal of Israel's dismal fate. In Joel 2:3 the prophet depicted Israel as transformed from a fertile land like the Garden of Eden into a desolate (שממה) wilderness. Now YHWH banishes the invaders to a desolate (שממה) land,[49] located away from the restored land of Israel. In a colorful hyperbole the prophetic poet describes the defeated force as so vast that its corporate body extends from the Dead Sea (the eastern sea) to the Mediterranean (the western sea). The foe is not just banished from the fertile area of Israel, but it lies stretched out as a vast stinking corpse. Of course, a corpse stretching from the Mediterranean to the Dead Sea would be within the boundaries of Israel—not far from it—but again, logic is no obstacle to poetic hyperbole.

Although many scholars view the lone line, *For he has magnified himself to act*, as a case of dittography (erroneous copying) from the following verse of the poem, where YHWH is described in the same words,[50] one could also interpret the line as meaningful in this context. We might recall that YHWH has been identified as Commander of the invading force, which was described as obedient to YHWH's word. So now one might ask: Why does YHWH turn against these obedient troops? *For he has magnified himself to act* might suggest that the army has exceeded expectations in the execution of its orders. Perhaps this army is like the Assyrian force which Isaiah depicted as the YHWH's "rod" that exalted itself beyond its mission (Isa 10) or the haughty Chaldeans from the passages in Habakkuk 1–2 discussed in the

---

47. Ahlström, *Joel and the Temple Cult*, 34.
48. Simkins, *Yahweh's Activity in History and Nature*, 196.
49. Simkins, *Yahweh's Activity in History and Nature*, 194.
50. Barton, *Joel and Obadiah*, 85; Wolff, *Joel and Amos*, 55. (Wolff also considers retaining the line.)

previous chapter,[51] although one can carry the comparison only so far. In the case of Joel 2, the mission of the locust army has never been clarified and has certainly not been represented as divine punishment.

In any case, the only one warranted to *magnify himself to act* is YHWH, and that is how the prophet describes the gracious actions of YHWH in the following hymnic passage with ornate parallels:

[21]<u>Do not fear</u>, *O soil*;

<u>rejoice and be glad</u>,

    for YHWH   has magnified
                     himself to act.

[22]<u>Do not fear</u>, *O beasts of the field*,

    for the pastures
         of the wilderness have sprouted;

    for the tree   bestows   its fruit,

        fig and vine yield   their wealth.

[23]*O children of Zion*

<u>rejoice and be glad</u>
in YHWH your God,

    for he   bestows to you early rain
                           for vindication.

       He   pours down for you a shower,

                          early rain

                          and late rain
                            as previously.

Like many Psalms of praise, this communal hymn includes: 1) imperative verbs calling for joyful celebration; 2) vocative address to particular groups, often including the natural realm; and 3) motives for praise introduced by *for* (Hebrew כי) and focused on YHWH's actions or attributes. Alternating commands, *Do not fear* and *Rejoice and be glad*; the parallel among the addressees—soil, beasts of the field, and children of Zion; and the extended motive clauses hold all these poetic lines together as a complex hymnic unit. The parallel among the soil, beasts, and children of Zion links the fate of

---

51. Also Crenshaw, *Joel*, 152–3.

these three together. As these groups mourned in a sympathetic response to one another in Joel 1:9–10, here they are called to rejoice together. The subject and verbal column in the motive clauses once again suggest the cosmic slide between the earthly and divine realms. Parallels link the subjects (*YHWH/He, the pastures of the wilderness, the tree, fig and vine*) and the actions (*has magnified himself to act, have sprouted, bestows, yield, pours down*), implying that YHWH's magnificent acts are not abstractions or nostalgic reminders of past history, but are rather the concrete blessings of fertile fields and trees and vines. YHWH *has magnified himself to act* in the rains and in the sprouting of the plants and budding of the trees. In the perspective of Joel 2, this is how the Israelite community and the nations will know that *YHWH is your God* (*YHWH ʾElôhêkem*).

In a reversal of the description of ruin in Joel 1:10 (*For grain is devastated, / new wine dries up, / fresh oil languishes*), the poet conveys YHWH's blessing by once again listing the three traditional economic resources of the land:

²⁴The threshing floors	will be full of	grain,
and the vats	will overflow with	new wine
		and fresh oil.

Also recalling Joel 1, which listed the four kinds of locusts devastating the land (1:4), the voice of YHWH now explicitly identifies the invading army of the poem:

²⁵I will recompense you
   for the years

              which   the *ʾarbeh*-locust   devoured,

                      the *yeleq*-locust,

                      the *ḥāsîl*-locust

                      and the *gāzām*-locust—

                      my great army,
                            which I sent against you.

The column of five parallels again exemplifies the cosmic slide, language which makes a direct connection between the concrete, historical world and the transcendent realm. The invading horde of Joel 2 is now explicitly disclosed as a locust plague, the same infestation as in Joel 1. (There is no satisfactory way of translating the different kinds of locusts, which are identical to those in 1:4 but in a different order.) But on the cosmic level, the locust swarm is *my great army, which I sent against you*. With no revelation of motive but with a promise of recompense, YHWH acts freely and mysteriously. The occurrence of *sent* (Hebrew שׁלח) in that line recalls the earlier appearance of the verb in YHWH's promise, *See, I am sending (*שׁלח*) to you / the grain and the new wine and the fresh oil* (2:19). Together these two assertions present YHWH as responsible for both bane and blessing. Such is YHWH your God (*YHWH ʾElôhêkem*), according to Joel 2.

The prophet develops that theme in lines which might seem disconnected[52] but which we can recognize as meaningfully parallel:

²⁶You	will surely eat to satiety,			
and you	will praise	the name of YHWH your God,		
			who has dealt with you wondrously.	
				(And my people will never again be put to shame.)
²⁷You	will know	that in the midst of Israel I am,		
		and I am YHWH your God		
		—and there is no other.		
				(And my people will never again be put to shame.)

The three parallel verbs, *(you) will surely eat to satiety / will praise / will know*, provide the skeletal shape to this section of parallel lines. The sequence of the verbs is significant. First the starving community will enjoy the blessings of YHWH—the heaping grain and the overflowing vats—and will *eat to satiety*. In response to these blessings and in answer to the taunting question of the nations, *Where is their God?* (*ʾayyeh ʾElôhêhem*), the Israelites will then praise *the name of YHWH your God (YHWH ʾElôhêkem), / who has dealt with you wondrously*. But even further, they will *know*. Usually connoting more than

---

52. Crenshaw asserts, "This entire unit lacks parallelism. . . ." (*Joel*, 163). Of this whole section, Joel 2:18–27, Coggins writes, ". . . though this section is printed as poetry in both BHS and NRSV, it is by no means certain that it should be regarded as poetry" (*Joel and Amos*, 45). I am arguing that we benefit from a broader view of poetry in prophetic texts, as in this case.

intellectual grasp of the facts, that Hebrew word *yada'* suggests relationship, conviction based on experience. The three convictions, the objects of *know* here, are interrelated both poetically and conceptually. The prophet connects the first two objects with the literary device of anadiplosis, the repetition of the end of one line in the beginning of the next: *that in the midst of Israel I am / and I am YHWH your God*. In response to those who put Israel to shame by their mockery, YHWH will reveal the divine presence unmistakably, graciously, and distinctively as the one *who has dealt with you wondrously*. A sound play in the first Hebrew words of the last two lines also connects them: *wa'anî* וַאֲנִי (*and I am*) and *we'ên* וְאֵין (*and there is*). In answer to the shameful taunts, the prophet conveys YHWH's extreme self-assertion that not only is YHWH Israel's god, but there is no other god. Earlier the prophet hedged on the traditional confident expression of YHWH's repentance from disaster with the assertion of YHWH's freedom in the question, *Who knows [what YHWH will do]*? Appropriately the poem concludes with YHWH's revelation of what the Israelites *can know*: YHWH, the only god, is present in their midst—for better or for worse, for bane or blessing.[53]

Joel 2 envisions communal disaster as a locust plague devastates the land, leaving humans and animals without sustenance. If we add Joel 1 to the depiction of the community's dire situation, we learn that a drought following the plague has exacerbated the disaster, as vines and olive trees wither and the lowing of thirsty cattle adds register to the lamenting voices. In this urgent situation the prophetic voice in Joel asks these questions: *Who can endure it? Who knows [what YHWH will do]?* and *Why should they say among the peoples, "Where is their god?"* The poem supplies its own answer to all these questions. Not entirely rhetorical, the first is essentially about human agency: can the community do anything to endure the disaster and restore harmony (*shalom*) among the spiritual, social, and natural realms? In this poem the response is that the community *can* endure the disaster through communal rites of lamentation—weeping, wailing, fasting, rending of garments, and the right words in petition to YHWH. Yet there is no guarantee that YHWH will respond favorably—who knows? Although the poem affirms the mysterious ways of YHWH, who sends both bane and blessing, it concludes with convictions about what the Israelites can know—that YHWH, the only god, is present as Israel's god. The repute of YHWH among the nations, the writer

---

53. Barker ends with a similar conclusion, perhaps stated more eloquently: "The text constructs YHWH as both the source of the devastation and the means of salvation from it, and its call here [in vv. 12–17] is for the community to 'turn' to YHWH in lament while YHWH 'turns' and demonstrates covenant relationship through restorative action" ("One Good 'Turn' Deserves Another?" 131).

assures, will be restored as YHWH *deals wondrously* with Israel in restoring *shalom* and removing communal shame.

The prophetic poet does not address the kinds of questions we find elsewhere in many laments in the Psalms and in other prophetic texts dealing with communal disaster: Why . . . ? How long . . . ? As we will see in the next two chapters of this study, other biblical prophets take up the "why" question in an attempt to explore human and divine agency in the face of disaster. Some prophetic voices respond by indicting Israel for unfaithfulness to the covenant and commanding repentance and return to YHWH as a way to restore life. Other prophetic voices lash out in bold protest calling YHWH to account for the disaster. Yet other voices simply demand YHWH's attention to the magnitude of the community's suffering. As we will discover in the next section on voices in prophetic poems, response to communal disaster is a central issue, perhaps *the* central issue in prophetic poems; but there is not a univocal response.

Returning to the Whole Poem from a Binocular View

Appreciating the artistry of this rich poem, those who read both vertically and horizontally—or with binocular vision, to borrow a metaphor from Roman Jakobson[54]—will notice the variety of ways the writer employs parallelism, which Chapter 2 of this study surveyed. Sometimes the semantically and syntactically matched words and phrases line up clearly in bicola illustrating specification or intensification in the second line, as in these examples:

> Before it a fire devours,
> and after it a flame sets ablaze (v. 3).

> The threshing floors will be full of grain,
> and the vats will overflow with new wine and fresh oil (v. 24).

But parallels often extend well beyond the two- or three-line unit to exhibit narrative development, to construct lists, or to present a complex development of images and ideas. A remarkable narrative development occurs in the fantastic scene enacting the march of the locusts in verses 4–9, with extended parallel similes describing the sight and sound of the troops and their relentless advance over the tops of the mountains, over the wall of the city, and into the houses through the windows. The parallelism assumes

---

54. Jakobson, "Grammatical Parallelism, 402.

an iconic function; that is, the poetic structure imitates the action, as the description of the leaping band "leaps over" a set of lines about people's reactions to them (v. 6) to resume in the following lines (vv. 7-9). The list of seven staccato commands calling the community to lamentation in verses 15-16 is an effective illustration of another kind of extension of parallelism, here to convey the urgency of the summons and to suggest the horn blasts signally the worshipers. The extension of parallels through complex "sprawling" structures is especially effective for more deliberative lines, such as those in which the prophet negotiates between traditional affirmations of YHWH's character as *gracious and merciful / slow to anger and great in ḥesed* (despite commanding a locust attack!) and uncertainty about YHWH's actions (*Who knows?*) and then carefully suggests that YHWH consider acting out of self-interest to preserve the sacrificial cult (v. 14). Another example of complex parallel structures appears in YHWH's closing promise that the Judeans will eat, praise, and know, extended with the self-characterization of *your God* as the one *who has dealt with you wondrously* and the refrain *And my people will never again be put to shame.*

Among the other functions of parallelism introduced in Chapter 2 of this study is the presentation of shocking revelations, as in the correspondence between the different kinds of locusts with *my great army, which I sent to you* (Joel 2:25). In one case the prophetic poet grammatically uncouples a traditional semantic pair, *your nation* and *your heritage*, to connect *your nation* instead to *a reproach* and *a byword among the nations* in order to express the disjunction between what *should* be the status of Israel and what has become of YHWH's people. Sometimes the poet also constructs lone lines for emphasis, as in the directive *Let all the inhabitants of the land quake!* (v. 1), the exclamation *There is absolutely no escape from it!* (v. 3), or the question *Who can endure it?* (v. 11). In addition to those functions of parallelism surveyed in Chapter 2 of this study, we have seen a benefit for translators, that is, clues for deciphering obscure words like פָּארוּר in verse 6.

The poet also employs parallelism for a smooth slide in perspective between the cosmic and the earthly realms. Beginning in the transcendent realm with YHWH's command to *blow the šôfār in Zion* and the prophet's announcement that the Day of YHWH approaches, parallels connect that ominous Day to a dark cloud descending toward the mountains. As the prophetic poet's vision shifts downward, the cloud comes into view as a vast, unprecedented horde devastating the land. After the detailed description of the invading horde, the end of the first stanza moves up again from the windows of Jerusalem to the heavenly realm, as parallels identify the "troops" as YHWH's own army and the invasion as a Day of Lord/Locust. Another example of the smooth slide between the earthly and transcendent realms appears in the lines of the hymn, in which the reference to YHWH's magnanimous actions parallels the sprouting of pastures, trees, and vines and the coming of the seasonal rains (vv. 21–23).

Discussion and interpretation is, of course, fruitless unless the reader returns to the poem with a richer appreciation for its meaning and artistry. Hebrew readers can return to BHS or BHQ and English readers to a good translation, such as the NRSV or, even better, Alter's new translation in his three-volume *Hebrew Bible* for smooth line-by-line progression through the poem, that is, horizontal reading. Ideally, though, readers could put together the diagrams above or construct their own for a binocular view of the poem. Those who experience Joel 2 two-dimensionally will undoubtedly enjoy their own discoveries, for the riches of the poem are inexhaustible.

Part II

Voice

4

Hearing Voices in Prophetic Poetry

Script Rather than Transcript

IF WE THINK OF prophets as messengers of the divine, we might expect prophetic books to read as transcripts of oracles originally delivered orally and clearly marked as divine speech through the messenger formula, *Thus says YHWH*. Although oracles introduced in this way do appear as represented speech from YHWH,[1] more often prophetic poems read like dramatic scripts with several characters presented as speakers or listeners: YHWH, a prophet, Israel, Jerusalem/Zion, other nations and cities, enemy invaders, heavenly beings, groups of mourners, watchmen, personified heavens and earth, prophetic rivals, and more. Different from dramatic scripts, however, biblical prophetic texts often do not explicitly label the speakers or audiences. Recognizing the challenge of identifying voices in biblical texts, scholar Sjef van Tilborg aptly described the task of the interpreter as "hearing voices while reading."[2] In this chapter I will consider selections from short prophetic poems to expose issues in "hearing voices while reading" and to propose interpretations of some ambiguous passages. Chapter 5, then, will examine the particularly rich, many-voiced, or *polyphonic*, poem in Jeremiah 4:5–31 and offer a script for dramatic reading.

---

1. Alter, *Art of Biblical Poetry*, 175–6, clarifies that all speech from YHWH is *mediated* by prophets and, one should add, by their scribal representatives. Hence, the words of YHWH in prophetic texts are *represented* speech.

2. Address by Sjef van Tilborg; quotation translated from the Dutch, reported, and used effectively by van der Woude in her chapter, "'Hearing Voices while Reading,'" 149–73.

The Notes Are not the Music: Subjective Judgments in Hearing Voices

Recently I attended a concert by the Israeli Goldstein-Peled-Fiterstein Trio, in which clarinetist Alexander Fiterstein played a modern solo piece, "For an Actor: Monologue" by composer Shulamit Ran.[3] In the discussion following the concert, someone asked Fiterstein about the composer's intention for the piece and what sort of instructions she had given him. He replied that Ran had given him very little direction but wanted him to make the piece his own. Presumably Fiterstein played the notes from the score, but he himself *made the music* in his performance.

Perhaps we might compare reading a prophetic poem to performing a musical composition. Although musicians usually play the notes as written, the score certainly does not direct all aspects of the performance. Some manuscripts might not even indicate instrumentation. Musical directors and performers interpret the scores for their performances and thereby *make* the music; the notes are not the music. Likewise, interpreting a biblical text involves making subjective judgments (and even deciding which text to interpret involves judgments, since there are multiple manuscripts and translations from which to choose). Although interpreters must be able to defend their judgments, the "notes" can be "played" in different ways. Certainly one reason for variance is the multiple possibilities for identifying unlabeled voices in prophetic poems, as we will see in all of the examples I discuss below. Some "performances" will, of course, be more compelling than others; but overconfidence in a singular interpretation would be similar to the claim that there is only one way to play a musical piece.

As an example of two different ways of hearing voices in a text, we can consider Mark Biddle's and Joseph Henderson's interpretations of Jeremiah 8:18—9:2 (Heb. 8:18—9:1), a poem with several unnamed speakers, one who weeps *a fountain of tears* over the impending ruin of Judah.[4] According to Biddle, YHWH is the speaker who weeps; and this passage is evidence that the book of Jeremiah portrays YHWH as an ambivalent character, often exploding in anger—even violence—against the people, but also suffering with them. However, if Jeremiah is the weeping figure, as Henderson believes, then YHWH is portrayed as consistently angry, and the prophet is the anguished mediator between YHWH and the people. Here is Biddle's script version of the text, using the NRSV translation of Jeremiah 8:13—9:1 and supplying his own labels for the speakers:

---

3. Goldstein-Peled-Fiterstein Trio, Wittenberg Series Concert, Wittenberg University, February 16, 2017.

4. Biddle, *Polyphony and Symphony,* 28–31; Henderson, "Who Weeps?" 191–206.

YHWH
> My joy is gone, grief is upon me, my heart is sick.
>> Hark, the cry of my poor people from far and wide in the land:

People
> "Is the Lord not in Zion? Is her king not in her?"

YHWH
> Why [then] have they provoked me to anger with their images,
>> with their foreign idols?

People
> "The harvest is past, the summer is ended,
>> and we are not saved."

YHWH
> For the hurt of my poor people I am hurt,
>> I mourn, and dismay has taken hold of me.

People
> "Is there no balm in Gilead? Is there no physician there?"

YHWH
> Why then has the health of my poor people not been restored?
>> O that my head were a spring of water,
>> [and my eyes a fountain of tears,
>> so that I might weep day and night
>> for the slain of my poor people!][5]

Such a reading has important theological meaning, as Biddle concludes: "God, by far the most interesting character in these dialogues, voices pathos and conflict, an internal struggle between anger and sympathy. In dialogue with personified Jerusalem, YHWH adopts an angry, almost vengeful tone. . . . In sharp contrast, YHWH also expresses sorrow over the suffering inflicted on the people."[6] In Biddle's script, YHWH is a god who suffers with the people.

Critiquing Biddle's interpretation, Henderson proposes this script version of the passage (slightly modified NRSV translation and extending through one more verse than Biddle's version above; labels are Henderson's):

---

5. Biddle, *Polyphony and Symphony*, 30. Biddle does not continue his script version through the lines in brackets, but his comments on the passage clearly indicate that he assigns the lines to YHWH.

6. Biddle, *Polyphony and Symphony*, 42–43.

Daughter People laments:
>My joy is gone, grief is upon me, my heart is sick.

Jeremiah responds:
>Hark, the cry of my Daughter People from far and wide in the land.

Yahweh lays the blame:
>Is Yahweh not in Zion? Is her King not in her?
>Why [then] have they provoked me to anger with their images,
>>with their foreign idols?

Daughter People laments:
>The harvest is past, the summer is ended
>>and we are not saved.

Jeremiah responds:
>For the hurt of my Daughter People I am hurt,
>>I mourn and dismay has taken hold of me.

Jeremiah lays the blame:
>Is there no balm in Gilead? Is there no physician there?
>Why then has the health of my Daughter People not been restored?

Jeremiah's wish:
>O that my head were a spring of water,
>>and my eyes a fountain of tears,
>so that I might weep day and night
>>for the slain of my Daughter People!

Yahweh's wish:
>O that I had in the desert
>>a traveler's lodging place,
>That I might leave my people
>>and go away from them!
>For they are all adulterers,
>>a band of traitors.[7]

---

7. Henderson, "Who Weeps?" 205–6. I've omitted the verse numbers and Hebrew terms in Henderson's script.

This reading of the passage supports Henderson's theological conclusion: "Throughout these chapters [Jeremiah 2–20] Yahweh is consistently portrayed as the wrathful deity who is bent on destroying his people and refuses to be moved to compassion by their cries."[8] Reading the same words in the text, Biddle and Henderson offer very different "performances" based on their identification of the voices, which the poem itself does not label.

At the heart of their interpretive controversy is the question: which speaker—YHWH or Jeremiah—characteristically refers to the people with the personification *bat-ʿammî, my Daughter People* (NRSV translates *my poor people*)? It is not my purpose here to survey those arguments but rather to think about the nature of opposing interpretations. In his rather sharp critique of Biddle's view, Henderson concludes, "The poetry cannot be read as drama without *consistent* characterization and *objective* criteria for identifying speakers" [italics mine].[9] Logical as this might sound, this is the point of Henderson's otherwise strong reading that I would challenge. We should first note that both Biddle and Henderson offer rationale for their judgments and both do indeed see the poetry as a kind of drama. Henderson might label his interpretation consistent and objective, but he has made some judgments which are open to challenge, for example, proposed emendations for Jeremiah 6:14 and 9:6 when the Hebrew MT does not support his arguments about the speaker in *bat-ʿammî* passages[10] and his reliance

---

8. Henderson, "Who Weeps?" 198.

9. Henderson, "Who Weeps?" 192.

10. Henderson argues that Jeremiah is the speaker in passages which use *bat-ʿammî* (*my Daughter People*), a phrase that "almost always occurs in speeches which express sympathy for the people"; and YHWH speaks in passages which simply call the people *ʿammî* (*my people*), a designation that "often occurs in speeches which harshly criticize the people" ("Who Weeps?" 195). In the list of the fifteen biblical passages using *bat-ʿammî*, however, he omits Jeremiah 9:6 (English 9:7), in which YHWH is clearly the speaker ("Therefore thus says YHWH Ṣebaʾoth: / I am now refining and testing them, / for what else can I do for the sake of *bat-ʿammî*?"), and adds Jeremiah 6:14, which has only *ʿammî* but is a doublet of 8:11, a passage using *bat-ʿammî* ("Who Weeps?," 195–96). In the case of 9:6, the Hebrew text is somewhat awkward and might be corrupt. Henderson's proposed change without *bat-ʿammî* is supposedly supported by the LXX; but LXX has πονηρίας θυγατρὸς λαοῦ μου (*wickedness of Daughter, My People*— adding *wickedness* but not omitting *my Daughter People/ Daughter, my People*). That 6:14 (with *ʿammî*) is a doublet of 8:11 (with *bat-ʿammî*) does not necessarily mean that *bat-* was inadvertently lost from the former passage; it could equally mean that *bat-* was added to 8:11 or that the writer of the text did not make the careful distinction between *ʿammî* and *bat-ʿammî* which Henderson proposes. Pilarski offers a significant argument for YHWH as the speaker in the *bat-ʿammî* passages. She bases her argument in the study of the Mesopotamian city laments, in which goddesses grieve over the destruction of their cities. In the Hebrew Bible, she contends, a process of hypostatization results in the change of gender of the lamenter (i.e., from the goddess to YHWH). See

on evidence from Lamentations for understanding that phrase in Jeremiah. My point is that both interpreters have made judgments which are not absolutely objective, since both have chosen and weighed the evidence they admit for their arguments. Working from the same "notes"—the words of the text—the two scholars have heard the voices differently for variant "performances." As we will continue to see in the examples below, there are usually several possibilities for "hearing voices while reading" a prophetic poem with unlabeled speakers. A compelling reading requires neither certainty nor rejection of other views.

Is the Dialogue Dialogic?

As we have noted in the previous chapter on Joel 2, some prophetic poems present at least two speakers—most often YHWH and the prophet—but the voices do not necessarily address one another. Much of that poem alternates between YHWH's words to the Judeans and the prophet's address to them (including people, animals, and soil). The voices of the two characters YHWH and Joel are so much in accord with one another that the words of one echo and reinforce those of the other, as if each "hears" the other. After YHWH commands the people of Jerusalem to blow the *šôfār* and shout an alarm, Joel describes the coming invaders. When Joel details the horrors of the locust invasion and asks, "Who can endure it?" YHWH follows with a prescription for endurance through turning to YHWH in prayer, fasting, and mourning. Joel promptly instructs the Judeans to turn to YHWH as directed. When YHWH vows to send the blessings of grain, wine, and oil, Joel calls the soil, the animals, and the people to praise YHWH for the blessings of grain, wine, and oil. The poem does not really present a dialogue between two speakers so much as a scenario of perfect sympathy between YHWH and Joel, expressing the conviction that the prophet-priest is a reliable minister for the people, guiding them in how to live in the presence of YHWH, whether in disaster or blessing. We can describe this kind of text as *monologic;* that is, it arrives at closure and expresses a singular sense of truth. That does not mean the text is without complexity, but rather that the themes are not challenged by voices which remain unmerged, or independent, from the dominant viewpoint.

In many prophetic poems, multiple characters appear—some unidentified, as we have noted above—and they do engage in dialogue with one another. But does dialogue necessarily mean that the text is *dialogic*? Discussions about monologic and dialogic truth in texts have engaged

---

her chapter, "A Study of the References to בת־עמי," 20–35.

many recent interpreters as scholars have recognized the value of applying the theories of twentieth century Russian philosopher and literary critic Mikhail Bakhtin to biblical materials, even though Bakhtin himself never applied his ideas to the Bible. I find Carol Newsom's article, "Bakhtin, the Bible, and Dialogic Truth," a particularly clear exposition of the difference between monologic and dialogic truth in biblical texts.[11] As she summarizes, monologic discourse expresses a singular truth because the voices are controlled to present the author's perspective or theme; the characters in the text are essentially representative of thoughts or propositions; and the text concludes with a sense of unity and closure. However, a dialogic text is like a genuine conversation which "requires at least two unmerged voices."[12] The meaning of the text is in the interaction between the participants, who emerge as distinctive characters rather than representatives of propositions. Arriving at no unified theme, a dialogic text remains open, or in Bakhtin's words (also quoted by Newsom), "Nothing conclusive has yet taken place in the world, the ultimate word of the world and about the world has not yet been spoken, the world is open and free, everything is still in the future, and will always be in the future."[13]

The distinction between monologic and dialogic texts is important for the way readers hear the voices in prophetic poems. Since these texts often present prophets conveying messages from YHWH, one would logically conclude that the poems are monologic. The writer, we assume, conveys a singular truth represented by the voice of YHWH delivered through a prophet. Other voices in the text will be in sympathy with YHWH, as is the case with the prophetic character Joel; will be persuaded to adopt the divine perspective if initially resistant; or will be exposed as foolish or evil opponents of all that is right and true. This assumption, however, proves to be too simplistic for the variety of prophetic poetry in the Bible. In the following discussion, I will consider three sets of poems with these questions in mind: How might we identify the unlabeled voices? Does the text present a monologic or dialogic sense of truth? How does attention to the literary, poetic features help us address these questions? How do identification of speakers and perception of the kind of truth claims in the text help us appreciate the poetry?

---

11. Bakhtin's most relevant works are *Problems of Dostoyevsky's Poetics* and *The Dialogic Imagination*. See Newsom, "Bakhtin, the Bible, and Dialogic Truth," 290–306.

12. Newsom, "Bakhtin, the Bible, and Dialogic Truth," 294.

13. Bakhtin, *Problems of Dostoyevsky's Poetics*, 106; quoted in Newsom, "Bakhtin, the Bible, and Dialogic Truth," 294.

Poems with Zion as Speaker in Isaiah 40–66: A Resistant Voice Persuaded to Rejoice

"The Former Things Have Come to Pass, /
And New Things I Now Declare" (Isa 42:9)

Much of the material in Isaiah 1–39 has its setting in Jerusalem in the second half of the eighth century BCE, when the prophet Isaiah addressed the kings Ahaz and Hezekiah of the Davidic lineage. The political threat to the land of Judah was the powerful Assyrian Empire, descending on the little nations to the southwest with brutal efficiency. This section of Isaiah closes with an extended account of the siege of Jerusalem by the Assyrian king Sennacherib in 701 BCE. While the Assyrian annals of the king claim victory with the capture of forty-six fortified cities and numerous small villages and the exile of 200,150 Judeans,[14] the narrative in Isaiah focuses on a story of the miraculous survival of the city of Jerusalem (37:30–38) according to YHWH's promise: *For I will defend this city to save it, for my own sake and for the sake of my servant David* (37:35). However, this section of Isaiah closes on an ominous note, as the prophet conveys a message to Hezekiah that in the days of Hezekiah's descendants the king of another empire—Babylon—will arise and carry off the treasures of his house and some of the royal family.

When we pick up the story of Jerusalem in Isaiah 40, Jerusalem *has received from the hand of YHWH / double for all her sins* (40:2). Among the "former things" that lie in the background to the latter chapters of Isaiah are not only the Babylonian seizure of palace treasures and some of the royal family, as threatened in the oracle to Hezekiah set over a century earlier, but also a Babylonian invasion of the city and deportation of leaders in 597 and the ruin of the city, burning of the temple, confiscation of temple treasures, exile of the king and other Judeans, execution of some of the royal sons and priests, and loss of Judean independence in 586. The foundations for Judean identity—land, Davidic king, and temple on Mount Zion—were lost. And many must have asked: what about YHWH and the covenant? Certainly YHWH's promise to *defend this city to save it, for my own sake and for the sake of my servant David* did not seem to apply to the Babylonian threat.

However, in Isaiah 40–66, YHWH declares a "new thing" for all creation, especially for Zion/Jerusalem. The poetry sings of the doom of Babylon (Isa 47) and the rise of a new conqueror, Cyrus of Persia (559–530 BCE), chosen by YHWH to return the exiles and rebuild Jerusalem (Isa 45–47). To

---

14. "The Siege of Jerusalem (704–681)," from Pritchard, *Ancient Near Eastern Texts*, 288.

distinguish these latter chapters from the oracles of Isaiah of Jerusalem over 150 years earlier, scholars often call the section Isaiah 40–55 "Second Isaiah" or "Deutero-Isaiah," and Chapters 56–66 "Third Isaiah" or "Trito-Isaiah," perhaps written by various scribes after some exiles returned to Jerusalem in 520 under the Persian king Darius and continuing throughout the century following the initial return.[15] No prophetic voice is named in any of these chapters, nor does the word *nabî'*, *prophet*, appear. One might think of this latter section of the book (as well as the final edition of Isaiah as a whole) as the work of anonymous scribal prophets reflecting on and reinterpreting the words of Isaiah for post-exilic audiences.

Even the geographical setting of the chapters—Babylon or Jerusalem—is uncertain and likely varies for different poems. Some poems, primarily in Chapters 40–48, highlight the experience of the exiles, who witness the Babylonian festivals, in which worshippers carry images of the gods Bel/Marduk and Nebo on parade, and who undoubtedly wonder about the power and care of their own god YHWH (Isa 46). To the exiles the prophetic voice declares YHWH the creator and sovereign of the whole cosmos and commands a return to the homeland: *Go out from Babylon; flee from the Chaldeans* (48:20). Other poems focus on witnesses to the devastation of the city of Jerusalem shortly after its fall:

> These two things have befallen you [feminine singular *you*; i.e., Jerusalem]—
> who will lament for you?—
> devastation and shattering, famine and sword—
> who will comfort you?
> Your children have swooned away;
> they lie at the head of every street
> like an antelope in a net,
> full of the wrath of YHWH,
> the rebuke of your [f.s.] God. (51:19–20)

Still others, primarily in Chapters 56–66, presume a later situation of struggles over the reestablishment of the cult after the rebuilding of the temple in Jerusalem in 515. For the purpose of this discussion, the most important point is that the focus of almost all the poems in Isaiah 40–66 remains on the city of Zion/Jerusalem after the catastrophe of the Babylonian exile,

---

15. Some recognize a major division between 40–48 and 49–55. Only the former section mentions Cyrus and Babylon. For a good recent summary of theories of the development of the book of Isaiah, see Berges, "Isaiah: Structure, Themes, and Contested Issues," 153–70.

whether the original audience was in Jerusalem or Babylon. The overriding theme is the renewal of the sacred center.

Isaiah 40:1–11: Lady Zion Called from Despondency

Isaiah 40 opens with a dramatic scene in which numerous voices, many of them unlabeled, engage in dialogue. While interpreters could choose to focus on the meaning of the indeterminacy of the characters and scene,[16] I will instead describe one particular way of hearing voices while reading Isaiah 40:1–11 without suggesting a critique of other possibilities. This reading highlights two kinds of evidence to identify the voices and the mysterious scene. First, the Hebrew text itself supplies a few clues to speakers and audience which are missing in English, since Hebrew marks number and gender of second- and third-person pronouns and verbs. Notes in the English translation and in standard commentaries often guide the English reader to this missing information. However, we will see that even in the Hebrew text the reader must make some choices about textual variants and the meaning of words with gender markers. Second, we can turn to the insights of form critics, who recognize patterns in similar biblical texts. Many interpreters see in Isaiah 40:1–11 the form of a call narrative or commissioning ceremony, the account of a person summoned by YHWH for a specific task. Noting similar elements in such stories as the calls of Moses (Exo 3–4), Gideon (Jud 6), Isaiah (chapter 6), Jeremiah (chapter 1), and Ezekiel (chapters 1–3), biblical form critics describe the narratives as consisting of these elements, with individual variations: *divine confrontation* through a theophany or audition, *introductory word* from the divine, a specific *commission*, an *objection* from the one being called, *divine reassurance*, and a *sign* verifying the call.[17] My hearing of the voices is particularly influenced by the interpretation of David L. Petersen in *Late Israelite Prophecy: Studies in Deutero-Prophetic Literature and in Chronicles*[18] and Ulrich Berges's chapter, "Personifications and Prophetic Voices of Zion in Isaiah and Beyond."[19] I will also give attention to specific words and parallels which help us appreciate the way the voices interact in the poem.

---

16. See, for example, Landy, "Spectrality in the Prologue to Deutero-Isaiah," 131–58.

17. Habel, "Form and Significance of the Call Narratives," 297–323; Petersen, *Prophetic Literature*, 20–21.

18. Petersen, *Late Israelite Prophecy*, 20–21. Habel, "Form and Significance of the Call Narratives," 314–16, also discusses Isaiah 40:1–8 as a call narrative.

19. Berges, "Personifications and Prophetic Voices," 54–82.

HEARING VOICES IN PROPHETIC POETRY 117

Divine Confrontation and Introductory Word

The text begins with a grand audition, as a narrator reports the voice of YHWH commanding an unnamed group, identified only through masculine plural forms (m.pl.) of the imperative verbs and pronoun *your* in Hebrew, to speak words of consolation to personified Jerusalem:

¹Comfort (m.pl.),			
comfort (m.pl.)	my people,	says your (m.pl.) God.	
²Speak (m.pl.)	to the heart of Jerusalem		
and say (m.pl.)	to her		
that she	has fulfilled	her term of labor,	
that her penalty	has been accepted,		
that she	has received		from the hand of YHWH
		double	for all her sins.

Familiarity with the conventions of Hebrew poetry helps us to imagine the scene as taking place before the throne of YHWH, who addresses the heavenly creatures surrounding the throne. We might think of the six-winged *seraphîm*, the burning creatures whose "Holy, holy, holy" song stuns the prophet Isaiah in his commissioning vision in chapter 6. The vision of Ezekiel imagines these creatures from the divine realm as four-faced *cherubîm* commandeering the wheeled throne of YHWH (chapters 1–3). In other texts they are described as sons of God/gods, horsemen who patrol the earth, divine *malʾakîm* (often translated *angels*, but better, *messengers*), the Divine Council, or the host of heaven, whom YHWH summons to discuss administrative matters of life on earth (e.g., 1 Kgs 22:19–23; Ps 82; Ps 89; Job 1:6–12; Jer 23:18–22; Zech 1–6).

The reader can identify both verses as a speech of YHWH, who commands the divine attendants in four imperative verbs: *comfort* (repeated for emphasis), *speak*, and *say*. Even though verse 2 refers to YHWH in third person, YHWH likely remains the speaker. In prophetic poetry the voice of YHWH frequently shifts to the third person to refer to the divine self. Other clear examples of this appear in Zephaniah 1:8–9:

> On the day of YHWH's sacrifice
> I will punish the princes and the king's sons
> and all who dress themselves in foreign attire.
> I will punish all who leap over the threshold on that day,
> who fill their masters' house with violence and fraud;

and in Jeremiah 5:10–11, where YHWH invites the invaders to Jerusalem:

> Go up into her vine rows and spoil;
> but complete destruction you should not make.
> Take away her tendrils,
> for they do not belong to YHWH.
> For they have utterly committed treachery against me—
> the house of Israel and the house of Judah—saying of YHWH.

Personifying the city of Jerusalem as a woman in Isaiah 40:2, YHWH directs the divine assembly to *speak to [her] heart*, a phrase suggesting tenderness and even having erotic connotations in contexts in which a man addresses a woman (Shechem to Dinah in Gen 34:3; the Levite to his concubine in Jud 19:3; Boaz to Ruth in Ruth 2:23; husband YHWH to wife Israel in Hosea 2:16).[20] The voice of YHWH turns to the language of sacrificial offerings and legal proceedings to convey the message that her *penalty has been accepted*, since she has fully served her *term of labor* imposed by YHWH, likely a reference to her ruin and the exile of her population.

Then an unidentified voice from the divine assembly cries out with another command to prepare the way for a revelation of the glorious presence of YHWH. The authority, prescience, and lofty tone of the voice consonant with the will of YHWH suggest that the speaker here must be one of YHWH's attendants. The hearing of such singular voices from the Divine Council might remind us of the scene in which the Israelite prophet Micaiah ben Imlah reports a throne vision: *I saw YHWH sitting on his throne with all the host of heaven standing over him to the right and to the left of him. . . . Then one said one thing and another said another . . .* (1 Kgs 22:19–20). Here the speaker uses geographical symbolism to suggest that the transformation of Jerusalem is a cosmic event of reversal:

---

20. This is contrary to Berges, "Personifications and Prophetic Voices," 65, who argues that the phrase *speak to the heart* refers to "rational argumentation," as it does in Genesis 50:21, in which Joseph consoles his fearful brothers after the death of father Jacob.

³A voice cries out:

"In the wilderness   clear (m.pl.)   the way   of YHWH.

                   Make straight (m.pl.)

in the desert   a highway for our God.

⁴Every valley   shall be lifted up,

and every mountain and hill   shall be low.

The steep ground (העקב)   shall become   a level place,

and the rough places   a plain (בקעה).

⁵Then the Glory of YHWH shall be revealed,

and all flesh shall see it together;

for the mouth of YHWH has spoken."

What a majestic speech linking the past Exodus event in references to the wilderness and desert, the movement of YHWH between Babylon and Jerusalem, and the transformation of the world to be witnessed by all flesh! The clear, strong parallels in verses 3–4 suggest a chant or song. Many scholars have noted how the mirror imaging of letters in the Hebrew words for *steep ground* and *plain* enacts the theme of reversal in nature.[21] Foregrounded by the parallels in the previous lines, the last three non-parallel lines acquire an emphatic quality as separate and assured pronouncements.

Commission

In the context of this grand throne vision, another voice from YHWH's entourage conveys a simple command, "Cry out!" (m.s.), to an individual. The commission can be succinct because the content of the proclamation has already been specified in the previous words shared among members of the Divine Council. But who is the individual receiving the commission? Here the text becomes complicated with many opportunities for interpretive decisions.[22] Three different textual traditions offer variant readings relevant

---

21. For example, Berlin, *Dynamics of Biblical Parallelism*, 120.
22. For a good survey of the possibilities, see Seitz, "Book of Isaiah 40–66," 336.

to identification of the addressee. The Hebrew MT renders the following line, "But *he* said, 'What shall I cry?'" (v. 6). The Septuagint translation of a Hebrew version reads, "But *I* said, 'What shall I cry?'" The oldest textual witness, the large Isaiah scroll from the Dead Sea collection (1QIsaᵃ; second century BCE), has a Hebrew verb form that could be either first person cohortative or third feminine singular, "But *she* said . . . ." If we read *he* with the Hebrew MT, the implication might be that the addressee is another member of the Divine Council or the symbolic character called the "servant" in later chapters of Isaiah. If one chooses the first-person subject from the Septuagint, the one being commissioned might be the prophet responsible for many of the poems in the book or the servant, who speaks of his prophetic role in first person in Isaiah 49 and 50. If the reading is *she*, the divine voice would be commissioning the personified Zion/Jerusalem. The masculine singular form of the command, "Cry out!" does not necessarily eliminate this possibility, since the divine attendant might be addressing any one of the hearers in general, and a female voice could answer. It is also possible that the text could originally have had a feminine singular imperative verb, which differs from the masculine singular imperative(קרא) by the addition of one letter at the end of the Hebrew word for *Cry out* (קראי). Perhaps we will find some clues to the identity of the addressee as we proceed.

Objection and Reassurance

Most significant for the present discussion of "hearing voices while reading" is the unfolding call narrative, which takes the form of a dialogue between the divine attendant and the one being called. In the text below, the words of the divine messenger are underlined, and the addressee's response is in italics:

[Commission]		
⁶A voice	says,	"Cry out!"
[Objection]		
But he/I/she	said,	"*What shall I cry?*"

All flesh	*(is)*	*grass,*	
and its goodness	*like*	*a flower of the field.*	
		⁷Grass	withers,
		a flower	droops

*when the wind/
spirit of YHWH
blows upon it."*

[Reassurance]

⁸"Grass   withers,

a flower   droops;

but the word of our God   will stand   forever.

[Reassurance and elaboration of commission]

⁹Ascend (f.s.)   you (f.s.)   to a high mountain,

                            herald of good tidings, Zion.

Lift (f.s.)   your voice   with strength,

                            herald of good tidings, Jerusalem.

Lift (f.s.)   [your voice];

fear (f.s.) not.

Say (f.s.)   to the cities of Judah,

                            'Behold your God!'"

In verse 9 the addressee is finally identified as the personified Zion/Jerusalem.[23] So we might choose the one reading in 1QIsaᵃ, "But *she* said, 'What shall I cry?'" in verse 6. The personification of the city as a woman has ancient roots in Near Eastern portrayals of patron goddesses lamenting over the ruins of their cities or the abandonment of the god.[24] Perhaps Biddle

---

23. Berges, "Personifications and Prophetic Voices," 65, also recognizes Zion as the one being commissioned in Isaiah 40. One could also read the phrase which I have translated *herald of good tidings, Zion,* as *herald of good tidings to Zion/Jerusalem.* See Seitz, "Isaiah 40–66," 336–7. For evidence of this reading scholars often cite the occurrence of the masculine bearer of good tidings to Zion in Isaiah 41:27 and 52:7 and the occasional reference to masculine roles with feminine nouns, such as קהלת (*preacher, gatherer of an assembly*) in Ecclesiastes 1. In that case, however, the verbs for the subject קהלת are masculine. In Isaiah 40:9, however, not only is the form of the phrase *bearer of good tidings* feminine, but the five imperative verbs directed toward her are feminine as well.

24. Fitzgerald, "*Btwlt* and *Bt* as Titles," 167–83; and "Mythological Background," 403–16; Doobs-Alsopp, *Weep, O Daughter of Zion*; Biddle, "Figure of Lady Jerusalem."

conveys the meaning of the symbolism most succinctly in his comments on the use of the image in Jeremiah, also applicable to Isaiah:

> Despite the text's clear intention to personify the capital city, interpreters of the book [of Jeremiah] regularly treat her as if she were synonymous with collective portrayals of the people. Such interpretations overlook the ideological implications of the capital city personified as mother and queen in the society of other personified leading cities of the [ancient] world. Just as the Statue of Liberty, Lady Liberty, does not represent a personification of the American people, but of the political principles which Americans hold dear, Lady Zion personifies a concept.[25]

In this richly symbolic call narrative the spirit of Jerusalem is being called from despondency to become a herald of the good tidings of the coming of YHWH to the cities of Judah.

From the chart of parallels above, we might note how the poet works strategically through repetition, imagery, and parallelism to acknowledge the despair of Zion but then to override her words with the message of transformation from the divine attendant. The parallels highlighting the contrast between *grass / flower/ the word of our God*; *withers / droops / will stand*; and the adverbial time indicators *when the wind [spirit] of YHWH blows upon it / forever* draw attention to the way the divine voice repeats the words and imagery of despair and then sweeps them up into the message of confidence in YHWH's promises of restoration. Careful choice of words also works to persuade Zion to adopt the divine perspective. Referring to YHWH as "*our* God," the divine messenger includes Zion in community with YHWH and the heavenly host. The ambiguity of the Hebrew word *ruaḥ*, meaning both *wind* and *spirit* subtly connects Zion's image of grass and flowers withering from the hot wind of YHWH to the spirit of YHWH, which forever revives and reanimates. Repetition of בָּשָׂר (*bāsār*), *flesh*, in Zion's despairing line *All flesh is grass* carries an echo of the earlier exultant proclamation of the lone crier that *all flesh* will see the revelation of the glory of YHWH (40:5). The term also plays on the commission that Zion turn from despondency over the condition of all flesh, בָּשָׂר (*bāsār*), to become a מְבַשֶּׂרֶת (*mᵉbasseret*), a bearer of good tidings to the cities of Judah. As the divine attendant acknowledges Zion's objection, he seeks to merge her perspective with that of the divine in his reassurance and elaboration of her commission.

For an assessment and survey of the discussion of the roots of the symbol, see especially Maier, *Daughter Zion, Mother Zion*, 60–74.

25. Biddle, *Polyphony and Symphony*, 9.

Sign

To verify the call, the divine messenger points to a sighting of YHWH coming as both divine warrior and shepherd:

¹⁰Behold,	Adonai YHWH	comes	with might,
	and his arm	rules	for him.
Behold,	his reward	(is)	with him,
	and his recompense		before him.
¹¹Like a shepherd	he will tend	his flock.	
In his arms	he will gather	[his] lambs,	
and in his bosom	he will carry	[them].	
		The nursing mothers	
	he will lead.		

This is a joyful message designed for the hearing of devastated Judeans, who must have questioned both the power and care of their God. Ruling with his arm, symbol of divine power, YHWH comes forth bringing his reward for victory in battle, probably a reference to returning exiles and temple treasures. But also in the image of a caring shepherd, YHWH tends, gathers, carries, and leads the vulnerable of the "flock" of returnees. With such a sure sign of YHWH's care and power, we might think that Zion would be moved to carry out her commission. Despite nine more chapters of encouragement and songs of joy, however, her voice does not yet merge with the perspective of the One Voice dominating Isaiah 40–55.

Isaiah 49:13–21: YHWH Gives Mother Zion Words

Zion speaks once more in this section of Isaiah, shutting down a grand hymnic call to praise with a voice of hopelessness in Chapter 49:

¹³Shout,	O heavens,
and rejoice,	O earth;
break forth with a ringing cry,	O mountains!

> For YHWH has comforted his people,
> and will have compassion on his afflicted ones.
>
> ¹⁴But Zion said, "YHWH has forsaken me;
> Adonai has forgotten me."

As in the call narrative, the writer of this poem seeks to merge Zion's voice with the divine perspective. YHWH answers her directly with repetition of the image of a mother rejecting her children[26] and the verb *forget* in order to override her complaint with a reassuring vision of the opposite:

> ¹⁵Can a woman forget her nursing child,
> (forget) to have compassion on the child of her womb?
> Even these may forget,
> but as for me—I will not forget you (f.s.).
>
> ¹⁶See, upon my palms I have inscribed you (f.s.);
> Your (f.s.) walls are before me continually.

After several more lines on the rebuilding of the city and return of exiles, the poem continues with another strategy to merge Zion's voice with the One Voice: YHWH gives her words.

> ²⁰The children born in your bereavement
> will yet say in your hearing,
> "The place is too cramped for me;
> make room for me to settle."
>
> ²¹Then you (f.s.; i.e. Zion) will say in your heart,
>
> "Who has borne me these?
> I was bereaved and barren,

---

26. Berges comments on the unusual female image of YHWH: "It is interesting to see that in the response of YHWH (Isa. 49:15) the female image—now as mother—is applied to himself. The personification of Zion as a woman is so strong that God is presented in a female image" ("Personifications and Prophetic Voices," 68).

		exiled and put aside.	
So who has reared these?			
	Yea,	I was	left alone.
Where have these come from?"			

YHWH supplies for Zion these words of joyful astonishment at her repopulation in the embedded quotation.[27] To highlight the contrast between "former things" and "new things," the lines alternate between the parallel phrases describing her previous hopeless condition—*was bereaved and barren / (was) exiled and put aside / was left alone*—and her amazement at the inexplicable appearance of numerous children—*Who has borne me these? / So who has reared these? / Where have these come from?* But do we ever hear Zion *herself* speaking her *own* words of joyful astonishment in harmony with the message of restoration which dominates the text?

Isaiah 61:10–11 and 61:1–3b: The Bride Zion Rejoices and Accepts her Commission

Chapters 60–62 from the last section of Isaiah read like an elaborate epithalamium, a wedding song for YHWH and YHWH's bride, the personified Jerusalem/Zion. That is most explicit in 62:4–5, where the narrator addresses Jerusalem using marriage imagery:

⁴You (f.s.)	shall no longer be called	"Forsaken";
your land	shall not be called	"Desolate."
But you	shall be named	"My-Delight-is-in-Her"
and your land		"Married."

For YHWH delights in you,
and your land shall be married.

---

27. Berges, "Personifications and Prophetic Voices," 68, reads the quotation as a reflection of Zion's confusion; whereas I place the emphasis on the secondary nature of the quotation—YHWH as the primary speaker—to suggest that these rhetorical questions express joyful astonishment.

⁵For as	a young man	marries	a maiden,
	your Builder	shall marry	you.

And [as] the rejoicing of a groom over a bride,
your God shall rejoice over you.

An elaborate wedding is the controlling metaphor uniting the three chapters. Reminiscent of the trading center Tyre bringing gifts to the Davidic king's wedding in Psalm 45:12 (Heb. 45:13), ships and camel caravans bring lavish gifts to the wedding of YHWH[28] and Zion, including silver, gold, frankincense, sheep and rams for offerings in the rebuilt temple, and Jerusalem's sons and daughters. Images of fertility pervade the chapters: Jerusalem will bear numerous children (60:22); the population of the city eats and drinks abundantly (60:16; 61:6; 62:8–9); the earth produces shoots, and seeds sprout in gardens (61:11); YHWH's people are called his *shoots* (60:21), his *planting* (60:21; 61:3) and *oaks of YHWH* (61:3). As Solomon the groom receives a crown on his wedding day in Song of Songs 3:11, so the groom YHWH has a crown, in this case, Zion herself (62:3).[29]

While YHWH or a narrator speaks *about* Zion or *to* Zion in the previous poems of Chapters 60 and 61, an unnamed first-person voice responds in 61:10–11. In the context of the wedding imagery set up in the previous passages, we could most naturally recognize these poetic lines as the joyful song of the bride Jerusalem/Zion:

¹⁰I		will greatly rejoice	in YHWH;
my whole being		will exult	in my God.

For	he	has clothed me	in garments of salvation;
			with a robe of righteousness
	he	has wrapped me,	

as a bridegroom	dresses as priest	with a turban,
and as a bride	decks herself	with her ornaments.

28. Verse 5 also identifies YHWH as the groom if one repoints *bānāyik, your sons,* as *bōnêk, your Builder,* as many commentaries suggest.

29. For a discussion of the background of cities as crowns, see Maier, *Daughter Zion, Mother Zion,* 64–69.

¹¹As	the earth	brings forth	its sprouting,
and as	a garden	causes to sprout	what is sown,
so	Adonai YHWH	will cause to sprout	righteousness
			and praise before all the nations.

Finally Zion's own voice unites with the One Voice in this exultant song rich with imagery of wedding garments[30] and fertility. In this bold metaphor, underlined by the parallels between *earth / garden / Adonai YHWH* and *brings forth / causes to sprout / will cause to sprout,* the powerful and mysterious natural force of fertility that propels plants into life serves as the vehicle for the reader to imagine YHWH's spirit enlivening the community with salvation, righteousness, and praise.

One might also identify Zion as the speaker in the other passage from this chapter featuring an unlabeled first-person voice, Isaiah 61:1–3b. Usually this voice is identified with the prophet-narrator, the servant, or a representative of all the faithful servants of YHWH. However, recalling the commission narrative in Isaiah 40, in which Zion is called to be a *bearer of good tidings* (*mᵉbasseret*—40:9), this passage could represent her acceptance of the call to *bear good tidings* (*bāsar*—61:1).[31] Even though the passage once refers to Zion in third person, this would not rule out Zion as speaker, as this could simply clarify the previous reference to *all mourners* by specifying them as *the mourners of Zion*.

¹The spirit of Adonai YHWH is upon me,

for YHWH	has annointed	me.
He	has sent	me

---

30. The line which I have translated *as a bridegroom dresses as priest* (v. 10) causes much discussion among commentators. Scholars often emend *yᵉkahēn*, a verbal form of *kōhēn, priest*, to *yākîn, prepare,* to read "as a bridegroom *prepares* a garland." For example, see Hanson, *Dawn of Apocalyptic*, 52–53. There is, however, no support for this emendation in textual traditions. Furthermore, the relatively unusual noun *turban* (not garland) occurs two other times specifically referring to priestly headgear (Exod 39:28; Ezek 44:18). In this wedding image, the groom, then, is dressed in an elaborate turban as a priest would wear.

31. Berges, "Personifications and Prophetic Voices," 74, identifies Zion as the speaker and views her voice as merged with the group of faithful servants of YHWH.

to bear good tidings	to the oppressed	
to bind up	the broken-hearted,	
to proclaim	to captives	liberty
	and to prisoners	opening-of-eyes,
²to proclaim		a year of favor for YHWH,
		a day of vengeance for our God,
to comfort	all mourners,	
³to provide	for the mourners of Zion,	
to give	to them	a turban instead of ashes,
		oil of gladness instead of mourning,
		a mantel of praise instead of a faint spirit

The framing of the passage with *spirit* (*rûᵃḥ*) is significant: the *faint spirit* that characterized Zion at her commission is now animated by *the spirit of Adonai YHWH* as she accepts her calling, specified by the seven infinitives: *to bear good tidings / to bind up / to proclaim* (as in chapter 40) / *to proclaim / to comfort* (as in chapter 40) / *to provide / to give*. It might seem incongruous for Zion to be *anointed* (מָשַׁח *māšaḥ*; the verbal root for the term *messiah*), but even in the more literal nuance of Zion as city or sacral location of the temple, the term is surprisingly appropriate. In biblical passages the verb *māšaḥ*, *to anoint*, applies not only to priests, kings, and prophets, but also to cultic places, vessels, and offerings. Jacob anoints a sacred pillar at Bethel (Gen 31:13); and Moses anoints the tent of meeting and tabernacle, its altar, and the cultic vessels (Exod 30:26; 40:9–11; Lev 8:10–11; Num 7:1), the unleavened bread for offerings (Exod 29:2; Lev 2:4; 7:12; Num 6:15), and animal sacrifices (Exod 29:36) to consecrate them to YHWH. In the late text of Daniel 9:24, the divine messenger Gabriel announces an appointed time *to anoint a most holy place* in reference to rededication of the temple defiled under the Greek king Antiochus Epiphanes. As the richly symbolic city-sanctuary-community-spirit, Zion is appropriately consecrated to the service of YHWH through her anointment and the investment of the spirit of YHWH. Thus animated, Zion has a special role to lift up the vulnerable, those listed in the column of beneficiaries of her activity: the oppressed, the broken-hearted, captives, prisoners, mourners. In this carefully organized report of her protocol, she offers seven benefits to match the seven infinitives.

We might note the jarring *day of vengeance for our God* following the Jubilee reference to *a year of favor for YHWH*; but for a powerless people dominated by the great empires of Assyria, Babylon, and then Persia, this is good tidings. Among the favors to the vulnerable of Zion are wedding images linking the passage to its context: the *oil of gladness*, a phrase appearing only here and in Psalm 45:7 (Heb. 45:8), where the king is anointed on his wedding day; the turban (פְּאֵר) instead of ashes (אֵפֶר) also worn by the groom in Isaiah 61:10; and the *mantle* (מַעֲטֵה) *of praise*, recalling the *robe of righteousness* in which the bride was wrapped (same Hebrew root עטה as in *mantle*) in 61:10. If this is Zion's voice, she has finally accepted her role as joyful bride of YHWH and her mission as bearer of the good tidings about a community in which the vulnerable live in righteousness and praise. Her voice has been merged with the One Voice to express a monologic truth about the power of YHWH to reanimate dispirited communities.

Habakkuk: A Monologic or Dialogic Text?

The book of Habakkuk takes us back before the Babylonian conquest of Judah. Although the text offers only the briefest of superscriptions, *The revelation which the prophet Habakkuk envisioned* (1:1), the content of the first two chapters suggests a setting in which the powerful Babylonian (also called Chaldean) armies were sweeping across the lands of the ancient Near East. With the capture of Nineveh, capital of the Assyrian Empire, in 612 BCE, and then the victory over Egypt in 605, the Babylonians established themselves as the dominant superpower, demanding tribute and loyalty from Judah and its neighbors.

Perceiving danger from the imperial conquerors and corruption within Judah itself, the prophetic voice in Habakkuk engages in a pointed dialogue with YHWH in which he questions divine justice in the face of violence. This would be a prime set-up for a dialogic text, in which a voice of protest could be matched with divine responses, leaving the audience with an open-ended challenge to continue the debate about the nature of divine justice. However, the scribe who assembled this prophetic book attaches to the dialogue between YHWH and Habakkuk a prayer, a theophanic hymn, and a prophetic response in an attempt to merge the two voices for a satisfying, monologic resolution. We might ask: How well does the design of the book work to accomplish this purpose? Do the voices blend for a harmonious resolution?

The book opens with Habakkuk's lament over corruption within Judah itself, which we can infer from his complaint that *Torah has grown numb* (1:4).³² As I noted in Chapter 2, his address to YHWH includes a rich vocabulary for disorder and shifts in syntax in verse 3, which connote the growing agency of the forces of chaos:

²How long, O YHWH,   have I cried out,

　　　　　　　　　　　　　　　　　　　but you will not answer?

　　　　　　　　　　have I called out to you,
　　　　　　　　　　　"Violence!"

　　　　　　　　　　　　　　　　　　　but you will not deliver?

Why do you   make me see   *trouble*

　　　　　　　and look upon   *toil?*

　　　　　　　　　　　　Havoc

　　　　　　　　　　　　and *violence*   before me—

　　　　　　　　　　　　　　　Strife   appears

　　　　　　　　　　　　　　　and *contention*   arises.

⁴Therefore   Torah   has grown numb,

　　　　　　 and justice   never goes forth;

　　　　　　　　　　　　　　　　　　for wickedness surrounds
　　　　　　　　　　　　　　　　　　　the righteous.

Therefore   justice   goes forth perverted.

The strong, independent voice of the prophet challenges YHWH with questions expressing frustration and calling for response. In the formulation of the questions, he suggests—not too subtly—that YHWH is ultimately responsible for the havoc: *Why do you make me see trouble?* (v. 3). The special concerns of YHWH, Torah and justice, have been perverted, the prophet claims. The one lone line, which spins out of the tight web of parallels, summarizes the issues and lifts up that imperiled person or group for whom YHWH should be concerned: *For wickedness surrounds the righteous* (v. 4).

　　32. Not all scholars recognize the evil-doers in Habakkuk 1:2–4 as Judeans. For example, Johnson, "Paralysis of Torah," 257–66, argues that the numbness of Torah refers not to transgressions of Judeans but to the apparent failure of promises by YHWH, which are also part of Torah. The Chaldean invasions, in his view, are the reason that the prophet regards the promises in the Torah as perverted.

Then YHWH *does* answer. Although the masculine plural form of *you* indicates that the voice of YHWH addresses the community as a whole rather than the prophet alone, the repetition of the verbs *see* and *look* from Habakkuk's complaint suggests that YHWH has heard his lament.

⁵Look (m.pl.)   at the nations

and see!

And be astonished!

Be astounded!

For a deed is being done in your days

that you will not believe when it is recounted.

For look! I am rousing   the Chaldeans,

                      the nation   fierce

                                    and hurried,

                             marching

                                    over the breadth of the land

                                                       to seize dwellings not his.

⁷Dreadful and terrifying is he.

From himself his justice and his dignity go forth.

⁸His horses   are swifter   than leopards,

                  are keener   than evening wolves.

His steeds   gallop.

His steeds   come from afar,

                  fly   like an eagle hastening to devour!

⁹Each one   hastens   for violence. . . .

So here's the response: YHWH is rousing the violence (*ḥāmās*) of the massive Babylonian army, with its own sense of justice, presumably to deal with the violence (*ḥāmās*) of the Judeans, who pervert justice.[33]

Despite the disturbing content of the speech, the description of the Chaldeans is poetically majestic. The lines begin "tightly wound" with side-by-side repetition (*be astonished* and *be astounded* are two forms of the same Hebrew verb תמה; the clause *a deed is being done* uses two forms of the Hebrew פעל) and then stretch out into those sprawling parallels describing the Chaldean army as fierce (*hammar*), hurried (*hannimhār*), and marching over the whole land (see Chapter 2 on parallelism). The speed and eagerness of their war horses is dramatized through the vivid images of leopards, wolves, and eagles and the word play on the movement of the galloping steeds (*ûphāšû pārāšāw ûphārāšāw*), suggesting the rhythmic pounding of hooves.[34] The unmatched line describing the army as marching *to seize dwellings not his* (v. 6) finds an echo in the infinitive depicting the eagle as *hastening to devour* (v. 8). From the voice of YHWH, the compelling majesty of the description of the terrifying Babylonian army which YHWH has roused leaves the prophet—and the reader—with concerns about the character of YHWH. Does YHWH speak with just a hint of admiration for the terrifying instrument of judgment? In her reading of this passage as a script for performance, Jeanette Mathews aptly describes the depiction of YHWH here as "an authoritative and perplexing *persona*" who responds to the prophet's complaint about his passivity like an actor who "has suddenly woken up and remembered his lines, firmly taking center stage."[35]

So disturbing is this question about the persona of YHWH in these lines that Peter Perry, who also prepared the text of Habakkuk for oral performances, chose to "hear the voices while reading" in a different way. Since the text does not actually label the speakers, interpretive judgments

33. Johnson, "Paralysis of Torah," does not interpret YHWH's response as a judgment on Judean corruption but rather as "an intensification of the dilemma of i 2–4" (263). Sweeney also does not see the coming of the Chaldeans as a judgment from YHWH: "Thus, YHWH's response to Habakkuk's complaint presents a negative picture of the Chaldeans. They are established by YHWH, but there is no indication that they are to correct the injustice announced in Hab. i 2–4. Instead, they appear to be the cause of that injustice" ("Structure, Genre, and Intent," 68). I am, however, reading the juxtaposition of the complaint about numbness of Torah and injustice in Judah and this response about YHWH sending the Chaldeans as implying that the Chaldeans serve as judgment upon Judah, much as Assyria was the rod of YHWH's anger in Isaiah. Otherwise it is difficult to see any rationale in YHWH's announcement, *I am rousing the Chaldeans* (1:6).

34. Mathews also notes and comments on the alliterations in *Performing Habakkuk*, 116.

35. Mathews, *Performing Habakkuk*, 105–6.

seem warranted. Perry found the tone of 1:6b–11 "sarcastic and regretful" in the voice of YHWH, and the message that "God would suggest this is a solution to injustice in Judah" to be incongruous with the depiction of YHWH in Chapter 2.[36] Through his experience of oral performance, Perry concluded that the prophet Habakkuk, rather than YHWH, should be identified as the speaker in 1:6b–11:

> In this case, the prophet interrupts God, reacting in shock. Instead of a statement, [in my oral performances] I made 1:6b into a rhetorical question the prophet speaks in shock to God's revelation that God has raised up the Chaldeans: "That hurtful and hasty nation? The Man who marches across expanses of the earth to take possession of dwelling places that are not his own?" If the prophet is the speaker, it makes better sense of the description that God's tool is "terrible and fearful" and he sarcastically says, "[The king's] justice and dignity go forth," rather than the justice from God's Instrument that the prophet desires (1:4).
>
> Performing the text helped to clarify who was speaking and how the two parts fit together. God's announcement, "I am raising the Chaldeans!" (1:6a), is the jaw-dropper that triggers the prophet's unflattering description of the king of Babylon in 1:6b–11.[37]

This is certainly a reasonable option for "hearing voices while reading" Habakkuk 1, a text which leaves room for readers' judgments on identifying the voices.[38] Wresting those descriptive lines on the terrifying speed and efficiency of the Babylonian army from YHWH's part in the script removes the reader's or the performer's uncertainty and discomfort over YHWH's tone: Is YHWH regretful? Sarcastic? Admiring? Now the depiction of the Babylonian army (the king, in Perry's view) is part of the prophet's protest against YHWH's brief answer to Judean corruption. To YHWH are left only the lines announcing that YHWH is rousing the Chaldeans (1:5–6a), but

---

36. Perry, *Insights from Performance Criticism*, 97.

37. Perry, *Insights from Performance Criticism*, 97.

38. Haak offers yet another interpretation of the voices in Habakkuk 1. His view is that Habakkuk is essentially a pro-Babylonian text. YHWH answers Habakkuk's complaint about injustice in Judah (1:2–4) with the salvation oracle revealing that YHWH is sending the Babylonians to deal with inner-Judean corruption (1:5–6). Then Habakkuk responds in 1:7–11, stating "his knowledge of the overwhelming power of the Chaldeans" and his "confidence that this power has truly been established by Yahweh for the salvation of the people" (*Habakkuk* 14). Habakkuk also speaks in 1:13b–17, not complaining about the Babylonians but again targeting the corrupt leaders of Judah, particularly the enemies of King Jehoahaz and his pro-Babylonian supporters.

YHWH does not express any disposition toward them before the prophet interrupts in shock and protest.

In the end, however, I find Mathews' reading and the traditional assignment of the speech in 1:6b–11 to YHWH more compelling. In my view it is not just the summoning of the Chaldeans as an instrument of judgment but also YHWH's inscrutable attitude toward them and their victims which propels Habakkuk's protest as the debate continues. If those lines depicting the Chaldean army belong to YHWH's voice, YHWH is fully responsible and absorbed in the destructive march of the Babylonian horsemen and fully aware of their self-deification: *He is guilty whose own strength is his god"* (v. 11). The prophet's protest, which continues in 1:12–17, complains that YHWH, who offers many words to describe the advance of the army, simply looks on silently when *the wicked swallow those more righteous than they* (1:13). YHWH seems to regard people as indiscriminate swarms of fish caught in a net. Does YHWH even care about humanity? Habakkuk's complaint in those lines might fit the text best if it is a reaction to the enigmatic and offensive attitude which YHWH expresses in YHWH's own characterization of the Babylonian army and YHWH's disregard of the victims in 1:6–11.

If we adopt this way of identifying the speakers, the beginning of the book of Habakkuk sets up a sharp dialogue between two developed voices expressing different perspectives on the workings of divine justice. As the text continues, the writer attempts to merge these two voices to express a satisfying resolution for the enigma of divine justice. In the next round of dialogue in Chapter 2, Habakkuk stations himself to wait for a reply (v. 1—lines recorded without charting parallels):

> Upon my watch-post let me stand,
> and station myself upon a rampart,
> and keep watch to see what he will say to me
> and what I will bring back concerning my argument.

YHWH answers Habakkuk, addressing him individually in masculine singular imperative verbs, directing him to write down a vision which will appear and to wait patiently for a response. Contrary to the proud, says YHWH, *the righteous will live by his steadfastness* (2:4). In a series of five "woes," the prophet reports YHWH's message that acquisitiveness, violence, injustice, and idolatry—whether Judean or Babylonian[39]—collapse on themselves. Creditors will rise up against those who pile on heavy debts and confiscate the property of others (vv. 6–7); the plundered will rise up against

---

39. Many commentators regard the woes as addressed to the Chaldeans alone, but the emphasis is on oppressive and violent actions and idolatry, which might equally apply to those responsible for injustice and numbness of Torah in Judah. See the discussion of the refrain in Chapter 2 and see also Mathews, *Performing Habakkuk*, 127, 137.

plunderers (v. 8); the very stones and rafters will turn against those who build their houses with ill-gotten gain (vv. 9–11); those who attack their neighbors will face attack themselves (vv. 15–16); the trees of Lebanon, cut down for building war machines and palaces, and the animals of the forest will rise up against their exploiters (v. 17); idolaters will recognize the worthlessness of their gods (vv. 18–19). This is one kind of resolution to the problems of violence, exploitation, and injustice: wait patiently, for wickedness cannot endure the powerful forces of reversal.

To the dialogues the scribe who shaped the book of Habakkuk added another kind of response, a prayer and a majestic hymn describing a theophany of Elohim, who appears as a warrior armed with thunderbolts, driving horses and a chariot, shaking mountains and churning waters, trampling nations in anger, and saving his people. Perhaps this is intended to be the promised vision. Habakkuk responds with appropriate awe and confidence in YHWH's just vengeance:

> I heard and my innards quaked;
> my lips quivered at the sound.
> Rottenness entered my bones,
> and from beneath I quaked.
> I will rest for the day of distress
> to rise over the people who attack us. (3:16)

The text ends with a definitive resolution in a hymn expressing a conviction contrary to the common misperception that faithfulness to YHWH necessarily brings blessings (3:17–19b):

Though	the fig tree	does not blossom,	
			and there is no fruit on the vines;
	the produce of the olive	grows lean,	
	and the fields	do not produce food;	
	the sheep	is cut off	from the fold,
			and there are no cattle in the stalls;

| yet I | will exalt | in YHWH, |
| | and rejoice | in the God of my salvation. |

YHWH Adonai is my strength.

He sets my feet   like the hinds'.
                          Upon my heights
he makes me tread.

When we consider the design of the book of Habakkuk as a whole, the construction of voices is particularly intriguing. In broad outline the book seems to portray a process toward realization of a theme or monologic truth. It begins with a dialogue between the independent voices of YHWH and Habakkuk, who dispute about the workings of divine justice. Through continued dialogue and an awesome theophany, YHWH persuades the prophet to wait in confidence for YHWH's just vengeance on the wicked and rescue of the steadfast.

But is the book successful in expressing a monologic truth? Some scholars, such as Marvin Sweeney, are persuaded that the book "has a coherent structural unity" and expresses a consistent theme, "a Prophetic Affirmation of Divine Sovereignty and Justice, the purpose of which is to convince its audience that YHWH is maintaining fidelity in a crisis situation."[40] Not all readers, however, will be left singing the beautiful hymn of praise and resting in confidence of divine sovereignty and justice. First, we might note that the text offers not just one resolution but alternate responses to the problem of injustice in a world presumably under YHWH's control. One response comes from YHWH's message reported by Habakkuk in Chapter 2: evil sets up the conditions for its own collapse, as the oppressed—even animals, trees, and stones—rise up against their tormentors. From this perspective no special divine intervention in the historical or natural world is required to deal with the problems of violence and oppression. The elaborate theophany in Chapter 3 offers quite a different response: YHWH appears as the Divine Warrior to conquer the wicked and rescue the steadfast. These two convictions, while they can be harmonized, do not merge easily into a singular resolution. Furthermore, although the prophetic voice concludes with joy and restful assurance of divine justice, the extended imagery and skillful poetry depicting YHWH's disregard of victims of oppression linger in the mind of the reader. If YHWH is the speaker in 1:6–11, the tone of that detailed description enacting the advance of the Chaldean army, with their horses swifter than leopards and eagles and keener than wolves, remains

---

40. Sweeney, "Structure, Genre, and Intent," 80–81.

uncomfortably enigmatic. And who can forget the extended fishing metaphor questioning YHWH's care for humanity (1:14–17)?

You have made humanity	like the fish of the sea,		
	like swarming creatures who have no ruler.		

The lot of them	he [=Chaldeans]	brings up	with a hook,
	he	drags him away	with his net,
	and he	gathers him	in his seine.

Therefore	he	rejoices	
		and is glad.	
Therefore	he	sacrifices	to his net
		and burns incense	to his seine.

For in them	his portion	is fat,	
	and his food	is rich.	

Will he then	[continue]	to empty	his net,	
	and continue	to kill	nations	without sparing?

The vividness of the images in these powerful lines describing the violence of the oppressor and questioning the care of YHWH causes these thoughts to linger despite the confident resolution at the conclusion of the book of Habakkuk.

Though the scribe might have intended the book to be monologic, not all readers will be convinced that the voices fully merge in a single resolution. Instead, some will read Habakkuk as a dialogic text, in which several voices offer thoughts which remain unmerged. One voice sounds the theme of theophany: the Divine Warrior comes to conquer evil and rescue those who wait patiently for YHWH. Another says: be confident that evil will collapse on itself as the oppressed rise against their oppressors. Still another small voice nervously asks: does YHWH in some sense celebrate the fearful efficiency of YHWH's instrument of judgment? Yet another wonders if YHWH cares for the swarms of suffering humanity so easily caught up in the nets of oppressive powers. A final voice sings: though fields dry up, though vines do not yield their grapes, though flocks do not bear young—and presumably, though *wickedness surrounds the righteous*—yet I will rejoice in YHWH. Some readers will experience the text as an open-ended dialogue inviting thought, wrestling, and discussion, rather than a drama culminating in a secure resolution and urging assent to a single truth.

The Polyphony of Trauma in Jeremiah

For a truly polyphonic text expressing dialogic truth, one can turn to the book of Jeremiah, in which we hear a chorus of unmerged voices, frequently expressing different viewpoints.[41] To change to a symphonic metaphor, Biddle describes "prophetic music," most notably that of Jeremiah, as "symphonically complex."[42] His method of reading Jeremiah "resembles the task of the sophisticated concertgoer who hears not only the sound of the orchestra, but the voices of different instruments and the various melodies, countermelodies, and harmonies contributing to the whole."[43] From one viewpoint, that of biblical scholars identified as historical or source critics, this prophetic counterpoint or polyphony—sometimes cacophony—is the result of the complicated history of development of the text. One could imagine an enlightening, though conjectural, PowerPoint presentation with separate slides to display the layers of development of the book of Jeremiah, from oracles arguably delivered orally by the prophet himself prior to the fall of Jerusalem in 586 BCE through the various stages of reinterpretation long after the catastrophe. Such an analysis would demonstrate how Jeremiah's words were reshaped to address the changing circumstances of communities of YHWH worshippers and would illustrate the more general point that religious traditions grow and change to meet the needs of those who preserve them. However, this is not the approach I will adopt here. Instead, this literary introduction to voices in Jeremiah will focus on the final stage of the poetry as we find it in the textual tradition of the Hebrew MT (the main source for most English translations). The operating assumption

---

41. Recognition of the dialogic, polyphonic nature of Jeremiah is, of course, not a new insight. Many commentators have written about it. Besides Holladay, Biddle, and O'Connor—cited frequently in this and the next chapter—see also Carroll, "Polyphonic Jeremiah," 77–85; Stulman, "Jeremiah as a Polyphonic Response to Suffering," 302–18, among others.

42. Biddle, *Polyphony and Symphony*, 8.

43. Biddle, *Polyphony and Symphony*, 8.

is that the poet or scribal prophet who finally assembled the various pieces of the text worked with creative intention.

Even for a literary, synchronic approach, some basic introduction to the historical context of the book is essential for understanding and appreciating the voices we hear in Jeremiah. Though the final stage of the book of Jeremiah is undoubtedly post-exilic, there seems little reason to doubt that some of the poems have their origin in the preaching of a historical prophet Jeremiah, a priest from the Benjamite village of Anathoth,[44] who was active in Jerusalem around 625 to 580 BCE. The text tells the story of his conflicts with Judean kings and the priests, prophets, and population of Jerusalem as he conveyed YHWH's judgment against idolatry and social injustice; warned of the destruction of Judah, Jerusalem, and even the sacred temple; and sought to persuade the people to accept a long exile in Babylon. During his days Babylon invaded Jerusalem three times—in 597, 586, and 581—each time taking hundreds, perhaps thousands, of Judeans captives. As we noted in the sketch of background to Isaiah 40, Judean independence ended in 586 BCE with the Babylonian capture of the Davidic king Zedekiah, assassination of many priests and members of the royal household, exile of much of the population, ruin of Jerusalem, confiscation of temple vessels, and burning of the temple itself. According to the story, Jeremiah remained in the land of Judah after the exile until a group of Judeans forcibly took him to Egypt to escape Babylonian reprisals for the murder of the Babylonian-appointed governor of Judea.

Historians and archaeologists continue to debate the extent of the devastation of Judah as a result of the Babylonian invasions. One detailed archaeological survey, Avraham Faust's *Judah in the Neo-Babylonian Period: The Archaeology of Desolation* (2012) concludes that excavations show destruction of almost all urban Judean sites in the early sixth century; a break in settlement of about fifty excavated rural sites between the Iron Age and Persian Periods; disappearance of four-room houses and new burial caves typical of Iron Age Judean life; and a 85 to 90 percent decrease in the population of Judah from the seventh century (which would include earlier Assyrian incursions) to the Persian Period.[45] The reasons for the devastation, Faust concludes, would not only have been exile and death in war, but also the accompanying scourges of famine and epidemics, looting of food by armies,

---

44. That Anathoth was the site of exile of the priest Abiathar for his support of Solomon's rival Adonijah is an intriguing clue to Jeremiah's ancestry and his opposition to the Jerusalemite theology. One wonders about the activity of the banished priestly descendants of Abiathar after the days of Solomon.

45. Faust, *Judah in the Neo-Babylonian Period: The Archaeology of Desolation.*

flight to neighboring lands, and collapse of administrative structures.[46] What is important for our literary study of voices in Jeremiah is this context of devastation. Unfortunately, we twenty-first century readers, accustomed to our own contemporary images of the ravages of war—bombed buildings, scorched fields, flights of refugees, corpses in streets, captives herded off at gunpoint, tortured and beheaded bodies—will not require much imagination to enter the world of the book of Jeremiah.

If we can conclude that the setting in which the poems of the book of Jeremiah were created was this post-war world, with horrifying memories—some fresh and some passed on to the next generation—losses of family and property, hopelessness, and threats to identity, then the book's disjointed quality makes sense. With a background in recent analyses of the effects of trauma on community, Kathleen O'Connor's studies, "Reclaiming Jeremiah's Violence" and *Jeremiah: Pain and Promise*, offer helpful insights for understanding the literary form of the poems. One of the results of traumatic experiences, she observes, is "fractured memories."

> People cannot fully experience traumatic violence as it occurs. They cannot absorb it into consciousness as it is happening because violence overpowers the senses. At the same time the violent events are imprinted on the brain in fragmented pieces, in fractured memories of the events. In the aftermath of violence, memory fragments stomp around in the mind like menacing ghosts, as if they were alive with a will of their own.[47]

The poetry of Jeremiah, she contends, helped the post-exilic community heal from disaster because it

> brings up memories of invasions, but . . . "at a slant" [phrase from Emily Dickinson], in poetry and symbol. . . . To tell the truth slant means to put it at a distance, slightly outside of life, as if on a screen, in a poetic world, so the violence does not come back to strangle and re-traumatize readers. . . . War in Jeremiah's poetry is no ordinary war, no news report. It is mythic battle cast in a cosmic realm.[48]

O'Connor's suggestion also makes sense of the apparent disjointedness of the poetry, the cacophony of voices in Jeremiah. The very form of the poetry relates to the inner world of the audience. The poems present fragmented memories of war and feelings expressed symbolically in images like a well

---

46. Faust, *Judah in the Neo-Babylonian Period*, 246–47.
47. O'Connor, "Reclaiming Jeremiah's Violence," 39.
48. O'Connor, "Reclaiming Jeremiah's Violence," 41.

bubbling forth with wickedness, striking adders who cannot be charmed, a lion stalking a prey, a fire smelting metal; or sound bites like a woman shrieking in the pangs of childbirth, signaling trumpets, shouts of alarm. Such poetry does not offer a sense of resolution in simplistic ideas about suffering, the nature of God, or the meaning of community but challenges the audience through multiple voices, not always singing in harmony.

In the next chapter I will offer an interpretation of Jeremiah 4:5–31 as a whole poem, with particular attention to the perspective of the different voices. Here I will simply use Jeremiah 6 to exemplify two features typical of the play of voices in the poetry of Jeremiah: the frequent shifts in speaker and addressee, which create the fragmentary sense of the text; and, on the other hand, a strategy the writer employs to stitch the fragments together.

Jeremiah 6 includes a large cast of characters. Speakers include YHWH, the prophet Jeremiah, invaders of Jerusalem, the people of Jerusalem, and some watchmen/prophets. To these we add Daughter Zion, Benjamites, and all nations of earth as addressees without voice. Although identification of characters is sometimes ambiguous, a list of the probable speakers and addressees or subjects demonstrates the frequent shifts in the text:

- YHWH (or divine messenger) to the people of Benjamin (v.1)
- YHWH about Daughter Zion (vv. 2–3)
- Invading commander to his troops (v. 4ab)
- Jerusalemite army (v. 4cd)
- Invading commander to his troops (v. 5)
- YHWH to invaders (vv. 6–7)
- YHWH to Lady Jerusalem (v. 8)
- YHWH to invaders (v. 9)
- Jeremiah about the people of Jerusalem (vv. 10–11ab)
- YHWH to Jeremiah (vv. 11c–12)
- YHWH about the people of Jerusalem (vv. 13–15)

  (with secondary quotation from the prophets of Jerusalem)

- YHWH to the people of Jerusalem (vv. 16–17)

  (with secondary quotations from the people and the watchmen/prophets)

- YHWH to the nations of earth (vv. 18–19)
- YHWH to the people of Jerusalem (v. 20)

- YHWH to the nations of earth (v. 21)
- YHWH to Daughter Zion (vv. 22–23)
- People of Jerusalem about invaders (v. 24)
- YHWH to people of Jerusalem (vv. 25–26a-d)
- People of Jerusalem about invaders (v. 26ef)
- YHWH to Jeremiah (v. 27)
- Either YHWH or Jeremiah about the people of Jerusalem (vv. 28–30)

With all these changes in speaker or addressee, the text reads like a drama. The main actions—an impending invasion of Jerusalem and a metaphorical smelting—are enacted through the words of the characters. Although YHWH's voice clearly dominates the drama, we do hear independent voices of invaders, Jeremiah, and the people of Jerusalem.

Even though the shifts in speaker and addressee cut the poem into segments, and the characters rarely engage in direct conversation with one another, the craftsmanship of the poet is revealed in the particular way the fragments are connected. As Biddle has noted in *Polyphony and Symphony,* the poet frequently uses an ABA structure[49] to alternate between different fragments, creating a layered, polyphonic text. Many interpreters have noted the first example of this in the chapter, the alternation between the voices of the invaders and the terrified Jerusalemites in 6:4–5.[50]

[*Invaders:*]

Consecrate war
   against her!

Arise   and let us go up   at noon!

---

49. Biddle, *Polyphony* and Symphony, 23–24.

50. As in the example of different possibilities for reading of Jeremiah 8:18—9:2, which I discussed in the beginning of this chapter, there are different options here. Some scholars read all the lines in 6:4–5 as spoken by the invaders. For example, Brueggemann, *Commentary on Jeremiah,* offers this interpretation: "Verses 4–5 offer three quotes allegedly from the principals in the battle to come. The alleged statements are from the mouth of the invading army, designed to escalate and dramatize the sense of danger and threat. It is as though the poet takes us into the commander's tent to hear the specific strategy. The second of the three quotes ['Alas, for the day has declined,/for the shadows of evening have lengthened!'] shows the chagrin the successful army has at the setting of the sun, for it means the end of the battle for the day (v. 4b). The winners never want darkness to come . . .'"(70).

[Jerusalemites:]

<u>Alas</u>   <u>for the day</u>   <u>has declined;</u>
<u>for the shadows
of the evening</u> <u>have lengthened!</u>

[*Invaders:*]

Arise   and let us go up   at night,
     and let us destroy her citadels!

The A B A structure is indicated not only by the alternation of voices but also by the parallels linking the two shouts of the invaders. Here the poet contrasts the invaders' enthusiastic rise to attack both day and night with the terror and helplessness of the Jerusalemites as darkness, both literal and metaphoric, descends. The alternation enacts a mini-drama taking the audience from the commander's tent, then to the Jerusalemite camp, and back to the tent. The dramatic scene effectively captures the emotions of attack and implies that the fearful defenders of Jerusalem stand little chance against the consecrated army, aroused to attack at any time of day or night.

Immediately following this scene another A B A structure associates YHWH's invitation to the invaders with YHWH's warning to Jerusalem (6:6–9).

[YHWH to Invaders:]
For thus says YHWH Seba'oth:
Cut wood,
and pour out over Jerusalem a siege mound.
She is the city to be punished.
As for all of her—oppression is in her midst.

As   a well   keeps fresh   its waters,
so   she   keeps fresh   her wickedness.

Violence and devastation   are reported   within her;
                                            before me continually
sickness and wounds.

[YHWH to Lady Jerusalem:]
Take correction, O Jerusalem,

lest my presence	*be torn away from*	*you,*	
lest I	*make*	*you*	*a desolation,*
			an uninhabited land.

[YHWH to Invaders:]
Thus says YHWH Seba'oth:

Glean thoroughly	*as a vine*	
		the remnant of Israel.
Turn your hand	*like a grape gatherer*	
	over her branches.	

The alternation between these fragments expresses a sense of urgency for Jerusalem to act, since YHWH seems to address the invaders and Jerusalem simultaneously. It also conveys the message that YHWH is sovereign of both the invaders and the people of Jerusalem. However, the juxtaposition also suggests a certain ambivalence in the character of YHWH. On one hand, the deity wrathfully invites the invaders to destroy the city and any remnant of the land of Israel. On the other, YHWH holds out the possibility that Jerusalem could actually take correction and avert disaster. If we set the two outer units together, we also can appreciate the irony of the metaphors. Usually fresh well water and grape harvest are positive images of refreshment and fertility, a contrast to the desolation threatening Jerusalem. Here the well bubbles forth with Jerusalem's wickedness, and the harvest with its final gleaning provides a vision of Israel's demise.

In a third example of ABA structure, YHWH invites the people of Jerusalem to walk in *the ancient paths . . . the good road* (6:16). The voice of YHWH then quotes their obdurate responses along with a warning cry from watchmen (6:16f–17).

But they said, "We will not walk [in it]."

> I raised over you watchmen:
> "Heed the sound of the *šôfār*!"

But they said, "We will not heed."

The watchmen here could refer metaphorically to truthful prophets delivering YHWH's call to repentance or more literally to the men stationed on the city walls to warn of invasion; in the polyvalence of poetic language, both meanings could apply. The people's words that they will neither act according to the ways of YHWH nor hear the warning surround and "swallow up" the words of alarm. Clearly the watchmen have not been able to wake them to the peril of their situation.

Immediately following this exchange is another ABA arrangement (6:18–21), in which YHWH's address to all the nations as witnesses to the judgment of the obdurate people (A) surrounds YHWH's angry words to the Jerusalemites rejecting their shallow efforts toward appeasement through sacrificial offerings (B).

[YHWH to Nations:]

[18]Therefore   hear,   O nations,

     and know   O assembly,

              what will happen to them.

    [19]Hear,   O earth:

Behold I am sending   evil   to this people,

       the fruit of their own devices;

for my words   they did not heed,
and my Torah   they rejected.

[YHWH to People of Jerusalem:]

[20]What is this to me—   frankincense coming from Sheba,

      aromatic cane   from a distant land?

Your burnt offerings	are not acceptable,
and your sacrifices	are not sweet to me.

[YHWH to Nations:]

²¹Therefore thus says YHWH:

Behold I am giving   *to this people*

       stumbling blocks.

And   they   shall stumble   over them—

      fathers and sons together—

      neighbor and friend   shall perish.

Recognition of the A B A pattern helps the reader identify the addressee in verse 21 as the nations of earth; as in verses 18–19 they are called to witness the disaster coming to Jerusalem. Noting this structure, we can also appreciate the parallels between *Behold I am sending / Behold I am giving* and *evil / the fruit of their own devices / stumbling blocks*. That latter set of parallels reveals that the enigmatic "stumbling blocks" refers to the evil which is coming as a consequence of the people's rebellion against YHWH. The ABA structure expresses the connection between the people's rejection of Torah, announced to all nations, and YHWH's rejection of their sacrifices. Since the relation between YHWH and the people of Israel was intended to be a witness to the nations of earth about who YHWH is, the divine message functions as a vindication of YHWH's treatment of "this people." The voice of YHWH announces that the whole earth should know that the coming destruction of Judah is not evidence of the inefficacy of the YHWH cult but rather YHWH's own judgment against the people for their rejection of Torah.

     Finally, the poem weaves a fragment on the Jerusalemites' terror at the impending invasion together with YHWH's report that *terror is all around* and YHWH's command that the people mourn their own inescapable death (6:24–26).[51]

---

51. Biddle, *Polyphony and Sympathy*, 23.

[People of Jerusalem:]
We have heard report of him [the invader];
our hands fall slack.

Distress   *has seized us,*
anguish like one in labor.

[YHWH to People of Jerusalem:]

Do not go out   into the field;
do not walk   in the road.

For the enemy has a sword!
Terror is all around!

O My-Daughter-People,

gird yourself   in sackcloth;
roll yourself   in ash;
make for yourself   mourning as for an only child,
                                      bitter wailing.

[People of Jerusalem:]
                Suddenly will come over us
the devastator!

In this polyphonic, dramatic scene the poet presents a sympathetic view of the people, as we hear their own words of terror, intensified in the parallels between *distress / anguish like one in labor / the devastator*. Their terror is juxtaposed with YHWH's words confirming their fears and finally expressing a hint of sympathetic connection to them in the address *O My-Daughter-People*.

The voices throughout Jeremiah 6 enact a drama of YHWH's dealings with Jerusalem that does not conclude in a single resolution or simple truth. In the chorus of voices we hear YHWH's wrath, divine self-justification, a hint of pity for the people, and an effort to hold on to the possibility of Jerusalem's repentance. We hear the people's terror and obduracy, the enemy's aggression, and the prophet's frustration (vv. 10–11b, concluding, *With the wrath of YHWH I am filled / I weary myself to contain [it]*). The poet carefully links the speeches but does not harmonize the voices so that the poem resonates with the complexity of experience of the traumatized audience. In the next chapter we will see how this polyphonic, dialogic quality of the poems of Jeremiah is even more pronounced in the earlier poem in 4:5–31, in which Lady Zion has a voice and a more prominent role.

In this chapter I have attempted to show that readers of prophetic texts, who might expect to find a singular and clear Word of God in oracles introduced *Thus says YHWH*, will instead discover rich, but often bewildering scripts of dramas with numerous, sometimes unlabeled speakers. One major challenge for anyone attempting to interpret these prophetic dramas is "hearing voices while reading." Sometimes the different speakers will sound like voices in unison, as in the book of Joel, where the prophet and YHWH speak as one. In other cases initially dissonant voices will eventually merge for a harmonious, monologic perspective, as the voices of YHWH and Zion do in Isaiah 40–66. Occasionally we readers might sense that a writer's attempt to create a monologic text leaves some dissonant, unmerged voices, as in Habakkuk. In other texts, such as the poetry of Jeremiah, the writer skillfully manages a cacophony of unmerged voices to reflect traumatic experience and to remain open-ended. There are other good, compelling ways to identify the voices, recognize literary features, and understand the meaning of all the texts I have considered in this chapter. The words of the text are the "notes," but each interpreter takes up the challenge of "making the music."

5

Reader's Theater for the Traumatized

An Interpretation of Jeremiah 4

IN THE PREVIOUS CHAPTER I characterized the setting of the poems of Jeremiah as a time of trauma with a devastated land; fragmented memories of Babylonian invasion; and losses of kin, Davidic kingship, political independence, the Jerusalem temple, and trust in YHWH's care and power. Although parts of the war poem in Jeremiah 4:5–31 might have originated in oral proclamation of the prophet Jeremiah as the invasion began, the text as we have it is a post-war scribal product woven together creatively in a form we might label a *reading drama*. Whether or not the poem was actually performed in ancient Israel, modern audiences might best hear the different voices and perceive the power of the poem if we think of it as a script for a Reader's Theater presentation, with individual voices reading the roles of the various speakers. In this chapter I will divide the poem into eighteen sections according to sets of parallels or changes in speaker or addressee, chart the parallels, offer a brief commentary focused on vertical reading and hearing voices, and finally propose a script version for a Reader's Theater presentation of the whole poem.

In her chapter "'Hearing Voices while Reading': Isaiah 40–55 as a Drama," Annemarieke van der Woude uses literary theory to arrive at her conclusion that the dramatic poetry of Isaiah 40–55 cannot be classified as a drama meant for staged performance but as a reading drama.[1] Her discussion of the characteristics of a reading drama applies well to Jeremiah 4:5–31, as we will discover in our analysis of the text. Reading dramas, she explains, lack a narrator, although rubrics like *saying of YHWH* (נְאֻם־יהוה) or a brief identification of the speaker might appear as "a kind of stage

---

1. Van der Woude, "'Hearing Voices while Reading,'" 149–73.

direction"[2] for readers. Instead of being described by a narrator, actions unfold through the speech of the characters. Therefore the language of reading dramas is *performative*: "the pronouncement of the utterance coincides with the performance of the action."[3] For example, in Jeremiah 4:13 the approach of the Babylonian army towards Jerusalem is enacted in the watchmen's announcement:

> Look! He [the invader] rises like clouds!
> Like a whirlwind his chariots—
> His horses are swifter than eagles!
> Woe to us, for we are devastated!

The destruction of the city itself happens in the poem as Lady Zion reports it several verses later: *Suddenly my tents are devastated, / in a moment my curtains* (v. 20). In a reading drama the dialogue is the primary means for developing a story. Although van der Woude recognizes that Isaiah 40–55 is essentially monologic, with YHWH being the dominant speaker, she notes that a story about YHWH's relation to Zion and to the servant unfolds dramatically in YHWH's words rather than through a narrator's description. YHWH is the dominant speaker in Jeremiah 4 as well, but the city watchmen, the people, the prophet Jeremiah, and Lady Zion also have prominent speaking roles and independent perspectives which do not merge. As in Isaiah 40–55, the story develops almost exclusively through speech describing the action and its emotive affect, even though the characters do not engage in sustained dialogue with one another.

Another scholar, Nancy Lee, suggests that the poems of Jeremiah might reflect actual performance as a dialogue between the historical Jeremiah and a female communal lament-singer, whose voice expressed the suffering of the city Jerusalem.[4] As evidence of such oral performances in ancient Israel she cites "the dialogical nature of psalms," which implies priests playing various roles in temple liturgies; references to oral singers in city gates; texts like Jeremiah 9:16–21, in which YHWH calls the mourning women to sing a dirge for Jerusalem; and 2 Chronicles 35:25, which reports that Jeremiah and *all the singing men and women* lamented the death of King Josiah of Judah.[5] Although such an oral performance might lie behind Jeremiah 4, I am more persuaded that the scribal poem which is available to us as a written text reflects various stages of development beyond the time of the historical

---

2. Van der Woude, "'Hearing Voices while Reading,'" 168.
3. Van der Woude, "'Hearing Voices while Reading,'" 169.
4. Lee, "Prophet and Singer in the Fray," 190–209.
5. Lee, "Prophet and Singer in the Fray," 195.

Jeremiah and might therefore be better characterized as a reading drama. Nevertheless, Lee's intriguing suggestion provides further reason for modern readers to access the power of the poem through oral performance of Jeremiah 4 as a Reader's Theater piece. Through such re-enactment the words of the ancient scribal prophet continue to have relevance for responding to traumas of war, natural disaster, violence, spiritual crisis, and loss of meaning.

YHWH Summons the Watchmen to Prepare for "Evil from the North" (vv. 5–6)

In Jeremiah 4:5–9, the beginning of this war poem, we can recognize the voice of YHWH. Although only the rubric *saying of YHWH* in verse 9 explicitly identifies the speaker of the opening sections, the authority of the voice commanding Judah to prepare for attack and the first-person motive clause, *For I am bringing evil from the North* (v. 6), suggest that YHWH speaks in these first verses of the poem as well. The poem begins on an urgent note with lines governed by eleven imperative verbs. Although the addressee is identified only by the masculine plural form of all the Hebrew verbs, there seem to be two levels of command in the lines: YHWH commissions one group to speak, and that group commands another to prepare for war. The poem sets up an imagined scene in which the divine voice summons the watchmen guarding Judah's fortified cities and dictates what they must say to the inhabitants. Untangling the speakers and addressees involves subjective judgments, but charting the parallels might help us distinguish YHWH's direct command to the watchmen (in regular print in the chart below) from the words they are commanded to proclaim to their cities (in italics); and an analysis of the columns also highlights associations we might not otherwise notice.

⁵Declare (m.pl.)   in Judah

                  and in Jerusalem;

proclaim

and say:

                           "Blow the *šôfār*   in the land!

Cry out;

raise full voice

and say:

                           "Assemble together
                               and let us go

                                                     to the fortified cities

                           ⁶Raise a signal   toward Zion.

                           Take refuge!

                           Do not tarry!"

For I am bringing   evil from the North

                         and great shattering.

In this interpretation, YHWH summons the watchmen in two sets of three imperatives related to speaking out: *declare, proclaim, and say; cry out, raise full voice,*⁶ *and say.* YHWH then dictates the urgent commands which the watchmen must convey to the people of Judah and Jerusalem. As in Joel 2, the first command, *Blow the šôfār*, is initially ambiguous, since it could call the people to worship or to war. The next set of parallel commands clarifies the meaning: *assemble together, raise a signal, take refuge, do not tarry* (in addition to the cohortative *let us go*). The effect of this command-within-a-command is to suggest that YHWH has full control

---

6. The meaning of the Hebrew verb מַלְאוּ, usually translated "to be full, to fill," is uncertain here. The LXX translates adverbially as μεγα, understood as a modifier of the previous verb "cry out." In my chart of parallels it is significant that the MT renders the word as an imperative verb, perhaps understood adverbially but having the connotation of raising the voice fully.

of events; there are no other independent agents at this point in the poem. Here YHWH's role is to send disaster and to summon the watchmen to announce it. We will see that direct and secondary quotations from watchmen throughout the poem serve to enact a plot, as they report the speedy approach of the invaders toward Jerusalem and express the growing panic of the people. Reading vertically through the column of prepositional modifiers in the secondary quotations, we note that the focus narrows from the whole land of Judah to the fortified cities to the temple site of Jerusalem/Zion. This focalization prepares for similar moves throughout the poem and more immediately for YHWH's direct address to the personified city in the next section of the poem.

YHWH's voice identifies the threat in startling ways. First, we note that the invaders themselves are also subject to the commands of YHWH: *I am bringing evil from the North*. While the historical threat at the time of the first audiences was the empire of Babylon to the northeast of Israel, the poetic abstraction *from the North* points, at the same time, to a location on the mythic/cosmic as well as the geographical map. As in the previous prophetic poems we have examined, this is another example of the slide between the historic and the cosmic. We can recall the locusts as the defeated "northern army" in Joel 2:20. In biblical poetry the North is not only the location of the threatening great empires of Assyria in the eighth and seventh centuries BCE and Babylon in the late seventh and sixth centuries, but also of awesome appearances of YHWH. Mount *Ṣāphôn* (=Mount North) is where the Canaanite Baal sat on his throne, a site co-opted by the psalmist who located Zion *in the far North* (48:3). From here the Daystar god *Hêlēl ben Šaḥar* attempted to take over the throne of Elohim (Isa 14:12–14), and Job shielded his eyes from *the golden splendor* of Elohim (Job 37:22). From the North came Ezekiel's vision of the wheeled chariot throne of YHWH uplifted by the four living creatures (Ezek 1); and from the North the chariot throne of YHWH would reenter the rebuilt Zion in Ezekiel's vision (Ezek 44). Certainly the original audience recognized the *evil from the North* as the Babylonian destroyers—first threatened and then a reality—and later readers could reinterpret the unnamed political foe as the situation warranted. However, the poetic expression invites ambiguity, since *from the North* in the lines above could modify not only *evil*, but also *I am bringing*. In the latter case, it suggests the ultimate source, YHWH, who brings destruction upon Judah and Jerusalem from the divine dwelling in the North.

Parallel to the threat of *evil from the North* is one of the key terms in Jeremiah, *a great shattering* (שֶׁבֶר). Appearing twenty-six times in Jeremiah, the vivid word conveys the smashing of pottery (19:11), the splintering of a wooden yoke (28:4, 11; 30:8), the fracturing of bone at a blow (14:17), the shattering of Egyptian obelisks (43:13), the snap of scepter (48:17) and bow (49:35), all appropriate to survivors' memories of tumbling walls, shattered homes, broken bodies, ineffectual defenses, and false assurances, as well as their hopes for YHWH's power over oppressive empires.

While modern readers are likely troubled by these images of YHWH as the terrifying deity who brings destruction to YHWH's own people, some of the ancient audience of survivors of the traumas of war and exile might have resonated with this portrayal of YHWH, as suggested in O'Connor's studies applying trauma theory.[7] She contends that the metaphors of a violent God are a way of "keeping God alive" in the crises of faith that are common to survivors of tragedy:[8]

> Defeat by Babylon meant for Judah, among other things, that God lost the war to superior deities, to the more powerful Marduk [chief Babylonian deity] and his pantheon. Defeat meant that Judah's God is ineffectual and disappeared.... [The portrayal of God as violent] says that Judah's God is powerful, active, and present, lord of the world and not a defeated lesser being. To make God the active agent of Judah's humiliation is to insist that Babylonian deities have not triumphed, nor has ungoverned Fate propelled events.[9]

When the poet later in the chapter adds communal wickedness as a divine motive to this portrayal of a violent God, the result is the troubling sin-punishment theology so frequently and easily misappropriated today by onlookers blaming victims for their suffering. To some of the defeated ancient Judeans, however, acknowledgement of communal guilt might have served to lend the community a sense of agency and hope for change. As O'Connor suggests, "Jeremiah's rhetoric of human responsibility is a survival strategy, another way to make sense of incoherent, inexplicable events. When the poetry lays responsibility for toppling Judah upon the people, it moves victims out of despairing passivity . . . and shows them how to avoid similar perils in the future."[10] As we will see, however, not all the voices in this polyphonic poem will adopt this theology.[11]

7. O'Connor, "Reclaiming Jeremiah's Violence," 37–49; and *Pain and Promise*.
8. O'Connor, *Pain and Promise*, 42.
9. O'Connor, *Pain and Promise*, 55.
10. O'Connor, *Pain and Promise*, 56.
11. Mandolfo's intriguing study *Daughter Zion Talks Back to the Prophets* views the prophets as essentially monologic: "Allowing for their differences, all the prophets assume that Zion is to blame for her loss of subjectivity, that she has abandoned her *true* identity and selfhood through her rebellion" (54). Her discussion of the prophets focuses mainly on the marriage metaphor, about which the above statement rings true;

YHWH Warns Jerusalem: "A Lion Has Risen" (v. 7)

Now YHWH turns to direct address to the personified Jerusalem, the presumed antecedent of the pronoun *your*, a feminine singular form in the Hebrew phrases translated *your land* and *your cities* in verse 7. As we have discussed in the previous chapter, the personified Jerusalem/Zion is more than the physical city itself or its population, although it includes both. It poetically connotes the transcendent significance of the city as the site of YHWH's temple, or the spirit of the city. In the lines below, *your land* can refer to the whole land of Judah, with its capital and spiritual center Jerusalem; and *your cities* could designate the fortified cities protecting the geographical Jerusalem and embracing the principles symbolized by the city.

A lion	has risen	from his thicket.
A destroyer of nations	has set out	
	has gone	from his place
		to make your land a desolation.

Your cities will fall to ruin,

without inhabitant.

In this personal address to Lady Jerusalem, the *evil from the North* becomes the metaphorical lion setting out with purpose from his den. The verbal column, arranged in narrative sequence—*has risen, has set out, has gone*—and with the deliberative term *has set out*, develops an unusual image of a lion's planned, rather than merely instinctual, progress from his rise to his hunt for a particular prey.[12] We note how the parallels in the first three

---

but generalization to all prophetic texts, in my view, is too extreme. Also interested in polyphony or dialogic theology, Mandolfo turns to Lamentations 1–2 to find a voice of protest. I will argue that we can find polyphony even within individual prophetic texts, such as Jeremiah 4.

12. Holladay notes that the Hebrew נָסַע, *to set out*, conveys deliberate movement: "Its connotation is of schedules and itineraries, being used of nomads starting out, of Israelites moving out from one camping spot to another in the wilderness. But never elsewhere is it used for a wild animal; this lion moves not as a wild animal does, by impulse, but deliberately, by plan, for this lion is the foe from the north" (*Jeremiah 1*, 154).

lines "unravel" in the next three non-parallel lines, each simply moving forward in specification:

> ... to make your land a desolation.
> Your cities will fall to ruin,
> without inhabitant.

In Hebrew each line is rhythmically shorter than the previous one (7–6–4 syllables), appropriate to the imagined progress of the lion stalking, approaching, and seizing the prey. Who is this lion, identified by the parallel as *a destroyer of nations*? The first exilic and post-exilic audiences probably heard the phrase as a reference to Babylon, the destroyer of Judah and its neighbors; but the ultimate agent of destruction has already been identified as YHWH. Some might even have heard an echo of the supernatural Destroyer (same Hebrew term מַשְׁחִית), the instrument of Death slaying the first-born of Egypt in the plague story. While the immediate prey in Jeremiah 4:7 is Jerusalem, the fortified cities, and the whole land of Judah, the image of the deity as a lion is not without solace to defeated peoples. From the perspective of the post-exilic community, the first audience of the whole poem in Jeremiah 4, they have already been prey to the furious lion; but the one who is *destroyer of nations* could also turn against the oppressor. A ferocious, dangerous deity, who even turns against his people, might be—in the view of a traumatized community—preferable to a complacent or powerless god.

YHWH Commands Communal Mourning (v. 8)

Ironically balancing the sets of three imperatives calling the watchmen to prepare the Judeans for invasion (vv. 5–6), now three masculine plural imperatives command mourning, as if the death of the community is inevitable.[13] Fleeing for refuge to the fortified cities will be ineffective against the Northern foe.

---

13. Holladay notes the irony here in *Jeremiah 1*, 147.

Because of this	gird on (m.pl.) sackcloth,
	lament
	and wail:
	"The fierce wrath of YHWH
	has not turned from us."

While the speaker might possibly have shifted from YHWH to the prophetic persona, who often has the role of calling the people to repentance or mourning,[14] there seems no compelling reason to imagine a change in speaker here. The pattern of three imperatives and a dictated speech (italics) continues YHWH's manner of address from verses 5–6. Here YHWH addresses the people as a whole, rather than the watchmen, explicitly commanding them to link their ruin to divine anger. These opening sections of the poem do not focus on the specific reason for YHWH's wrath, only the raw force of it and its effects.

Hearts of Leaders Fail on That Day (v. 9)

After YHWH addresses the watchmen, Lady Jerusalem, and the general population of the city, a short oracle of YHWH, introduced by the "doomsday" signal *on that day*, rhythmically pronounces the failure of Judah's leaders.

It shall happen on that day—saying of YHWH—

the heart of the king	will fail,
and the heart of the officials.	
The priests	will be appalled,
and the prophets	will be astounded.

---

14. Holladay, *Jeremiah 1*, 137, 146.

As we have seen in Joel, *that day* signifies the Day of YHWH, identifying the disaster of invasion as a time of divine judgment. Critique focusses on the leaders of the Judean community—the king, officials, priests, and prophets—all stunned and ineffectual in the face of disaster. *Courage,* the frequent translation of the literal *heart,* captures the general meaning; courage of the leaders will fail. But Timothy Polk's explanation is richer: ". . . 'heart' is used in addressing and characterizing people as moral agents responsible for what they make of themselves through their exercise or neglect of the capacities proper to and constitutive of human subjects. This use of 'heart' . . . [relates] to the moral agency of selfhood. . . ."[15] The intense verbs *will fail, will be appalled, and will be astounded* suggest the surprise and extremity of the leaders' response to the Day of YHWH.

Jeremiah Objects (v. 10)

One of those prophets is astounded not into silence but into speech. Just as we imagine the shock of the king, officials, priests, and prophets, the poet abruptly turns the focus on a new unnamed first-person speaker, which we might identify as one of those prophets—the brazen Jeremiah himself—crying out urgently against YHWH.

Then I said, "Ah, Adonai YHWH,
surely you have utterly deceived this people and Jerusalem,
saying, '*You shall have peace,*'
when the sword has reached to the throat!"

The poet presents the words of Jeremiah as one continuous utterance without parallels—just a smooth slide from accusation of divine deceit to the evidence.[16] How bold and intense is his protest! He begins with the interjection *Ah,* enhanced by assonance of the initial *aleph* (א) in three

---

15. Polk, *Prophetic Persona,* 49.

16. We could as easily record this verse as prose, as many translations do. In my view poetic lineation seems preferable because of the surrounding poetic context; the recognition that poetic lines do not always include parallels; and the significance of each one of the four sections of Jeremiah's extended sentence, which readers can attend to more carefully with the division into phrases or clauses.

of the first four words of the Hebrew (אֲהָהּ אֲדֹנָי יהוה אָכֵן). The Jeremiah persona rhetorically calls for YHWH's assent with *surely*, and he intensifies the verb *deceived* with a Hebrew construction which repeats the verb in two different forms, here rendered as *utterly deceived*. The strong accusatory verb (the same one applied to the serpent's deception of Eve in Genesis 3:13 and to the false prophets in Jeremiah 29:8) and the alleged quotation of YHWH attribute to the deity the deceptive promise of peace for Jerusalem, coming from the mouth of the false prophets elsewhere in the book of Jeremiah. Jeremiah's protest concludes with an image opposite to peace—a sword poised to slice throats.

So bold is this accusation that some ancient translators and modern commentators "correct" the identity of the speaker here from Jeremiah (the *I* of the text) to *they*, the false prophets who oppose Jeremiah and YHWH.[17] Certainly that change would be consistent with the rest of the book of Jeremiah, in which it is the false prophets of Jerusalem—not Jeremiah—who claim YHWH has promised, *You shall not see the sword, nor shall you have famine, but I will give you true peace in this place* (14:13). When Jeremiah complains about these prophets, who contradict his own warnings of impending disaster to the city, YHWH affirms Jeremiah, saying that his opponents *are prophesying lies in my name* (14:14). But in 4:10 Jeremiah accuses *YHWH* of promising peace. Consistency is not a hallmark of the polyphonic book of Jeremiah. The text does not offer confident pronouncements, consistent dogmas, or unchanged personae but gives voice to community struggles to understand the role of YHWH in the face of the ruin of YHWH's beloved city and disaster to the covenant people. The verse can stand without emendation. In Jeremiah 4:10, then, it is the voice of the Jeremiah persona himself who attributes to YHWH deceptive promises of peace and conveys the sense of betrayal by YHWH, which the Judeans must have felt in the disasters of defeat and exile. After YHWH's voice commands flight from coming invasion, warns of inevitable ruin of all the cities of Judah, orders lamentation, takes responsibility for the attack, and shuts down communal leaders in open-mouthed astonishment, this bold prophetic persona expresses the vigorous protest of those in the traumatized audience who find no solace in the power of YHWH and even wonder if YHWH

17. Greek Codex Alexandrinus; see notes in BHS; Carroll, *Jeremiah*, 161, also supplies names of other commentators. Even Biddle, who otherwise takes care with identification of speakers, offers no defense of his view that Jeremiah 4:9–10 is "a prose comment on false prophets.... Jeremiah 4 does not portray a prophet participating in his people's sorrow and anguish" (22). Biddle's concluding chapter summarizing the voices throughout the book of Jeremiah is, however, helpful in recognizing a consistent prophetic persona, whose "complaints all reflect the concern that YHWH be proven just" (117). The voice I have identified as Jeremiah's in 4:10 fits this characterization.

can be trusted. The prophet receives no direct answer; the poet refuses to mitigate the force of Jeremiah's protest or harmonize it with other voices but lets it stand as an independent witness.

A Sirocco Saying (vv. 11–12)

A narrative voice now briefly introduces a saying with an echo of YHWH's previous speech; the opening to this section, *At that time* . . . , recalls the introduction of the saying of YHWH from verse 9: *It shall happen on that day*. That YHWH is the speaker of this saying about the wind is admittedly disputable. I am taking my cue from the reference to *My-Daughter-People* as YHWH's own designation for the covenant people of Judah.[18]

---

¹¹At that time it will be said

      to this people

      and to Jerusalem:

"A glowing wind   from the bare heights
                           in the wilderness

              toward My-Daughter-
              People,

                          not to winnow

                          and not to cleanse,

¹²a wind too
  strong for
  these   has come from me."

Now it is I also who will speak

judgments against them.

---

18. Others attribute the saying to the Jeremiah persona. See, for example, Berridge, *Prophet, People, and the Word of Yahweh*, 111–2; Lee, "Prophet and Singer in the Fray," 196; Henderson, "Who Weeps?" 195–6. Pilarski, "Study of the References to בת־עמי in Jeremiah 8:18—9:2(3)," 20–35, offers a convincing discussion arguing that YHWH is the speaker in the בת־עמי passages.

As most readers recognize, the glowing wind refers to the sirocco coming from the desert toward Jerusalem, bringing scorching heat and sand. It is not the useful wind which helps farmers separate grain from the chaff or cleanses the air from pollutants and rank odors but the hot, stifling air that saps strength, withers vegetation, and covers all things with grit. We note how the poet lingers on the description of the movement of the wind from the bare heights of the desert toward YHWH's beloved people, personified as My-Daughter-People,[19] and on the destructive power of the wind before identifying it as coming for YHWH's own purposes.[20] Although the image is clear, there is some ambiguity about whether we should read the lines as literal or metaphorical. Is the text suggesting that a literal sirocco should be regarded as judgment from YHWH, or is the scorching wind a metaphor for the destructiveness of the Babylonian invaders? The multivalent language of poetry does not require a choice. Perhaps it is both in this poem; a literal sirocco could even be a harbinger of the human terror to come. Of course the more difficult ambiguity is the character of YHWH, who recognizes the people as "Daughter" and yet sends the withering wind and prepares to speak direct judgment against them.

The Watchmen Cry, "Woe!" (v. 13)

Before YHWH can speak those words of judgment announced in verse 12, another voice cries out in panic. The lines in this new verse read like a continuation of the words YHWH has commanded the watchmen to cry to their cities at the beginning of the poem:

> "Blow the *šôfār* in the land! . . .
> Assemble together and let us go to the fortified cities.
> Raise a signal toward Zion.
> Take refuge! Do not tarry!" (vv. 5–6)

Now in direct speech these watchmen spy the approaching army.

---

19. For recent discussions of בת־עמי (here translated *My-Daughter-People*) as YHWH's designation for the people in Jeremiah, see O'Connor, *Pain and Promise*, 63; Biddle, *Polyphony and Symphony*, 30–31; Maier, *Daughter Zion, Mother Zion*, 88; and Pilarski, "Study of the Reference to בת־עמי in Jeremiah 8:18—9:2(3)," 20–35.

20. This interpretation involves a translation of לי as *"from me"* in the line *A wind too strong for these has come from me*. More literally the preposition means *to me* (appropriate if the speaker is the prophet) or *for me*. I am interpreting the prepositional phrase to mean *for me* in the sense of "for my purposes." See discussion in Holladay, *Jeremiah 1*, 156.

Look!	He		rises	like clouds!
				Like a whirlwind
	his chariots—			
	His horses		are swifter	than eagles!

Woe to us, for we are devastated!

Although this cry of the watchmen separates the announcement of YHWH's judgment in verse 12 from the words of that judgment in the next section of the poem, it connects to the previous speech through the image of wind. The scorching wind from the desert becomes the cloud of dust and the whirl of chariots here. Throughout the poem the terrifying drama of invasion unfolds through the voice of the watchmen, twice in secondary quotations (vv. 5–6, 16) and here in direct speech. With the watchmen we see the approach of the invading army and feel the panic of the people of Jerusalem. The chart of parallels highlights the rich visual imagery of the description of the coming army—*like clouds, like a whirlwind, (swifter) than eagles*—and effectively exposes the lone, emphatic line: *Woe to us, for we are devastated!* Because the voice of YHWH is silenced for the unmediated speech of the watchmen, this memory of the terror of invasion gains a forceful and independent hearing in this rich, polyphonic poem.

YHWH Calls Jerusalem to Repentance (v. 14)

As the army approaches, YHWH addresses Lady Jerusalem personally (feminine singular *you/your*) for a second time, now with a call to repentance as well as a word of judgment.

> Wash your heart from evil, O Jerusalem,
> in order that you might be delivered.
> How long will there lodge in your midst
> your troublesome schemes?

To be sure, identification of YHWH as speaker is a subjective judgment, since the text does not label the speaker. Many interpreters recognize the voice of the prophet Jeremiah here, for it is often a prophet's role to call people to repentance in the light of YHWH's judgments.[21] Paying attention to poetic style, we could also note that a set of four non-parallel lines describes the earlier protest speech of Jeremiah (v. 10; see also v. 18, if we were to assign those lines to the prophet). Since YHWH, as depicted in this poem, has not previously called for repentance or held out any hope for deliverance, it would be reasonable to attribute these lines to the persona of Jeremiah. That would certainly be a compelling option for reading these lines. However, another possibility is to hear the voice of YHWH here, primarily on the basis of the direct address to the personified Jerusalem. In this reading of the poem, one of its layers is the story of the tortured relationship between YHWH and "his" beloved Jerusalem.[22] Therefore when the speaker addresses Jerusalem directly as a woman, I will hear in the lines the voice of YHWH. Apparent in the physical images of *your heart* and *your entrails/ innards* (the literal translation of *your midst*)[23] is the metaphor of a person-to-person encounter between YHWH and Lady Jerusalem.

If one interprets YHWH as the speaker, the content of the passage is mystifying. How does the invitation to repent *that you might be delivered* relate to the earlier pronouncements of inevitable doom? The lion has already set forth, and YHWH has already pronounced that *your cities will fall to ruin, / without inhabitant* (v. 7). The sword has already *reached to the throat* (v. 10), the watchmen can see the chariots approaching, and Jerusalem's people know they are devastated (v. 14). How can there be any hope for deliverance? One possibility is to interpret the passage diachronically, highlighting the layers of editing. In this case the call for repentance and hope for deliverance could be attributed to the first pre-disaster rendition of the prophet's words, or, alternatively, this could be a post-exilic addition giving survivors hope for restoration. Passages on the inevitability of invasion, while perhaps delivered before the event, would have been preserved and repeated after the defeat of Jerusalem.[24] Consistency of thought is not likely to be characteristic of a text which grows through reapplication of prophetic words to new situations.

21. For example, Holladay, *Jeremiah 1*, 147.

22. O'Connor offers a very perceptive discussion of the family metaphor and its effects in her chapter "A Family Comes Undone: The Metaphor of a Broken Family (Jeremiah 2:1—4:4)," in *Pain and Promise*, 35–45.

23. Holladay, *Jeremiah 1*, 158: "Jrm plays on the image of baneful schemes lodging both in the geographical middle of the city and also of their lodging deep within the character of the city."

24. For a diachronic interpretation, see Carroll, *Jeremiah*, 164.

Another possibility is to try to make sense of the poem as a literary whole. As suggested above, one way of handling the apparent contradiction would be to regard YHWH as the speaker of passages threatening inevitable doom and the prophet as the voice calling for repentance and holding out hope for deliverance. However, another reading, the one proposed here, recognizes the ambivalence in the depiction of YHWH throughout the book of Jeremiah. From this perspective the same wrathful divine persona which threatens—and knows—Jerusalem's inevitable fate also never abandons the call to communal repentance and renewed covenant.

A Narrator Hears YHWH's Command to Proclaim, "Here [They Are]!"[25] (vv. 15–17)

Before YHWH's accusatory address to Jerusalem resumes, the dramatic reporting of the approach of the invaders intensifies, with a narrator overhearing YHWH's command that watchmen announce the arrival of the invading army.

[15]For a voice	declares		from Dan
	and reports	trouble	from Mount Ephraim:
[16]Proclaim	to the nations:	"Here [they are]!"	
Report	against Jerusalem:		
"Guards	are coming	*from a distant land.*	
They	raise their voices	*against the cities of Judah.*	
		[17]*Like watchmen of a field*	
they	have become	*against her round about."*	

---

25. The translation below accepts the frequent suggestion to repoint the MT הִנֵּה "look"—never otherwise standing alone—to הֵנָּה "Here [they are]." See Holladay, *Jeremiah 1*, 158.

<u>For against *me* she has rebelled—</u>

<u>saying of YHWH</u>

Appropriate to the dramatic and polyphonic nature of the poem, in which the plot is enacted through speech, this section is multi-layered. A narrator overhears a voice from afar; the voice, later identified as YHWH's, commands the watchmen what to say; and their words will report the invasion as it progresses. So we have three layers of alarm here:

Narrator's audition (plain type above)

YHWH's command and motive (underlined words)

Words the watchmen are commanded to proclaim (italics).

Although this section interrupts YHWH's direct accusatory speech to Lady Jerusalem, the poet links this new fragment to the previous lines through the spotlight on Jerusalem and the Hebrew term *'āwen*, (אָוֶן, "trouble"). Jerusalem's unspecified *troublesome schemes* (probably better translated *evil schemes* in verse 14, but with the loss of the connection between verses 14 and 15 in the translation) are related to the *trouble* coming from Dan and then Mount Ephraim. Although the exact crimes of Jerusalem remain vague in this poem, the narrator's voice here nevertheless relates the evil deeds of the city to the consequences. Through the narrator we hear the enemy's approach from the North to Dan, the northernmost city of Israel; then further south to the Ephraimite hill country; and finally—in the voice of YHWH and the watchmen—to the city of Jerusalem itself.

Echoing the opening of the poem, YHWH first enters this fragment as a voice directed to the watchmen. They must not only make proclamation to Jerusalem, the ultimate target of the attack from the North, but also to all the nations as witnesses of the invasion of the city (recall 6:18–19, where YHWH also addresses all nations to witness the demise of Jerusalem). As in the opening commands, the words the guards must speak narrow the focus from *a distant land* to *the cities of Judah* and finally to Jerusalem herself. The identification of the invaders as נֹצְרִים, here translated as *guards*, and sometimes used of keepers of vineyards (Isa 27:3; Job 27:18) or fig trees (Prov 27:18), relates well to the following simile for the invaders, who are *like watchmen of a field*. Here the poet compares the enemies to farmers who set up booths, temporary shelters, in fields and vineyards at harvest time to be near their work and to maintain vigilance against thieves. Ironically, the "watchmen" from the North have laid claim to Jerusalem by surrounding her and maintaining a vigilant siege until she surrenders. The voice of YHWH then links the invasion to Lady Jerusalem's rebellion: *For against me she has rebelled.* It is important to note here that the voice of the narrator who introduces YHWH's words—or even the voice of YHWH itself—is not necessarily equivalent to the view of the writer of the poem, who presents a multivalent perspective by giving voice to personae with different viewpoints. Not all voices in the poem adopt the rebellion-punishment theology conveyed by YHWH in this section.

YHWH Rebukes Jerusalem for Misery of Her Own Making (v. 18)

Now YHWH returns to addressing Jerusalem directly with a rebuke linked to the previous third-person indictment of rebellion through a word-play between *mārātāh, she has rebelled* (מָרָתָה) and *mār, surely bitter* (מָר), once again connecting deeds and consequences.[26]

> Your way and your deeds
> have done these things to you.
> This is your misery—surely bitter—
> for it has reached to your heart.

Although the rebellious deeds of Jerusalem remain unspecified at this point, the metaphorical language personalizes the relationship between YHWH and Lady Jerusalem, suggesting that both the problem and the pain it causes are deeply entrenched as matters of the heart (*Wash your heart from evil*—v. 14; *[Your misery] has reached your heart*—v. 18).

---

26. Without comment on the word-play here, Miller nevertheless emphasizes the "direct connection between the conduct and its consequences" in these verses in "Book of Jeremiah," 613. Translators face a couple of challenges with the phrase כִּי מָר, rendered here as *surely bitter*. I am reading this first appearance of כִּי in the verse as asseverative, *surely*. The adjective מָר appears as masculine, which does not agree with the feminine form of *misery*, the noun it modifies.

Lady Jerusalem Cries from the Heart (vv. 19–21)

In one of the most intense fragments of the text, the poet finally summons up Lady Jerusalem herself, who cries from the heart. She does not acknowledge YHWH's accusation of evil deeds, cry for help, or repent; instead her independent voice bears witness to her terror and agony.

---

¹⁹My anguish!
    [lit., my belly]

My anguish!   I   writhe!

The walls of my
    heart!

        My heart   is tumultuous
                              within me!

        I   cannot be silent;

   for   I   hear   the sound of the
                                          šôfār,

                                        the alarm of war.

²⁰Shattering upon shattering is proclaimed!

For   the whole earth   is devastated!

   Suddenly   my tents   are devastated,

   in a moment   my curtains.

²¹How long   must I see   the signal,

                must I hear   the sound of the šôfār?

That it is Lady Jerusalem who speaks here requires some argument, since many commentators have assigned the lines to the prophet Jeremiah.[27] The

---

27. For example Bright, *Jeremiah*, 34; Miller, "Book of Jeremiah," 614; Volz, *Prophet Jeremia*, 56; Holladay, *Jeremiah 1*, 137; Polk, *Prophetic Persona*, 35–57; Brueggemann,

passage most closely resembles Jeremiah 10:19-21, where the image of a woman setting up the curtains of a tent for her children applies better to Lady Jerusalem's activity than to childless Jeremiah:

> Woe is me because of my wound!
> My injury is severe.
> But I have said, "Surely this is my sickness,
> and I must bear it."
> My tent is devastated,
> and all my tent-cords are snapped.
> My children have left and are no more.
> There is no one stretching out my tent any longer,
> nor setting up my curtains. . . .
> For the shepherds are stupid. . . .

For a positive use of the same image, we can turn to Isaiah 54, where YHWH commands the barren woman Jerusalem to *broaden the place of your tent; / stretch out the curtains of your dwelling* (v.2). Furthermore, the writhing[28] and pain in the belly or womb in Jeremiah 4:19—Hebrew *mēʿeh*, which I have translated as *anguish* for a less jarring English reading than the literal *belly*—suggest labor pains (see also Gen 25:23; Isa 49:1; Ps 71:6; Ruth 1:11 with מעה as *belly* or *womb*; חול as the writhing of labor in Isa 13:8; 21:3; 23:4; 26:17-18; 45:10; 54:1; 66:7-8; Jer 6:24; 22:23; 50:43; Mic 4:9-10; Ps 48:7). The identity of the speaker as Jerusalem rather than Jeremiah here also helps us perceive the movement of the poem, which progresses from a third-person announcement of doom (*Like watchmen of a field / they have become against her round about*—v. 17) to second person accusation (*Your way and your deeds / have done these things to you*—v. 18) to a climax, the anguished cry of Jerusalem herself here. We experience the painful intensity of the poem in the visceral references to the stomach and heart and the sensations of feeling, hearing, and seeing. The dense repetition of the poem suggests that Jerusalem cries out in an urgent stutter: *My anguish! My anguish! . . . my heart / my heart . . . shattering upon shattering . . . earth is devastated . . . tents*

Commentary on Jeremiah, 57-59. Carroll, *Jeremiah*, 167, argues for the land or city as speaker; O'Connor identifies Jerusalem as the speaker in *Pain and Promise*, 51; as do Biddle in *Polyphony*, 21; Kumaki, "New Look at Jer 4,19-22 and 10,19-21," 113-22; and Korpel in "Who Is Speaking in Jeremiah 4:19-22?" 88-98. I have previously made the case for Jerusalem as speaker in my article, "Poet as 'Female Impersonator,'" 166-74. Some of the defense here borrows from that earlier article.

28. With many commentators I am emending the MT אוֹחִילָה *I wait* to אָחוּלָה *I writhe* in verse 19.

are devastated . . . I hear the sound of the šôfār . . . I hear the sound of the šôfār. Reading vertically through the columns of verse 20, we also notice the kind of focusing we have seen earlier in the columns. Jerusalem hyperbolically sees the whole earth as devastated; then the dwellings, the tents of the city, are devastated; and finally the lens focuses on the curtains of the tents. Later her focus will zoom outward again toward the broadest possible portrayal of ruin—the devastation of the whole cosmos.

YHWH the Sage Declares the Children Foolish (v. 22)

Jerusalem's urgent cry incongruously[29] summons the voice of YHWH the Wisdom Teacher, delivering a critical evaluation of Jerusalem's children rather than responding to her pain.

My people	are stupid.		
		Me	they do not know.
They	are foolish sons.		
They	are not discerning.		
They	are wise	to do evil;	
		but *to do good*	they do not know.

Reading vertically through the second column, we can appreciate the effect of the rhetorical strategy of foregrounding, establishment of a pattern, so that the audience feels the jolt when expectations are overturned. YHWH describes the people as *stupid / foolish / not discerning*, but finally *wise*. Of course, the irony is that the wisdom they exhibit is wisdom *to do evil*. The structure here is quite ornate, with all six lines linked in some way to others in the section. Repetition and syntax link *Me they do not know* with *but to do good they do not know*, with the infinitive phrase *to do good* functioning as an object parallel to *Me*. Not to know (i.e., be in relationship to) YHWH is equivalent to not knowing how to act with goodness. At the same time, the

---

29. Korpel, "Who Is Speaking in Jeremiah 4:19–22?" adduces manuscript evidence to support her view that v. 22 is a later addition to the text (95–97). While this is probably correct, the effort here is to interpret the final poem as a whole, finding some significance in the discontinuities.

infinitive phrase *to do good* links to its opposite, *to do evil,* which completes the line *They are wise to do evil.* The lines are organized as an intricate network, appropriate to the discourse of the Wisdom Teacher here.

Jerusalem Envisions Cosmic Collapse (vv. 23–26)

Nothing in YHWH's distant, critical assessment of YHWH's people has prepared us for the intense first-person visionary account of cosmic collapse that follows:

I looked	at the earth			
	and lo!	—*tōhû wābōhû*—		
	and to the heavens	and there was no light.		
I looked	to the mountains			
	and lo!	[they were] quaking,		
			and all the hills	shook to and fro.
I looked	and lo!	there was no human,		
			and every bird of the heavens	had fled.
I looked	and lo!	the fertile land [was] a wilderness,		
			and all its cities	were torn down

before YHWH,

before his fierce wrath.

Identification of the speaker of these lines once again invites interpretive judgment. Usually commentators assign the lines to Jeremiah, whose account of a visionary experience, introduced by the phrase *I looked and lo!* resembles those of Ezekiel (chapters 3, 8, 10, 37), Daniel (chapters 8, 12) and Zechariah (chapters 1–6).³⁰ Robert Carroll regards the section as a later apocalyptic vision added by a post-exilic writer to reflect the experiences of Babylonian destruction.³¹ Although the poet who constructs the disparate fragments of Jeremiah 4 into a whole poem likely writes from a post-exilic perspective, the persona who speaks here could be the previous first-person voice, Lady Jerusalem, rather than Jeremiah or an anonymous post-exilic voice. Certainly there is nothing particular to female experience in these lines to identify the image of a woman here, but there is no reason for a male voice to be the default in a poem in which the YHWH-Jerusalem relationship is central. The Hebrew Bible attests to women prophets (e.g., Miriam, Deborah, Huldah, Noadiah, the prophetess in Isaiah 8, the vilified women prophets who have visions in Ezekiel 13, the daughters who will prophesy in Joel 3) and others with access to the divine (e.g., Hagar, who sees a manifestation of YHWH in Gen 16; Rebekah, who seeks YHWH and receives an oracle in Gen 25; the necromancer of En-dor in 1 Sam 28).³² The ancient audience would likely be able to imagine a woman—the metaphorical Jerusalem, in this case—having a visionary experience. But more specifically, Lady Jerusalem has just spoken in the poem (vv. 19–21), linking the devastation of her tents and curtains to the devastation of the whole earth (v. 20). Now we can imagine her lens zooming out to view the chaos of the whole cosmos on the basis of her vision.

I have left the phrase *tōhû wābōhû* without translation not only because of its great rhyme and rhythm, but also because it is the distinctive, untranslatable phrase describing the primordial chaos in Genesis 1:2

30. Holladay, *Jeremiah 1*, 151; Miller, "Book of Jeremiah," 614; Lee, "Prophet and Singer in the Fray," 196. On the basis of the observation that רָאִיתִי (*I looked*) has YHWH as the subject in the other four occurrences of the verb in Jeremiah, Korpel judges these to be words of YHWH. "[T]hat YHWH is spoken of in third person in v. 26 is not a decisive argument against attributing vv. 23–26 to God" because YHWH frequently refers to the divine self in third person ("Who Is Speaking in Jeremiah 4:19–22?" 92). However, those other four passages do not use the formulation רָאִיתִי וְהִנֵּה (*I looked and lo!*), most often indicative of a vision. While reference to YHWH in third person in v. 26 certainly doesn't rule out identity of YHWH as speaker, the formulaic introduction to a prophetic vision and the relative awkwardness of the third-person reference to YHWH in YHWH-speech argue against YHWH as speaker here and in favor of a prophetic voice. The argument here is that the "prophet" speaking in vv. 23–26 is not Jeremiah but Jerusalem.

31. Carroll, *Jeremiah*, 168.

32. See Gafney, *Women Prophets in Ancient Israel*; Stökel and Carvalho, *Prophets Male and Female*; and Hamori, *Women's Divination in Biblical Literature*. Hamori notes that in the biblical tradition "most women with special access to divine knowledge are depicted as living outside of other social norms as well" (220). Lady Jerusalem, however, is depicted as a wife and mother; but she is a special metaphorical character with unique access to YHWH.

(rendered *a formless void* in NRSV; *formless and empty* in New International Version; *a vast waste* in Revised English Bible; *welter and waste* in Alter's translation). The implication is that the speaker envisions the cosmos returning to the original chaos; this is a vision of the "virtual dismantling of creation."[33] Nevertheless, I do not view the poem as apocalyptic but rather as an example of the characteristic prophetic slide from the historic to the cosmic, conveying the terrible significance of the ruin of the holy city from the perspective of the traumatized audience. Ironically Lady Jerusalem's description of *tōhû wābōhû* is the most orderly—almost formulaic—section of the poem. One senses that Jerusalem feels compelled to contain the chaos through formalism in language. The anaphoric line *I looked . . . and lo!* repeats four times, each iteration introducing two images of collapsing creations: earth and heavens, mountains and hills, humans and birds, fertile land and cities. With a glance at the chart, we notice the increasing length of each verse, creating a quickening pace as a reader crams more and more words into the blocks created by the repeated formula. We also note that the speaker reserves the "punch line" for the conclusion—all events of this cosmic collapse are due to the fierce wrath of YHWH. The parallelism between *YHWH* and *fierce wrath* suggests that the salient characteristic of YHWH from Jerusalem's perspective is wrath.

As Biddle concludes in his book *Polyphony and Symphony*, Jerusalem's voice sounds a consistent note throughout the book of Jeremiah:

> Lady Zion, herself, speaks only in cries of despair and mourning. These exchanges, then, engender an impression of immediacy—an angry and cuckolded deity, a frightened and imperiled spouse and mother. Notably, Lady Zion offers no defense of her actions, either by way of excuse or explanation. She merely reacts to her fate. Whether by calculated intent or as an expression of an immediate context of crisis, the dialogue between YHWH and Lady Zion merits appreciation for its dramatic, violent, and emotive force.[34]

Although Biddle does not identify Lady Jerusalem as the speaker in Jeremiah 4:23–26, his description of her consistent voice in the book of Jeremiah as despairing, mourning, dramatic, violent, and emotive would be additional evidence for recognizing her voice in these lines.

---

33. Miller, "Book of Jeremiah," 614.
34. Biddle, *Polyphony and Symphony*, 118.

YHWH Reveals Plans for Cosmic Desolation (vv. 27–28)

Addressing the general audience rather than Jerusalem herself, an oracle of YHWH delivered by the prophet (*Thus says YHWH* being the technical introduction to a prophetic speech) responds to Jerusalem's vision report, affirming that the cosmic disaster she has envisioned is consistent with YHWH's plans.

---

²⁷For thus says YHWH:

	The whole earth	shall become a desolation.		
			But a full end	I will not make.
Because of this	the earth	shall mourn,		
	and the heavens above	shall be dark.		
			For	I have spoken;
				I have planned;
				I have not relented;
				and I will not turn back from it.

Echoing the first sightings of Jerusalem's vision in the previous section, the subject column here—*the whole earth, the earth, the heavens above*—suggests that the coming disaster for Judah has cosmic significance. The Hebrew text of verse 27 highlights the term *desolation* (שְׁמָמָה *šemāmāh*) by placing it as the first word in the line, more literally rendered *A-desolation shall-become the-whole-earth*. In the interpretation proposed here, the passage is not an apocalyptic threat of future cosmic collapse but a God's-eye perspective on the *significance* of the historical events of the desolation of Judah, particularly the temple site of Jerusalem, mythical center of the whole earth. On this perspective Lady Jerusalem and YHWH agree.

The four final parallel clauses strike like blows to identify YHWH as the source of the collapse and to emphasize its inescapability: *I have spoken,*

I have planned, I have not relented, and I will not turn back from it [i.e. the planned desolation]. The outlier in this section is the line *But a full end I will not make*. Poetically the clause links both to the previous line through the rhyme between *šᵉmāmāh*, *desolation*, and *kālāh* (כָּלָה), *a full end* (also in first position in the line); and to the last four lines with YHWH as the first-person subject. The semantic tension, however, is great. How can YHWH both insist that there can be no reconsideration of the planned desolation of earth and heaven and then hold out a promise not to make a full end? Commentators usually propose changes to the Masoretic Text, such as Holladay's suggestion that the text should read, *None of it shall I remake*[35]; or they regard the line as a later addition from a post-exilic writer, who knows not all was lost.[36] Although it might well be the case that these occasional notes of restrained hope throughout Jeremiah 4–6 come from a late strand of editing (see also 5:10, where YHWH addresses the invaders: *But a full end do not make*; and 5:18: *Yet even in those days—saying of YHWH— / I will not make a full end of you*), this synchronic literary analysis considers the final poem, with all its jagged-edged fragments of traditions, memories, and reflections of traumatized people at various stages of their experience of disaster. Consistency is not a hallmark of such compositions. Not only do we hear a polyphony of contending voices; but even the voice of individual personae—notably YHWH and the prophet later in Jeremiah 5–6—can shift to reflect qualifications, new thoughts, and changes in perspective. And the most "shifty" of those personae in the book of Jeremiah is YHWH—depicted as a raging husband, ardent lover, wronged father, warrior, fountain of living water, etc.—sometimes threatening the collapse of the cosmos and sometimes calling for reconciliation. Just as the poetic devices of rhyme and syntactic parallelism hold the promise *But a full end I will not make* together with the absolutist threats of collapse, so the poet holds these contradictory thoughts together in the grand, polyphonic construction which is Jeremiah 4.

Every City Abandoned (v. 29)

As in Lady Jerusalem's visionary narrowing of focus from heavens and earth to the fertile land and its cities in 4:23–26, now YHWH—or perhaps a narrator or Jeremiah—turns from the cosmic perspective to report on the scene in the cities of Judah.

---

35. Holladay, *Jeremiah 1*, 166.
36. Carroll, *Jeremiah*, 170–1. Carroll uses the image of the text as a patch-work quilt, from a source-critical view.

At the sound of the horseman and the archer,

> every city   flees.
>
>   They   enter   into the thickets;
>
>   climb   among the rocks.
>
> Every city   is abandoned,
>
>   with no one dwelling in them.

Holladay notes the irony that the usual flight in warfare is toward the protection of the fortified cities, to which the watchmen were commanded to summon the Judeans in the opening verses of the poem; but here the city dwellers flee for safety out of the cities toward caves and thickets in the countryside.[37] Perhaps there is not so much irony here as a chronicling of the progress of the invasion throughout the poem and in historical reality. Initially the inhabitants of the countryside were summoned to flee to the cities: *Assemble together and let us go to the fortified cities* (v. 5). Then the watchmen spied the chariots coming like a whirlwind in the distance (v. 13) and later reported that the cities of Judah and then Jerusalem herself were surrounded by troops *like watchmen of a field* (v. 17). It fell to Lady Jerusalem herself to report the ruin of the city in the metaphor of her devastated tents and curtains (v. 20) and her vision that all the cities of Judah were torn down (v. 26). With no defenses left, everyone remaining has now fled to the thickets and rocks of the countryside, as YHWH had warned in YHWH's initial address to Jerusalem: *Your cities will fall to ruin / without inhabitant* (v. 7). With this echo of the earlier threat to Lady Jerusalem in the lines above, YHWH now turns to address personified Jerusalem once again.

---

37. Holladay, *Jeremiah 1*, 169. The meaning of the Hebrew term translated *thickets* is uncertain.

YHWH Rebukes Jerusalem for Her Desperate Vanity (v. 30)

Seeing all her tents and curtains ruined and her population fleeing, Lady Jerusalem retains a desperate hope that her beauty might yet save her; but YHWH rebukes her for vanity.

And you—O Devastated One—what are you doing

that you put on	scarlet,
that you adorn yourself with	ornaments of gold,
that you enlarge your eyes with	kohl?

In vain you beautify yourself.

Those who lust after you	despise	you;
they	seek	your life.

In some ways the writer has prepared the audience for this climactic shard of poetry. The narrowing of the lens from a wide angle to the city of Jerusalem has characterized much of the poem from the beginning: *in the land / toward the fortified cities / toward Zion* (vv. 5–6); *from a distant land / against the cities of Judah / against her [=Jerusalem] round about* (vv. 16–17); *the whole earth / my tents / my curtains* (v. 20); and *the whole earth / every city* of YHWH's oracle in vv. 28–29 before the present verse on Jerusalem. YHWH has previously addressed Lady Jerusalem directly to warn her about the coming destruction (v. 7), to call her to a "heart washing" (v. 14), and to register the doom which has reached to her heart (v. 18). The thematic word *devastated* (שדד) has appeared in the watchmen's cry of panic, *Woe to us, for we are devastated!* (v. 13) and in Jerusalem's description of the condition of the earth and her own tents (v. 20). Now this term is YHWH's appellative of the city herself: *O Devastated One.*[38] What renders this sec-

---

38. Korpel also recognizes these connections in "Who Is Speaking in Jeremiah 4:19–22." 98.

tion unique within the poem is the detailed development of the metaphor. We note how the poet lingers on Jerusalem's elaborate preparations to meet *those who lust after* her, highlighting the rich colors of her scarlet clothing, gold jewelry, and black eye powder. The metaphor of Jerusalem desperately beautifying herself for lovers functions here as a critique of her dependence on foreign alliances. In later chapters of the book of Jeremiah we read the stories of Jerusalem's attempts to secure her safety through alliances with Edom, Moab, Ammon, Tyre, and Sidon (Chapter 27) and her unstable diplomatic relations with Egypt and Babylon. The description of the invaders as lovers turned vicious intensifies and personalizes the story of Jerusalem's foreign affairs. Through the metaphor the audience feels the shock and pain of Jerusalem's ruin and senses the disdain of the rejected Protector YHWH, who calls her efforts vanity.

A Cry like a Woman in Labor (v. 31)

The poem shifts again as a first-person speaker, whom I identify as YHWH,[39] turns away from direct address *to* Jerusalem to a report *about* her. Here YHWH names Jerusalem *Daughter Zion*, an endearing title for the city, calling attention to the personification of Jerusalem as a woman, her close relation to her Father-Protector YHWH, and the temple on Mount Zion.[40]

---

39. Another possibility, however, is to imagine the speaker of these lines as the persona Jeremiah. In this case, one reads the Hebrew *kî* as the untranslated particle denoting a change of speaker. Holladay, *Jeremiah 1*, imagines this shift to a new speaker and a different, more sympathetic image of Jerusalem—from the whore of YHWH's speech (more accurately, wayward daughter) to the woman in labor: "[O]ne must take account of the curious way in which Jrm 'corrects' Yahweh's imagery by his own. Jrm has offered the tenderer image of the woman in labor instead of the more brutal image of the whore perceived to be voiced by Yahweh. But both images are communicated to us through Jrm's perception, both his perception of Yahweh's utterance and his perception of his own utterance. . . . [O]ne is duty-bound to listen to Jrm's perception and become aware of the tension within him between what he would like to say and what he hears Yahweh say" (172). (Holladay views Jeremiah as the prophet-speaker rather than a poetic persona.)

40. There is a lively discussion of the meaning of the title בַּת־צִיּוֹן *Daughter Zion* or *Daughter of Zion*). See Floyd, "Welcome Back, Daughter of Zion!" 484–504, and "Daughter of Zion Goes Fishing," 177–200; J. Andrew Dearman, "Daughter Zion and Her Place in God's Household," 144–59; Maier, *Daughter Zion, Mother Zion* and "Daughter Zion as Queen and the Iconography of the Female City," 147–62. I will not engage the arguments here, but I am reading the title as *Daughter Zion* and recognizing her as the same entity as Lady Jerusalem, the metaphorical woman who is being attacked by her lovers in v. 30 and now cries in terror.

For I hear	a voice		as of one in labor,
	distress		as of one bearing her first-born,
	the voice of Daughter Zion.		
She	gasps;		
she	stretches out	her palms.	

In the chart above we can observe the poetic skill in construction of the lines. Reading vertically, we observe the gradual clarity of the audition. First the speaker YHWH hears a voice; then it emerges as a call of distress; finally YHWH identifies the voice as that of Daughter Zion. In the next section we will hear her words. The parallel between the similes also exemplifies intensification. The voice of Daughter Zion sounds the shrillest note of pain in the repertoire of Hebrew poets—the cry of one in labor. And this is not just any labor but the sharp, new experience of a young woman bearing her first child. Her cry is accompanied by a gasp and a stretching out of empty palms.

In this interpretation the poet imagines YHWH turning away from direct address to Lady Jerusalem/Daughter Zion with these lines on her painful cry to verify to the general audience the revelation that her lovers are treacherous and seek her life. A Hebrew word-play between *gasp* (תִּתְיַפֵּחַ *tityappēₐḥ*) and *beautify* (תִּתְיַפִּי *tityappî*–v. 30) underlines YHWH's angry irony that Jerusalem's attempts to beautify herself have indeed been futile.[41] The controlling image continues to be that of Jerusalem the desperate woman attempting to charm her lovers; it is only her cries of desperation—not Jerusalem herself—that resemble the sound of a woman in childbirth. This is a simile within a metaphor:

> Jerusalem the city beset by invaders, with whom it has troubled diplomatic relations
>> compared to a woman betrayed by her lovers, who seek her life (metaphor)
>>> woman's cry sounds like the cry of a woman in labor (simile).

41. Holladay, *Jeremiah 1*, 149.

The identity of Jerusalem here as *Daughter Zion* highlights the relationship between the personae of YHWH and Jerusalem. Keeping that troubled relationship in mind, we might hear more than angry irony and self-confirmation in YHWH's voice here. Previously YHWH's words commanded, rebuked, warned, threatened, and admonished. Only toward the end of the composition does the poet offer a couple hints that the persona of YHWH "hears" the voice of Jerusalem. YHWH's words, *The whole earth shall become a desolation. . . . / Because of this the earth shall mourn, / and the heavens above shall be dark* (vv. 27-28), echo Jerusalem's previous vision, *I looked at the earth, / and lo!—tōhû wābōhû— / and to the heavens, / and there was no light* (v. 23). Also YHWH's appellative for Jerusalem, *O Devastated One* (v. 30), picks up her own description of her tent dwellings as devastated (v. 20). Now YHWH explicitly "hears" Daughter Zion's cry of pain, lingering over the sound of her voice; YHWH recalls her status as *Daughter Zion* rather than simply *Devastated One*; and YHWH recognizes her desperate gesture as outstretched palms, the usual posture of prayer (Exod 9:29, 33; 1 Kgs 8:22, 38; 2 Chr 6:12, 13, 29; Ps 44:21). Elsewhere within the book of Jeremiah, YHWH will grieve over Daughter Zion (8:21—9:3, if we identify YHWH as speaker in those lines);[42] in this poem she at least gets a hearing at its close.

Daughter Zion Gets the Last Word (v. 31)

At the level of greatest intensity, Daughter Zion gasps the last words of the poem, a cry of anguish as she is set upon by her assailants. The scream as of one in childbirth is ironically a death wail.[43]

Woe is me!
My life faints away before murderers!

The cry has been anticipated earlier in verse 13, where the watchmen, seeing the approaching chariots, yell in panic, *Woe to us, for we are devastated*; but it intensifies here where the named female persona of Daughter Zion is the victim. The poet does not leave the audience with moral admonition,

42. O'Connor, *Pain and Promise*, 59-68.
43. O'Connor, *Pain and Promise*, 52.

resolution, or hope but with the raw panic of Daughter Zion as the sword reaches to her throat. How will YHWH respond? Will Lady Zion and YHWH finally enter into dialogue just as the one partner expires? Certainly this is an open-ended, dialogic poem; the story of YHWH and Jerusalem must continue.

Shaping the *Tōhû*: Order and Disorder in Jeremiah 4

With attention to the literary features of Jeremiah 4, we can conclude that the poet or scribal prophet, the one who assembled these eighteen pieces into a whole, was not simply an editor but a *creative* artist. That is, the poet's task was to begin shaping the *tōhû wābōhû* experience of the traumatized Judeans into meaningful order. Too much order, however, would betray the victims of violence, as the poem would lack integrity and not resonate with their lives. On the other hand, too much chaos would subvert the aims of a creative work, as no one would be able to apprehend communal meaning in the piece. The polyphonic arrangement of Jeremiah 4 masterfully negotiates between the experience of disorder and the urge for order.[44]

In several ways the polyphony lends order to the piece. For example, a survey of the voice of the watchmen, either in secondary speech from YHWH or in direct speech, reveals a dramatic sequence of events: the horn sounds to alert the Judeans of impending invasion, and the Judeans are summoned to flee to the cities (vv. 5–6); the watchmen see the clouds of dust of the coming chariots and know the Judeans are doomed (v. 13); and then the army arrives from the north and surrounds Jerusalem (vv. 16–17). This is performative language characteristic of drama, in which the utterances of the speakers enact the plot. The narrator has little to do besides occasionally providing some "stage directions" identifying the voice of Yahweh, because the plot unfolds steadily through the words of the watchmen, either direct or dictated by YHWH. The experience of invasion is not a descriptive but an emotive report; through the voices of the watchmen, the progress of the invasion connects with the rising panic of the Judeans.

The voice of Lady Jerusalem continues developing the story where the watchmen left off. Her sensual speeches enact the destruction of the city itself as she *feels* panic (*My anguish! My anguish! / The walls of my heart!*—v. 19), *hears* the sound of the *šôfār* (v. 19); and *sees* her ruined tents and curtains and the battle signals (v. 21). She tries to shape the chaos in formulaic

---

44. Perhaps this is most eloquently expressed by Stulman: "Prophetic meaning-making places disjunction and disaster within a context of meaning" ("Reading the Prophets," 163).

speech (*I looked . . . and lo!* four times—vv. 23–26) reporting a vision which links the destruction of the Judean cities to the collapse of the cosmos. The invasion has undone the world of the traumatized audience. Finally the spirit of the city of Jerusalem itself is snuffed out, as her voice enacts her death: *Woe is me! / My life faints away before murderers!* (v. 31). In these two voices—that of the watchmen and of Jerusalem—there is an unfolding plot capturing memories of Babylonian invasion; and each voice has its own emotional register, a kind of personality. These features of the polyphony lend order to the poem.

In addition, thematic words, word-plays, or images serve to modulate from one section to the next in much of the poem. We can discern a conscious effort to forge these connections if we bring together the examples noted in the paragraphs above. The *evil from the North* in vv. 5–6 becomes the metaphorical lion in v. 7; and the set of three imperatives commanding lamentation followed by a speech dictated by YHWH links v. 8 to the opening call to prepare for war with a similar syntactic structure. YHWH's oracle that *the prophets will be astounded* on *that day* (v. 9) ironically generates a protest from the prophetic persona (v. 10). The image of the *glowing wind* coming from the desert (v. 11–12) shifts to the cloud of dust and whirlwind of approaching chariots in the next section. The *troublesome schemes* which YHWH finds in Jerusalem (v. 14) link to the consequences—*trouble* coming from Dan to Mount Ephraim and then toward Jerusalem (vv. 15–17); similarly, it is because Jerusalem has rebelled (מָרָתָה *mārātāh*) against YHWH (v. 17) that she will meet a bitter (מָר *mār*) fate (v. 18). After YHWH tells Jerusalem that her misery has reached her heart (v. 18), the poet has Lady Jerusalem utter her own heart-rending cry (vv. 19–20). As mentioned above, Jerusalem's visionary report that the earth is *tōhû wābōhû* and the heavens have no light (v. 23) is affirmed by YHWH's following oracle that *the whole earth shall become a desolation . . . / and the heavens above shall be dark* (vv. 27–28). The word-play between *beautify* (*tityappî*—v. 30) and *gasp* (*tityappēªḥ*—v. 31) ironically links YHWH's angry address to Jerusalem for her vain efforts to save herself and the report that YHWH hears her gasp of distress. Finally, the parallel among *a voice, distress,* and *the voice of Daughter Zion* at the beginning of verse 31 prepares us to hear the words of her cry which conclude the poem. These links between sections; the sense of an unfolding plot; and the development of consistent personae of Lady Jerusalem and the watchmen, as well as the protesting prophet (who plays a surprisingly small role in the piece), lend the poem a sense of order and bear evidence of conscious, careful arrangement of the fragments.

However, several other strategies disrupt the order. YHWH's announcements of doom complicate the plot sequence because YHWH reveals the end already before the words of the watchmen and Jerusalem enact the invasion. At the beginning of the poem YHWH threatens Jerusalem with the lion, *the destroyer of nations* who *has gone from his place / to make your land a desolation./ Your cities will fall to ruin, / without inhabitant* (v. 7). YHWH commands lamentation, as if the death of Judah has already occurred (v. 8), and announces the coming of the Day of YHWH (v. 9) even before the watchmen sight the arrival of the chariots. The effect of such plot disruptions is to suggest that the fall of Judah, the unfolding human drama, is working according to a preconceived divine plan, not according to a natural sequence or the determination of invading Babylonian armies.

Despite all the threads connecting the eighteen sections outlined above, there are also notable discontinuities from section to section. Perhaps most important, Jeremiah's sharp protest, *Ah, Adonai YHWH, / surely you have utterly deceived this people and Jerusalem . . .* (v. 10), receives no answer or even acknowledgement from YHWH; and the prophet's challenge interrupts two sections describing what will happen *on that day / at that time* (vv. 9, 11). The watchmen's sighting of the chariots and cry, *Woe to us, for we are devastated!* (v. 13)—a recognition of inevitable doom—is followed incongruously by YHWH's suggestion that deliverance might be possible: *Wash your heart from evil, O Jerusalem, / in order that you might be delivered* (v. 14). But Lady Jerusalem's anguished cry of pain which follows does not respond to YHWH's indictment or call to repentance (vv. 19–21). She neither repents nor calls for help but intensely voices her terror. The distant tone and wisdom vocabulary of YHWH's denunciation in the next verse,

> My people are stupid.
> Me they do not know.
> They are foolish sons.
> They are not discerning.
> They are wise to do evil;
> but to do good they do not know (v. 22)

ignore Lady Jerusalem's anguish of heart in the preceding section and have little semantic connection to her cosmic vision of collapse which follows. Finally the poem ends on a dissonant note with Daughter Zion's death cry, which receives no response.

While the voices of Jerusalem, the prophet, and the watchmen establish consistent personae, the speeches of YHWH complicate the poem, as noted in the discussion of each section. Most often we hear the thundering of *the fierce wrath of YHWH* (v. 8; see also v. 26) in all its threatening and accusatory power. YHWH is *bringing evil from the North / and great shattering*

(v. 6) so that all the cities of Judah will *fall to ruin / without inhabitant* (v. 7). So significant will be the devastation that *the earth shall mourn, / and the heavens above will be dark* (v. 28). And there is no escaping YHWH's determination to destroy: *For I have spoken; I have planned; / I have not relented; and I will not turn back from it* (v. 28). YHWH also reveals a singular motive for this wrathful devastation: Jerusalem's heart is evil, full of schemes (v. 14); she is rebellious against YHWH (v. 17); her deeds have brought on the misery of invasion (v. 18); she is like a promiscuous woman preening to meet her lovers (v. 30); and all God's people are *foolish sons* who do not know YHWH, but are *wise to do evil* (v. 22). However, despite YHWH's thunderous wrath, warnings of inescapable doom, and sharp accusations against Jerusalem and Judah, we occasionally hear a subtle note of longing for reconciliation in YHWH's voice. Inconsistent with the threats of inevitable doom, YHWH once calls Jerusalem to repentance and offers a hope for deliverance (v. 14). In the same section in which YHWH vows not to turn back from plans to devastate the whole earth is the line *But a full end I will not make* (v. 27). At the climax of the poem, YHWH finally hears the voice of Daughter Zion and interprets her last desperate gesture as a stretching out of palms, the posture of prayer. We are left with the question: How will YHWH respond as Jerusalem gasps her dying words? There is no resolution within the limits of this poem, nor perhaps in all of the book of Jeremiah. Instead we might recognize in this polyphonic poem the community's unresolved struggle to understand the ways of YHWH, their need to bear witness to their pain, and their intent listening for a faint note of hope in the light of their traumatic losses.

Jeremiah 4 for Reader's Theater: A Script for Performance

One way to appreciate the polyphony and power of this poem would be to create a musical composition rendering the voices with different instrumentation or vocal styles. In a general sense Leonard Bernstein has already done that brilliantly in his Symphony No. 1, *Jeremiah* (1942),[45] in which the first two movements ("Prophecy" and "Profanation") depict the prophet's struggles against his people, with particular instrumentation distinguishing between the voices of Jeremiah and the Judean people. The last movement, a piece for orchestra and mezzo-soprano solo voice singing select verses

---

45. Description based on attendance at a performance of Bernstein's Symphony No. 1 by the Dayton Philharmonic Orchestra in Dayton, Ohio, on January 21, 2018, and comments by artistic director and conductor Neal Gittleman.

from Lamentations, traditionally attributed to Jeremiah, concludes with a protest that YHWH has forgotten the people and a plea that they might be reconciled. In his music Bernstein captures the open-ended spiritual struggle that would have been particularly poignant for the Jewish audience of 1942. He presents to the listeners a rendition of Jeremiah that is dialogic, disturbing, and relevant. With the exception of that last movement, Bernstein's piece is not an attempt to render a particular biblical passage, but rather to capture the emotions of the struggle between prophet, people, and God throughout the book of Jeremiah (and Lamentations). Taking a cue from Bernstein, a composer might now attempt to render all the individual voices in the one text Jeremiah 4:5–31, giving prominence to the voices of YHWH and Lady Zion. I present that idea as encouragement and a challenge to someone with composition skills.

Another possibility for hearing the voices would involve performance of Jeremiah 4:5–31 as a Reader's Theater piece, a reading drama with different speakers rendering the voices of the personae. Peter Perry's *Insights from Performance Criticism*, cited in Chapter 4 in the discussion of voices in Habakkuk, describes the practice of performing a biblical text, and suggests the benefits for both the performer and the audience. Examples he offers envision individual performers of an entire text. A polyphonic piece like Jeremiah 4:5–31, however, might be most effectively presented by several voices, as in a Reader's Theater performance. Such presentations require no movement, costumes, or stage setting but readers whose voices convey the script thoughtfully and expressively. I offer the analysis of the poetry above as a way to help readers deepen their understanding of the lines and appreciate their place in the broader dramatic poem. Below is a proposed script for the performance, omitting the few rubrics identifying speakers and changing the translation only slightly for smoother reading, while retaining perception of the parallels and rhythm of the lines. Readers should feel free to identify the voices differently; but, in any case, listeners should be able to hear the wrath and ambivalence of YHWH, the protest of Jeremiah, the terror of the watchmen, and the agony of Lady Zion as independent voices with integrity and power.

Script for Jeremiah 4:5–31

Characters:

YHWH

Lady Jerusalem/Daughter Zion

Watchmen (secondary or direct speech)

Judeans (secondary speech)

Jeremiah

Narrator

[*YHWH to Watchmen*]

Declare in Judah,

and in Jerusalem proclaim and say:

> [*Watchmen (secondary quotation, read by YHWH, Watchmen, or both)*]
>
> *Blow the šôfār in the land!*

Cry aloud and say:

> [*Watchmen (secondary quotation)*]
>
> Gather together and let us go
>
> to the fortified cities.
>
> Raise a signal toward Zion.
>
> Take refuge! Do not tarry!

For I am bringing evil from the North

and great shattering.

[*YHWH to Lady Jerusalem*]

A lion has risen from his thicket.

A destroyer of nations has set out,

has gone from his place

to make your land a desolation.
Your cities will fall to ruin,
without inhabitant.

[*YHWH to Judeans*]
Because of this gird on sackcloth,
lament and wail:
> [*Judeans (secondary quotation)*]
> The fierce wrath of YHWH
> has not turned from us.

[*YHWH*]
It shall happen on that day—
the heart of the king will fail,
and the heart of the officials.
The priests will be appalled,
and the prophets will be astounded.

[*Jeremiah to YHWH*]
Ah, Adonai YHWH,
surely you have utterly deceived this people and Jerusalem,
saying, "You shall have peace,"
when the sword has reached to the throat!

[*Narrator*]
At that time it will be said

to this people and to Jerusalem:

> [*YHWH (secondary quotation from narrator)*]
> A glowing wind from the bare heights in the wilderness
> toward the My-Daughter-People,
> not to winnow and not to cleanse,
> a wind too strong for these has come from me.

[*YHWH*]
Now it is I also who will speak
judgments against them directly.

[*Watchmen*]
Look! The invader rises like clouds!
His chariots are like a whirlwind!
His horses are swifter than eagles!
Woe to us, for we are devastated!

[*YHWH to Lady Jerusalem*]
Wash your heart from evil, O Jerusalem,
in order that you might be delivered.
How long will there lodge in your midst
your evil schemes?

[*Narrator*]
For a voice declares from Dan
and reports trouble from Mount Ephraim:

[*YHWH*]

Proclaim to the nations:

> [*Watchmen (secondary quotation)*]
>
> Here they are!

Report against Jerusalem:

> [*Watchmen (secondary quotation)*]
>
> Guards are coming from a distant land.
>
> They raise their voices against the cities of Judah.
>
> Like watchmen of a field
>
> they have surrounded her.

[*YHWH*]

Against *me* she has rebelled.

[*YHWH to Lady Jerusalem*]

Your way and your deeds

have done these things to you.

This is your misery—surely bitter—

for it has reached to your heart.

[*Lady Jerusalem*]

My anguish! My anguish! I writhe!

My heart races!

My heart is in a tumult within me!

I cannot be silent;

for I hear the sound of the *šôfār*,

the alarm of war.

Ruin and shattering is proclaimed!

For the whole earth is devastated!

Suddenly my tents are devastated,

in a moment my curtains.
How long must I see the signal,
must I hear the sound of the *šôfār*?

[*YHWH*]
My people are stupid.
Me they do not know.
They are foolish sons.
They are not discerning.
They are wise to do evil;
but how to do good they do not know.

[*Lady Jerusalem*]
I looked at the earth, and lo!—waste and void—
and to the heavens, and there was no light.
I looked at the mountains and lo! they were quaking,
and all the hills shook to and fro.
I looked, and lo! there was no human,
and every bird of the heavens had fled.
I looked, and lo! the fertile land was a wilderness,
and all its cities were torn down
before YHWH, before his fierce wrath.

[*YHWH*]
The whole earth shall become a desolation;
(but a full end I will not make.)
Because of this the earth shall mourn,

and the heavens above shall be dark.

For I have spoken; I have planned;

I have not relented; and I will not turn back.

[*YHWH continues; alternatively the narrator speaks*]

At the sound of horseman and archer,

every city flees.

They enter into the thickets,

climb among the rocks.

Every city is abandoned,

with no one dwelling in them.

[*YHWH to Lady Jerusalem*]

And you—O Devastated One—what are you doing

that you put on scarlet,

that you adorn yourself with ornaments of gold,

that you enlarge your eyes with kohl?

In vain you beautify yourself.

Those who lust after you despise you;

they seek your life.

[*YHWH to general audience*]

For I hear a voice as of one in labor,

distress as of one bearing her first-born,

the voice of Daughter Zion.

She gasps; she stretches out her hands.

[*Lady Jerusalem*]

Woe is me!

My life drains away before murderers!

Part III

Design

6

Seeing Shapes in Prophetic Poetry

If understanding prophetic poetry involves learning to *hear voices*, another challenge for readers is *seeing shapes* in the poems. We might describe prophetic poetry as both "trance and craft,"[1] inspiration and conscious shaping. Reflecting on the term *poiēsis*, meaning "making," poet and literary critic Edward Hirsch offers insights on the relation between craft and inspiration and between readers and writers in his engaging study of lyric poetry:

> Poetry is a soul-making activity, and the reader in part authors that activity by responding to the form of the poem, its way of shaping itself. I have the idea that a certain kind of exemplary poem teaches you how to read it. It carries its own encoded instructions, enacting its subject, pointing to its own operation. It enacts what it is about—a made thing that indicates the nature of its own making. Poems communicate before they are understood and the structure operates on, or inside, the reader even as the words infiltrate the consciousness. The form is the shape of the poem's understanding, its way of being in the world, and it is the form that structures our experience. . . . The Greeks saw no contradiction (and I don't think we should, either) between the truth that poetry is somehow or other inspired and, simultaneously, an art . . . , a craft requiring a blend of talent, training, and long practice.[2]

Although Hirsch's subject is lyric poetry, his observations could also apply to prophetic poetry. Even if the rubric *Thus says YHWH* claims a divine encounter as the source of a poem, the prophetic poet must shape the message to reach and move an audience. The form of the poem works on the reader

---

1. Hirsch, *How to Read a Poem,"* 25.
2. Hirsch, *How to Read a Poem,"* 31.

and "enacts its subject," and a reader's role in the meaning-making process is to be attentive and responsive to the form of a poem. The interpreter's task is to find ways of describing that shape.

I prefer the words "shape" or "design" instead of "form" here in order to distinguish my subject from the work of form critics, biblical scholars who classify texts on the basis of recurring formal elements and propose an originally oral setting for each text type. A particular prophetic poem might therefore be classified as a judgment oracle, a disputation, a salvation oracle, a trial speech, a vision report, a call narrative (see chapter 4 on Isa 40:1–11), or some other form.[3] Certainly this kind of interpretation is valuable for understanding a poem and suggesting how the first audiences might have received it. In this section I am more concerned with the individual design of each poem rather than classification according to formal type. Also different from the form critic's endeavor to set a poem in its ancient oral context, my interest here is in the modern reader's access to the ancient poems through careful attention to patterns of verbal and structural repetition. While seeing shapes in prophetic poetry involves subjective observations, such insights are the result of the reader's attentiveness to the structures which the prophetic poet has constructed.

Since poetry involves metaphorical use of language, it seems appropriate to describe the design of individual poems metaphorically. I will employ an architectural metaphor to describe the design of two sections of Isaiah 40, a metaphor from the visual arts to characterize the structure of Hosea 6:1-6, and a musical metaphor to consider the shape of Micah 3. In each case, I will argue, the design is integral to the meaning of the poem. These metaphors are ways of responding to the verbal and structural patterns which I see in the poems and encouragement for interpreters to engage in attentive readings of other poems with an eye toward shape.

The Architecture of Isaiah 40:21–31: Building Frames of Reference

Most scholars recognize Isaiah 40:12–31 as a coherent prophetic poem consisting of several strophes or sections focused on the theme of YHWH as Creator. Many of the verbs for YHWH's actions in these verses evoke the image of God as craftsman, an architect and builder of the cosmos (*measured, marked off with a span, enclosed in a measure, weighed in a balance*), who contrasts with the artisan constructing an idol (40:18–20). Responding

---

3. For a useful survey of forms of prophetic literature, see Nogalski, *Interpreting Prophetic Literature*, 57–77.

to these images of craftsmanship as part of the *content* of the poem, the reader might be inspired to describe the *structure* of the poem itself with an architectural metaphor. Here I want to examine only two "rooms" of that complex poetic structure, the segments in verses 21–28d and verses 28e–31. Each of these sections is enclosed by a frame of repeated phrases, slightly but significantly altered in the second iteration: *Have you* (m.pl.) *not known? / Have you not heard?* and *Have you* (m.s.) *not known, / or have you not heard?* in verses 21ab and 28ab; and *[YHWH] does not faint nor grow weary* and *[Those who wait upon YHWH will] not grow weary / . . . and not faint* in verses 28e and 31cd.[4] If we think of these frames as enclosing the material between them, we might gain some insights on the relationships among the lines within the "room" and the significance of alterations to the frame itself. Furthermore, the image of an architectural frame serves as a metaphor not only for literary structure but also for a perceptual frame of reference. The burden of this prophetic poet is to persuade the dejected Israelite audience to adopt a different frame of reference, to see not from their limited and weary perspective but from the viewpoint of *the one who dwells above the circle of the earth* (v. 22) and to recognize that cosmic being as their own god YHWH.

Isaiah 40:21–28d: YHWH as Creator

Using an architectural metaphor to describe the structure of Isaiah 40:21–28d, we can envision the refrain about knowing and hearing, along with the pairs of reinforcing lines, as a frame enclosing the poetic segment or "room" in this way:

---

4. There is no claim here that this is the *only* way to view the structure of Isaiah 40:12–31 or a part of it. The reader will likely notice the repetition of the question *To whom will you compare God/me?* in verses 18 and 25 and perhaps wonder why I do not recognize these lines as a frame enclosing the material between the verses. Certainly one could, but I think proposals about structure should yield benefits for understanding and appreciating content. I have not been able to see such benefits from considering that repeated question a frame; but I will make a case for the value of viewing the verses I have indicated as frames.

> Have you (m.pl.) <u>not known</u>?
> Have you <u>not heard</u>? (v. 21ab)
>
> | Has it not been told to you | |
> | *from the beginning*? | The God *of Eternity* is YHWH, |
> | Have you not understood | Creator of *the ends of the earth*. |
> | *the foundations of the earth*? | (v. 28cd) |
> | (v. 21cd) | |
>
> Have you (m.s.) <u>not known</u>,
> or have you <u>not heard</u>? (v. 28ab)

Speaking with authority and from a transcendent perspective, the implied narrator can best be identified as a voice from the Divine Council, the same speaker who dominated the call narrative in Isaiah 40:1–11.[5] The divine herald begins by addressing all humanity (with the masculine plural form of *you* in the Hebrew), first calling for their attention through the rhetorical questions *Have you not known? / Have you not heard?* (v. 21ab). Then the voice specifies and intensifies these rhetorical questions with another set directing the listeners to recall what they should have heard and known from creation, envisioned both temporally (*from the beginning*–v. 21c) and spatially (*the foundations of the earth*–v. 21d). When the refrain returns in verse 28, the implied audience is no longer universal humanity but specifically Israel, identified by the masculine singular form of *you* in Hebrew and by the addressee of the previous verse (*Why do you say, O Jacob, / and speak, O Israel*–v. 27). The modified refrain, the rhetorical question about knowing and hearing, is once again followed by two lines directing the listeners' attention to creation, now an assertion identifying YHWH, god of Israel, as Creator, Lord of time (*God of Eternity*–v. 28c) and space (*Creator of the ends of the earth*–v. 28d).[6] Identifying the frame and noting the variations in it, readers can apprehend the development and purpose of the enclosed lines. The divine herald attempts to move Israel to reorient its perspective by first drawing the attention of all humanity to incontrovertible truths established at creation and then focusing on the relevance of those truths for despondent Israel.

---

5. For more discussion of the speaker in Isaiah 40, see Seitz, "Book of Isaiah 40–66," who introduces this section by identifying the speaker: "There is no reason to speak of another voice at work here than the voice that last spoke in v. 11. Thundering forth from the divine council is a statement reminding Israel who the Lord is" (341).

6. Westermann, *Isaiah 40–66*, 60.

Before we examine the poetic lines enclosed by the frame, we should briefly review the situation of the first Israelite listeners. As we recall from the study of voice in Isaiah 40:1–11 (see chapter 4), Isaiah 40–66 is a postexilic anthology originally addressed to a community defeated by Babylon in 586 BCE and later dominated by Persia. The Israelites had lost the traditional foundations of their identity—land, temple, and king—and undoubtedly questioned the care and power of their national god YHWH, who had not defended them from devastation. Judging by the polemics against the Babylonian god Bel/Marduk (e.g., Isa 44 and 46), we can surmise that the exiles must have been inclined or impelled to acknowledge the power of the Babylonian deity, who had apparently triumphed over Israel's god. Contrary to the prevailing view, the writers of Isaiah 40–55 assert the bold monotheistic claim that there really *exists* only *one* independent god, Israel's national god YHWH. Further, YHWH is not just a national god but the Creator and Sustainer of the entire cosmos. The framed section in Isaiah 40:21–28d is one masterfully constructed presentation of that radical claim, stated as an incontrovertible, universal truth that Israel has simply forgotten.

As we enter the "room" that is this poetic segment, we can imagine an inscription on the lintel that bears the weight of the structure. It expresses the theme of the enclosed lines in two matched nominal phrases (v. 22ab). Although one cannot translate these lines smoothly without adding words to form complete clauses, the more literal translation, with attention to the repetition and word-play in the Hebrew, expresses the stark contrast concisely:

The one who dwells (הַיֹּשֵׁב)	above the circle (חוּג) of the earth,
and its dwellers (יֹשְׁבֶיהָ)	like grasshoppers (חֲגָבִים)

These lines convey important information about the development, focalization, topic, and genre of the poem: that it will proceed as an alternation between scenes featuring heavenly and earthly dwellers; that the narrative lens is in the transcendent realm whence the divine herald, a member of the Creator's entourage, looks down; and that the topic is the distance between divine and human perspectives. Further, the lines begin a hymn of praise,[7]

---

7. Although Westermann labels Isaiah 40:12–31 a disputation, in my view his stronger form-critical observation is his emphasis on the hymnic style of this section: "[The prophet] reminds his people of the God whose praises they themselves had sung in the past in their hymns; he revives their forgotten praise. The passage taken altogether is modelled on the structure found in descriptive praise; in this God is extolled in respect of his majesty and of his goodness" (*Isaiah 40–66*, 49). Childs, *Isaiah*, 307, also notes that the focus of the passage is "unremittingly theocentric."

with a series of participles celebrating the actions of the Creator: *the one who dwells* (v. 22), *the one who stretches . . . and spreads* (v. 22), *the one who sets* (v. 23), and *the one who brings forth* (v. 26). From a stance above the firmament, the voice from the Divine Council will attempt to draw all humans, and most particularly the despondent Israelites, into praise of the Creator.

Continuing in the language of hymnody, the herald first focuses on activity in the heavens, where the Creator's establishment of the firmament appears as the pitching of a tent:

| ²²The one who | stretches | the heavens | like a curtain, |
| | and spreads | them | like a tent for dwelling. |

Then the narrative lens turns earthward, as the voice sings of the Creator's control over the most exalted of those living under the tent. This deity is

| ²³the one who | sets | rulers | to naught, |
| | makes | judges of earth | like *tōhû*. |

²⁴Hardly	are	they	planted,	
hardly	are	they	sown,	
hardly	does	their stem	root	in the earth—

when, yea, he blows upon them, and they wither;
and a tempest bears them away like chaff.

As the view shifts from the heavens to the earth, the poet links the two sections through alliteration (*hannôṭeh*, the one who stretches and *hannôtēn*, the one who sets). Also the structural parallels between verses 22cd and 23 connect the objects under the Creator's control—heavens, rulers, judges of earth—and highlight the deity's power as both benevolent (spreads out the heavens *like a tent for dwelling*) and destructive (sets rulers *to naught / like tōhû*, the primordial chaos controlled by Elohim at creation in Gen 1). Alliterative Hebrew verbs (נטה, to stretch; נטע, to plant) assist in the smooth transition from the metaphor of tent dwelling to planting. The image of rulers as seeds and the passive form of the first two verbs in v. 24—*are planted, are sown*—suggest that these earthly governors have no control over their own rise to power. Even as their stem/reign roots in the earth, the as-yet-unnamed deity blows upon them like a hot wind to wither and scatter them. The image recalls the words of the despairing Zion from earlier in Isaiah 40:6–7:

> All flesh is grass,
> and its goodness like the flower of the field.
> Grass withers, a flower droops,
>   when the wind/spirit of YHWH blows upon it.

While Zion acknowledges YHWH's control and receives a word of hope, these exalted rulers, presumably secure in their own power, are not just withered; but all trace of them vanishes like chaff blown away by the wind.

At the center of this poetic section, before continuing with another alternation between heavenly and earthly scenes, the prophetic poet offers thundering words from the Creator, here called the Holy One: *"To whom would you compare me that I might be alike?" / says the Holy One* (v. 25). The words link this section of the poem with the larger unit, vv. 12–31, where a similar refrain (v. 18) introduces a critique of idols. Here the divine narrator directs the general audience to consider some potential rivals in the heavens, the astral powers (v. 26):

[26]Lift your eyes on high and see:

Who created these?

The one who	brings forth	their host	by number,
	and calls	all of them	by name;

because [he is]	great of power
	and mighty in strength,

not one of them is missing.

Earlier the hymn celebrated the Creator's control over the rise and fall of earthly powers; here even the stars, often representative of deities, are part of the host, or celestial army, of the Holy One. We might note the contrast between the Creator's exercise of control over the earthly and heavenly powers. While the rulers and judges of the earth disappear without distinction like chaff in the wind, the Holy One commandeers the great star host, numbering and naming each member. Robert Alter appreciates the "beautiful instance of ... focusing and heightening" in that second set of lines above: "first, God musters the host of the heavens, the stars, as their supreme commander; then, going beyond what any terrestrial general could do, He is able to name each one of the vast multitude of the stars."[8] Although the concept of a god surrounded by a heavenly army represented by the stars is part of the most ancient mythology, these lines would speak with particular relevance to the exiles in Babylon, whose chief god Marduk was a sun god. Even the unnamed Marduk would not be an independent god in this scenario, but simply one of the great host numbered and named by the Holy One.

From this general directive to look to the heavens, the divine messenger now focuses attention on one particular earth-dweller, the despondent, defeated Israel:

> [27] Why do you say, O Jacob,
>
> and speak, O Israel:
>
> "My way is hidden from YHWH,
>
> and from my God
>
> my right is disregarded"?

In Israel's despairing words is the first personal naming of the god YHWH in this poetic segment. Israel identifies YHWH as *my God*, its national deity, who seems to have abandoned the people. Perhaps Israel, as part of the implied general audience in previous lines, has heeded the voice from the Divine Council and has marveled at the deity who stretches out the heavens like a tent, blows away earthly rulers like chaff, and summons every one of the starry host by name; but Israel has not recognized the awesome Holy One as Israel's own god YHWH. At the climax of this section, then, the refrain from the beginning repeats as a singular address to Israel specifically:

> [28] Have you (m.s.) not known,
>
> or have you not heard?
>
> The God of Eternity is YHWH,
>
> Creator of the ends of the earth.

---

8. Alter, *Hebrew Bible*, 752.

For sixth century Israelites, conquered by the powerful Babylonians and accustomed to recognizing gods as national deities, this new formulation of the framing words is not self-evident but revelatory. It is an audacious assertion that YHWH, seemingly defeated god of Israel, is the Holy One, Lord of all time (*the God of Eternity*) and space (*Creator of the ends of the earth*).

Isaiah 40:28e–31: YHWH as Sustainer

Although the frame in 40:21and 28a–d encloses a well-shaped poetic segment alternating between heavenly (vv. 22a, 22cd, 25–26) and earthly (vv. 22b, 23–24, 27) scenarios and arriving at a rousing conclusion, it also opens up to another "room" developing the theme of YHWH as Creator with its corollary, YHWH as Sustainer of the weary people. As in the previous poetic segment, this smaller unit opens and closes with repetition of a pair of negative verbs as a framing device. Here the verbs are repeated in reverse order to provide a definitive sense of closure:

[YHWH] *does not faint nor grow weary* (v. 28e).

[Those who wait upon YHWH] will run and *not grow weary.*

They will walk and *not faint* (v. 31cd).

As Sustainer, the transcendent Creator deity of 40:21–28d grants some of the divine attributes—not fainting nor growing weary—to those who maintain hope in YHWH.

Between the framing lines is a concatenation of clauses linked by repetition of the words *faint, strength, grow weary*; the triad of *strength, power,* and *might* from the previous unit (v. 26); and a block of parallel lines (including the closing frame) contrasting the natural vigor of youth with the renewed strength of those weary Israelites who trust in YHWH (40:28f–31):

[28]His understanding is unsearchable.

[29]He gives   to the faint   strength;

    and to the one without power

he magnifies   might.

[30]Youths   will faint and grow weary;

and young men   will surely stumble.

³¹But those who wait upon YHWH	will renew	strength.
They	will rise [on] pinions	like eagles.
They	will run and not grow weary.	
They	will walk and not faint.	

Whether the weary Israelites fly like eagles, run, or simply walk, the heavenly voice assures those who patiently maintain hope in YHWH that they will receive power, strength, and might to be "on the move." From the broader context of Isaiah 40–55, we can understand this movement to refer to a new exodus from Babylon to Israel. The two frames, one enclosing a poetic unit on YHWH as Creator and the other on YHWH as Sustainer, should be their new frame of reference for the journey.

Hosea 6:1–6 in Diptych Form

A reader attempting to discern shape in prophetic poems is not only looking for *verbal* patterns—repetitions of phrases or lines, as in a refrain or frame—but also for *structural* patterns. In some texts these structural patterns create balance, which is key to the meaning of the poem. Using an image from the visual arts, we might think of some balanced prophetic poems as diptychs. In early ecclesiastical contexts these two-panel paintings served as portable altarpieces inviting viewers to "read" each panel in light of the other. Analogously, some prophetic poems consist of two parts of similar size and line structure connected by a "hinge"—a common metaphor, refrain, set of key words, or a word play—holding them together. This poetic shaping invites the reader to view the poem as an artistic presentation in four pieces: the left panel, the right panel, the hinged panels together, and the hinge itself. Viewing Hosea 6:1–6 in this way, we can perceive the text as a rich portrait of the fraught relationship between the people of Israel and YHWH; and we can locate the tension between the two parties as we examine the relations between the panels and the content of the "hinge," the shared metaphor of YHWH's coming as the dawn.

Hosea 6:1–3—Confidence in the Dawn of YHWH's Presence

If we envisioned Hosea 6:1–6 as a diptych, its structure might look like the diagram below. The panel on the left takes the form of a liturgical call to

SEEING SHAPES IN PROPHETIC POETRY

return to YHWH, probably from a priestly or prophetic voice, inviting the Israelites to worship at one of the altars of the Northern Kingdom of Israel (=Ephraim) in the last decades before the nation fell to the Assyrians in 722/721 BCE, the original setting of the prophecies of Hosea. If this were a painted panel, we might imagine a background scene depicting the worshipers coming *with their flocks and their cattle . . . to seek YHWH* (5:6).

Come, let us return to YHWH;	
for he himself has torn, but he will heal us,	What shall I do with you, O Ephraim?
has stricken, but he will bind us up.	What shall I do with you, O Judah?
He will revive us after two days;	Your fidelity is like a morning cloud,
on the third day he will raise us,	like dew that disappears early.
that we might live before him and know,	Therefore I have hewn by the prophets;
might press on to know YHWH.	I have slain them by the words of my mouth.
His going forth is sure as dawn.	*And my judgment goes forth as light.*
He will come to us like autumn showers;	For fidelity have I desired and not sacrifice,
like spring rain he will water earth.	knowledge of God more than burnt offering.

After the initial call to return, the summons unfolds with rich imagery and clear parallels in three sets of lines,[9] a lone line, and then a closing bicolon. While obscuring the line structure somewhat, we can chart the parallels in this way:

¹Come, let us turn to YHWH;

for he himself   has torn,   but   he will heal us,
                  has stricken, but   he will bind us up.

---

9. My interpretation of the lineation in 6:2–3 differs from that in the BHQ. BHQ has יְחַיֵּנוּ מִיָּמִים / בַּיּוֹם הַשְּׁלִישִׁי / יְקִמֵנוּ וְנִחְיֶה לְפָנָיו / וְנֵדְעָה נִרְדְּפָה לָדַעַת אֶת־יהוה. I am reading this to create two more balanced lines with 2/3/3/3 words and 8/10/9/9 syllables: יְחַיֵּנוּ מִיָּמִים / בַּיּוֹם הַשְּׁלִישִׁי יְקִמֵנוּ / וְנִחְיֶה לְפָנָיו וְנֵדְעָה / נִרְדְּפָה לָדַעַת אֶת־יהוה.

⁲He will revive us　　after two days;
　　　　　　　　　　　　　on the third day
　　　　　　　　he will raise us,

that we　　might live　　　　before him
　　　　³and (might) know,
　　　　might press on to know　　　　YHWH.

His going forth is sure as dawn.

He will come　　　　to us　　like autumn showers;
　　　　　　　　　　　　　like spring rain
he will water　　earth.

  Considered by themselves, the words on this panel of the diptych seem devout and sincere, expressing confidence in YHWH's presence and power to revive a nation shattered by Assyrian domination and reprisals for rebellion; an intense desire to *know, . . . press on to know YHWH*; and a recognition of YHWH—not the Canaanite Baal—as the god of vitality who waters the earth. All this is consistent with the theological themes of the Hosean prophetic voice.

  If we examine this left panel, imagining that the words in the previous chapters of Hosea are part of a background scene, we view the invitation to come (הלך) and return (שׁוּב) and the line *for he himself has torn (ṭāraph), but he will heal (rāphaʾ) us* in light of the image of YHWH as a leonine deity mauling its prey and returning to its lair from the previous scene in Hosea 5:

> For I am like a lion to Ephraim,
> like a young lion to the House of Judah,
> I, I myself, will tear apart (*ṭāraph*) and go away,
> and carry off, with no one rescuing.
> I will go (הלך) and return (שׁוּב) to my place
> until they acknowledge guilt and seek my face;
> in their distress they will long for me. (vv. 14–15)

In the immediate context YHWH's anger was directed against Ephraim and Judah's crediting the Assyrian Empire with power over their livelihood, health, and restoration:

> When Ephraim saw his sickness,
> and Judah his wound,
> Ephraim went to Assyria
> and sent to the great king.
> But he was not able to heal *(rāphaʾ)* you;
> nor could he cure your wound. (5:13)

In response, the song of communal turning acknowledges YHWH as the one who has torn apart and the one from whom the people can now anticipate healing. If we think of the passage in the metaphor of artwork, the lines share the same palette with the larger book of Hosea; that is, they share the prominent play between the name *ʾEphraim* (אפרים) and the verbs *tear* (טרף, *ṭāraph*) and *heal* (רפא, *rāphaʾ*), conveying the Hosean theme of YHWH's violent manifestation as part of a process of healing (Hos 7:1; 14:4 [Heb. 14:5]).

The confidence that YHWH will heal and bind continues in the poetic parallelism with the following lines, in which the verbs with first-person plural object suffixes (-*ēnû*) create rhymes and "a forceful chant-like effect"[10] (*yirpāʾ ēnû*, יִרְפָּאֵנוּ; *yaḥbᵉšēnû*, יַחְבְּשֵׁנוּ; *yᵉḥayyēnû*, יְחַיֵּנוּ; *yᵉqimēnû*, יְקִמֵנוּ). The parallel among *heal, bind, revive,* and *raise* develops the image of Israel as a wounded body, descending to the realm of the dead, but then snatched up and restored to life. Perhaps the implicit sonic connection between *rāphaʾ* "to heal," and *rᵉphāʾîm*, lifeless shades in the realm of Sheol (not actually appearing here), also contributes to the development of the image. The time phrases, *after two days / on the third day* express assurance of the swiftness of YHWH's restorative action. As in Ezekiel's grand vision of dry bones reconnecting and rising (Ezek 37), this is not a promise of individual resurrection but of restoration of the nation of Israel, devastated in conflicts with its neighbors and reprisals from its overlord Assyria, an instrument of YHWH's wrath, in Hosean perspective. The time phrases, here connoting a short and perhaps divinely predetermined period, exemplify the poetic strategy of numbers parallelism, as in Amos's oracles against the nations (*For three transgressions / and for four*—Amos 1:3, 6, 9, 11, 13; 2:1, 4, 6) or the categorical sayings of Proverbs (*Three things are too wonderful for me; / four I do not understand*—Prov 30:18; see also vv. 15, 21, 24, 29).

---

10. Andersen and Freedman, *Hosea*, 420.

In response to the anticipated graciousness of YHWH, the communal song expresses a prominent Hosean theme: Israel will *know*, and even more intensely, *press on to know YHWH*. In the background to these words, we can recognize the dominant coloration of Hosean theology: what YHWH desires of Israel is knowledge of God (*daʿath ʾElohim*), that is, intimate relationship with YHWH. That idea is developed in the metaphor of the covenant between YHWH and Israel as a marriage, especially in Hosea 1–3. The song anticipates that the intense covenant relationship which YHWH desires will be Israel's response to divine restoration.

At the bottom of this panel of the diptych, we might see the image of sunrise to express the assurance of YHWH's beneficent presence: *His going forth is sure as dawn*. If we survey the background scene carefully, we also can detect a connection between this image of YHWH's presence as dawn (שַׁחַר) and the unusual occurrence of the verbal form of that word at the close of the previous chapter: *in their distress they will long* (שחר) *for me* (5:15). The verbal connection highlights the assurance that this beneficent presence of YHWH answers to Israel's fervent longing.

From the dependability of the life-sustaining sun, the image shifts to rain, the other natural element required for life and arriving with regularity in Palestine: *He will come to us like autumn showers; / like spring rain he will water earth* (6:3). The similes, modifying the verbs *come* and *water*, express confidence in the regularity and beneficence of YHWH's manifestation to Israel. In the context of the book of Hosea, they also assume a more literal meaning, the acknowledgment of YHWH, rather than the Canaanite god Baal, as the fertility god of Israel, who waters the ground with reviving rains. In the background to this panel are scenes of YHWH's struggle for recognition as the one who grants the gifts of grain, wine, and oil, which Israel has attributed to the potency of its lover Baal (especially Hos 2). The communal song, however, seems to offer the right words, expressing ideas which should be pleasing to YHWH: acknowledgement of divine wrath; confidence in YHWH's beneficent manifestation to Israel; a fervent desire to *know* and live before YHWH; recognition of YHWH rather than Assyria as the source of healing and power, and YHWH rather than Baal as the god of fertility and vitality.[11]

11. Many commentators regard the words of communal turning as inherently shallow and flawed. For example, Mays argues that the people arrogantly believe that "Yahweh's purpose is fulfilled in their mere existence"; that they "claim [Yahweh] by the act of worship"; and that they have abandoned the historical, covenant relation to Yahweh for a "Canaanized" belief in Yahweh's seasonal manifestation (*Hosea*, 95–96). In contrast, Yee understands the people's words as an initial step in a process of true repentance, "the first stage in a three-part movement from barrenness to fertility in chaps. 4–11" ("Book of Hosea," 250). I am interpreting their words as sincere and in

Hosea 6:4–6—Assurance of the Light of Divine Judgment

Shifting attention to the right side of the diptych, the viewer will likely be puzzled, or even shocked, by the oracle delivering YHWH's words of frustration instead of the expected oracle of salvation. Although YHWH's words are a direct response to the people's call to return in 6:1–3, the viewer might briefly examine the right panel by itself before considering the relationship between the two.

Despite the "agony of indecision"[12] at the beginning of YHWH's response, the clear parallels lend the speech a sense of grandeur, as each second line in the pair reinforces its counterpart:

⁴What shall I do with you,   O Ephraim?

What shall I do with you,   O Judah?

Your fidelity is   like a morning cloud,

like the dew that disappears early.

⁵Therefore   I have hewn   by the prophets;

I have slain   them   by the words of my mouth.

And my judgment goes forth as light.[13]

⁶For   fidelity   have I desired   and not sacrifice,

knowledge of God   more than burnt offering.

With bold personification, the poet imagines YHWH as a parent directly addressing the errant sons Ephraim and Judah, *What shall I do with you?* YHWH immediately identifies the cause of such divine agonizing: Israel and Judah's *ḥesed*, fidelity to the covenant with YHWH, is as ephemeral as morning fog or dew, which disappears as the sun rises. In themselves these

---

many ways consistent with Hosean theology. As we shall see, however, Israel's perspective is limited and different from that of YHWH.

12. Andersen and Freedman, *Hosea*, 426.

13. MT has וּמִשְׁפָּטֶיךָ אוֹר יֵצֵא, which I am reading, with the LXX and many commentaries, as וּמִשְׁפָּטִי כָּאוֹר יֵצֵא. The change requires only a shifting of the כ from the end of one word to the beginning of the next and a repointing of the verb.

images of fog and dew can connote refreshment and vitality to a parched land and dying people, as they do later in Hosea, where YHWH promises to *heal their apostasy, love them freely,* and *be like the dew to Israel* (14:4–5 [Heb. 14:5–6]), but the qualifier *that disappears quickly* specifies the ephemeral nature of the fog and dew as the point of comparison in 6:4.

Directing the viewer to the background scenes on this panel of the diptych, the voice of YHWH reminds the audience, now in third-person, that YHWH has a history with this people. YHWH has repeatedly delivered prophetic judgments, has *slain them by the words of my mouth* (6:5). In the background are images of an enraged husband whose wife keeps turning to lovers, a frustrated parent who keeps calling the rebellious child to return, and the prophet Hosea slashing the Israelites with sword-words of judgment for infidelity to the covenant. Assonance between the Hebrew words חָצַבְתִּי, *I have hewn,* and חָפַצְתִּי, *I have desired,* links the effect, the divine ferocity, to its cause; fidelity to the covenant and knowledge of God, what YHWH most desires—even more than sacrifices[14]—are not what Israel offers. Therefore YHWH must remind Israel that divine judgment, unlike Israel's fidelity, is as reliable as the rising sun.

Viewing the Panels Together: The Match and Clash of Perspectives

One of the benefits of imaging this poem as a diptych is that the reader views the two matching panels together to compare them and perceive meaning of the whole piece in the dynamics of their relationship. Although YHWH's view prevails, this is not a simple monologic text; rather its meaning *is* the clash of perspectives between YHWH and Israel. We can clarify the tensions as we open the hinge and examine the two panels together.

First we might notice the difference in tone between the speeches. YHWH does not emerge as a confident, finger-wagging deity whose voice entirely undermines Israel's flawed call to return, as a sequential reading of the text might suggest. In fact, confidence—albeit quite misplaced in the context of the end of the eighth century BCE—is on the side of Israel, while YHWH is caught in the "agony of indecision." Although Israel briefly acknowledges YHWH's wrath in the past (*he himself has torn . . . has stricken*),

---

14. I am interpreting the final lines not as rejection of the sacrificial system *per se* (as in Mays, *Hosea*, 98) but rather as a condemnation of offerings performed by worshippers who are not committed to the covenant (Yee, "Book of Hosea," 252). See also Andersen and Freedman: "[S]acrifice is not denigrated; it is simply put in second place" (*Hosea*, 430).

the communal voice focuses almost exclusively on confident hope for YHWH's beneficent action in the future: *he will heal us, he will bind us up, he will revive us, he will raise us, he will come to us like autumn showers, he will water earth*. YHWH, on the other hand, is not quite so certain what the divine response will be: *What shall I do with you, O Ephraim? . . . O Judah?* YHWH cannot so easily let go of the past history of "hewing and slaying" through the sword-words of prophets and the frustration of desiring *ḥesed* and receiving only burnt animals.

Perhaps one clue to YHWH's refusal to applaud Israel's confidence lies in the difference in connection between each panel and the immediate context, the leonine deity's resolution:

I will go (הלך) and return (שוב) to my place

until they acknowledge guilt and seek my face;

in their distress they will long (שחר) for me. (5:15)

As we have seen, the Israelite communal voice does invite, *Come* (הלך), *let us return* (שוב); does seek YHWH's face; and does express confidence that the God for whom Israel longs (שחר) will come like the dawn (שחר). YHWH, however, notes what is missing: the communal song nowhere expresses any acknowledgement of guilt. This YHWH supplies in the focus on *ḥesed*: *Your fidelity is like a morning cloud. . . . For fidelity have I desired*. Without Israel's acknowledgement of guilt over covenant unfaithfulness, YHWH remains indecisive about Israel's future.

Other relations between the two panels underline this fundamental difference in perspective. Both voices acknowledge YHWH's past wrath with graphic images of violence, but through word play the Israelites link the mauling (טרף) to the healing (רפא), but YHWH connects the hewing (חצב) to his frustrated desire (חפץ). While the Israelites are confident that the revival will occur in a short time (*after two days, on the third day*), YHWH focuses on the short duration of Israel's fidelity. The images of the morning cloud and dew to portray the transience of Israel's fidelity echo and contrast with the simile comparing YHWH's presence to the sufficiency and regularity of autumn and spring showers watering the earth. Both voices recognize knowledge of God as essential to the relationship between YHWH and Israel; but Israel connects such knowledge to the future revival of the community, while YHWH links it to the fidelity which YHWH desires but does not receive from Israel. Seen together the matching panels of the diptych portray a relationship fraught with tension that must be resolved as the story of YHWH and Israel unfolds.

The Hinge: The Ambivalent Image of Dawn

The panels are brilliantly balanced and held together by a structural and metaphorical "hinge," the two lone lines well exposed among the sets of parallels, one in the presentation of the people's words and one in YHWH's response.[15]

His going forth	is sure	as dawn. (v. 3)
And my judgment	goes forth	as light. (v. 5)

Besides their distinction as lone lines within sections of clear parallels, other similarities bring them together: the repetition of *going forth / goes forth* (both forms of the root יצא), the alliteration between the subjects *going forth* (מוֹצָא *môṣāʾ*) and *judgment* (מִשְׁפָּט *mišpāṭ*), and the image of the reliability of the rising sun. Reading the two lines as parallels highlights the significant difference between Israel's security and YHWH's standards. Israel acknowledges no failings here, but rather expresses its confidence that YHWH's blessing will surely come like the rising sun and the seasonal rains reviving the land. While YHWH answers that the divine presence is indeed as assured as the sunrise, YHWH offers a different understanding of what that means: YHWH's presence comes not only as beneficence but also as judgment. Just as surely as the sun rises, YHWH's justice goes forth, penetrating the depth of Israel's commitment and demanding fidelity from the covenant people. The tension between the assertions in the two matched lines, the "hinge" of the diptych, effectively summarizes the fraught relationship between YHWH and Israel throughout the book of Hosea. Viewing the text in this way forgoes a sense of closure and invites readers to engage in the dynamism of the whole book as the prophetic poet works to resolve the tensions in this story of thwarted divine love.

Micah 3 in Sonata Form

If one could use the visual metaphor of a diptych to describe the design of poems with two balanced parts connected by a common element or "hinge," a musical analogy might be appropriate for analyzing the more complicated verbal and structural patterning of three-part poems like Micah 3, in which

---

15. Andersen and Freedman also observe this hinge: "Is this coming forth of Yahweh, or of his word, like the light of dawn, beneficial or destructive? This is not easy to decide, and it is made more complicated by the insertion of the two lines of this bicolon (v 3aB and v 5b) like prongs into two different places in the discourse" (*Hosea,* 424).

the sections exhibit an A-B-A' relationship. The way musical ideas unfold and relate to one another in sonata form[16] offers some insight to help readers perceive an intelligible design and appreciate the dynamics of the prophetic poem. Very generally the sonata form begins with an *exposition*, which presents a main theme or subject in the tonic key and continues with a second theme or subject in another key, usually the dominant. The dissonance between the two themes creates tension, which is resolved by the end of the musical movement. The second section, the *development*, builds on material from the exposition and modulates widely to explore the two themes and add texture to the piece. Finally, the *recapitulation* restates some of the material from the exposition with variations anticipated in the development. The dissonance between the two themes from the exposition is resolved as the second theme is re-presented in the tonic key. Besides this general three-part structure, the modulation between each section and before key changes in sonata form offers an analogy to the strategies the prophetic poet employs to move between sections and ideas. The musical codetta, a preliminary closure at the end of a section, and coda, the climax of the whole movement, also have literary counterparts in prophetic poems like Micah 3. I offer the musical analogy, then, as a way of making the case that Micah 3 is a unified three-part composition which introduces tension, modulates creatively between ideas and images, and builds to a dramatic climax.

Exposition: Micah 3:1–4

The judgment speech in Micah 3:1–4 unfolds in five parts, which reappear with variations in the other two sections of the composition; we might consider this structure the basic "melody" which defines the piece[17]:

- identification of the speaker (v.1—first-person *And I said*)
- summons of an audience (v. 1—*heads of Jacob / chiefs of the House of Israel*)
- series of participles characterizing the audience (v. 2—*haters of good / lovers of evil / robbers of their skin*)
- development of the description in verb phrases (v. 3—*who have eaten / have flayed / have cracked / have scattered*)

---

16. For a description of sonata form, I have consulted Grove Music Online. See Webster, "Sonata Form."

17. Hillers notes the pattern and relates the elements to *hôy*-oracles in *Micah*, 42.

- sentence or consequence (v. 4—*[YHWH] will not answer/he will turn his face*)

It is, however, the relationship among the three parts of the composition as a whole (Micah 3) and the dynamics of the controlling metaphor of injustice as cannibalism that are best illuminated by consideration of certain aspects of sonata form.

A metaphor asserts a similarity between two subjects that normally belong to wholly different contexts, therefore creating tension as readers or listeners labor to make sense of the puzzling juxtaposition. We can compare this to the way a musical exposition of sonata form introduces two themes in different keys, creating tension that is developed and finally resolved at the end of the piece. In Micah 3:1–4 the first theme, metaphorically in the tonic key, is the tenor or target domain of the metaphor—injustice of Israel's rulers:

> And I said,[18]
> Hear now, O heads of Jacob
> and chiefs of the House of Israel:
> Is it not for you to know justice?—
> haters of good and lovers of evil, . . . (vv. 1–2a)

Very abruptly even shockingly, the prophetic poet shifts key and introduces the second theme, cannibalism, the vehicle or source domain of the metaphor. Parallelism among the three participles functions to modulate from the first to the second theme:

haters	of good	
and lovers	of evil,	
robbers	of their skin	from them
	and their flesh	from their bones. (v. 2)

Through very graphic imagery the Micah poet develops this second theme in a series of dependent clauses governed by dynamic, alliterative verbs:

| who | have eaten | the flesh | of my people, |
| | have flayed (פשט) | their skin | from them, |

---

18. This verb form is unusual at the beginning of a prophetic passage and might be an editorial addition to link Micah 3 to the rest of the prophetic book. If so, this fits the analogy to sonata form, which describes the structure of a particular movement that is part of a larger composition.

have cracked (פצח)	their bones,		
have scattered (פרש)	[them]	like flesh	in the pot,
		like meat	within a caldron. (v. 3)

The passage offers a vivid, if chronologically muddled, image of cannibals ripping the skin from their victims, "cracking open the bones in order to suck the marrow,"[19] and scattering the bones while the meat boils in the caldron. The portrait is sequentially disjointed, as it begins with the eating before the skinning, and the final similes suggest that the *bones* are scattered *like flesh*[20] *in the pot / like meat within a caldron*, a comparison that makes little sense.[21] However, those closing similes probably relate back to the initial line: *who have eaten the flesh of my people . . . like flesh in the pot*. The sequential disjointedness and the encasing of the three central lines with the general depiction of eating flesh of people like eating meat seem appropriate to the imagery of dismantling a corpse and cracking its bones for the marrow. The metaphor, then, functions like the themes in a sonata form in this way:

THEME 1 (tonic key)	THEME 2 (dominant key)
TENOR/TARGET OF METAPHOR	VEHICLE/SOURCE OF METAPHOR
injustice	cannibalism
heads and chiefs of Israel	eaters/cooks
people of Israel	meat

Tension builds as the second theme unfolds because the graphic image of cannibalism seems too brutal and rapacious for comparison with the faults of communal leaders and because Theme 1 remains vague compared to the vivid detail of Theme 2.

---

19. Alter, *Hebrew Bible*, 1305. The translation of פצח as "cracked" is also inspired by Alter's "cracked open." See also Hillers, *Micah*, 43.

20. With most commentaries and the Septuagint, I am reading כְּשְׁאֵר rather than the MT's כַּאֲשֶׁר.

21. Noting this difficulty, Hillers proposes to emend the verb פרש to פרס, *divide*, and read it in a derived sense of serving up. He translates: "[Who] break their bones and serve them up / Like flesh in a pot" (*Micah*, 41–42). The proposal of disjointed lines seems simpler and more suitable to the larger image in v. 3.

At the end of this exposition, the Micah passage returns to Theme 1, or the target domain of the metaphor, in a preliminary conclusion or "codetta" announcing the consequences for the heads and chiefs of Israel:

> Then they will cry out to YHWH,
> but he will not answer them;
> and he will turn his face from them at that time
> because they have done evil deeds. (v. 4)

This is, however, no resolution of the tension because the evil deeds of the leaders remain unspecified and the image of cannibalism reverberates with an excess of power.

Development: Micah 3:5–7

The middle section of Micah 3 is a variation on the same five elements of the previous passage:

- identification of the speaker (*Thus says YHWH*—v. 5)
- identification of the audience (*concerning the prophets*—v. 5)
- series of participles characterizing the audience (*the ones who lead astray / the ones who bite*—v. 5)
- development of the description in verb phrases (*they speak shalom / they consecrate war*—v. 5)
- sentence or consequence (*Therefore it will be night for you / . . . The visionaries will be ashamed/ . . . For there is no answer of God*—vv. 6–7)

The similarity to the structure of the previous passage is evident, but the variants suggest a development of the content of the exposition. The first-person prophetic voice from 3:1–4 yields to a report of an oracle from YHWH, and the direct summons of the audience of heads and chiefs shifts to an identification of a particular subset of leaders responsible for justice— the prophets, perhaps not only those of Israel/Jacob, a common designation of the Northern Kingdom, but of all YHWH's people.

Instead of the three participles characterizing the audience, as in the exposition, here the two participles describing the prophets link closely to their referent through rhyme and alliteration:

> Thus says YHWH concerning the prophets (הַנְּבִיאִים, *hannᵉbîʾîm*),
> the ones who lead astray (הַמַּתְעִים, *hammatʿîm*) my people,

the ones who bite (הַנֹּשְׁכִים, *hannōšᵉkîm*) with their teeth.

The final participial phrase adds metaphorical resonance to the judgment against the prophets with the word *bite*, most often used of poisonous snakes (Gen 49:17; Num 21:6, 8, 9; Amos 5:19, 9:3; Jer 8:17; Prov 23:32; Eccl 10:8, 11). These prophets do not simply mislead, but their activities are dangerous to the survival of the community. The participial metaphor of prophets as snakes who bite modulates to the more literal critique of those who render their services for food (v. 5):

And they	speak (קרא)	shalom;	
			but against one who does not give to their mouths
they	consecrate (קדש)	war.	

This depiction of the prophets, focused on biting, teeth, mouths, and eating, resonates with the theme of cannibalism from the exposition, suggesting that the abuse of the prophetic role is not just corrupt and regrettable but brutal, rapacious, and deadly. The interweaving of the vivid images of snakes and cannibals with a very specific indictment of corrupt, dangerous prophets moves toward a balance of the tension between the themes of the exposition.

YHWH's pronouncement of sentence against the prophets, *[it will be] night . . . without vision,* begins as a direct address to them and then modulates on the metaphor of darkness as it continues in third person through a series of clear parallels aimed against specific categories of prophets (vv. 6–7):

| Therefore [it will be] | night | for you | without vision, |
| | darkness | for you | without divining. |

| The sun | will go down | over the prophets, |
| and the day | will darken | over them. |

The visionaries	will be ashamed,	
and the diviners	will be disgraced.	
All of them	will cover themselves	up to their moustaches;

for there is no answer of God.

The judgment concludes in the vivid portrayal of disgraced prophets *cover[ing] themselves up to their moustaches*, apparently a practice of mourning (Ezek 24: 17, 22), focused on the prophets' lips, the source of offense and danger. The series of tight parallels unwinds in a conclusion or "codetta," the unmatched pronouncement *for there is no answer* (ענה) *of God*, recalling the end of the exposition, *but he will not answer* (יענה) *them* (v. 4).

Recapitulation: Micah 3:8–12

The third section of the poem opens with an ornate transition or bridge between the development and the recapitulation. As we have seen, the development section modulates from a general critique of rulers to a scathing judgment of one particular type of leader, the prophets. But since the first-person voice which now returns from the exposition is presented as the voice of the prophet Micah, he must distinguish between himself and the corrupt prophets.[22] The recapitulation, therefore, opens with an impressive list of this prophet's credentials and a statement of the integrity of his mission (v. 8):

> But indeed, as for me,
>   I am filled with   power,
>
>   the spirit of
>   YHWH,
>
>   and justice
>
>   and strength
>
>   to declare   to Jacob   his transgression
>   and to Israel his sin.

The prophet's claim to be filled with justice answers to the indictment of the leaders in the exposition: *Is it not for you to know justice?* (v. 1).

---

22. Sweeney notes that "the book of Micah nowhere refers to Micah as a prophet" and "verses 5–8 . . . might also suggest that he does not see himself as a prophet" (*Twelve Prophets*, 372). Sweeney compares Micah to Amos, who protests that he is not a trained professional. Nevertheless, Micah delivers oracles from YHWH and claims to be filled with the *rûaḥ YHWH* to expose sin. These are the qualities he cites to distinguish himself from the other prophets, rather than his unprofessional status.

Near repetition of the summons to the heads and chiefs from the exposition is the clearest indication that this new passage can be interpreted as a recapitulation. The addition of two words modifies the initial summons and changes the rhythm slightly so that it could be rendered in three lines rather than two, and the new object *this* adds a note of intensity:

> Hear now *this*,
> O heads of the *House* of Jacob
> and chiefs of the House of Israel. (v. 9)

After the identification of the speaker (first-person, as in the exposition) and the summons of the leaders of Israel, the passage continues with the familiar "melody" in the other three elements:

- series of participles characterizing the audience (vv. 9–10—who *abhor* / *twist*[23] / *build*[24])
- development of the description in verb clauses (v. 11—*Her heads judge* / *Her priests teach* / *Her prophets divine* / *they lean upon YHWH*)
- sentence or consequence (v. 12—*Therefore Zion shall be plowed* . . .).

In the participial characterization of the audience, the *heads of the House of Jacob* and *chiefs of the House of Israel*—who might originally have been clan elders of the Northern Kingdom—their identity has clearly shifted to the leaders of Judah, recognized by the new place names Zion and Jerusalem.[25] They are the ones

---

23. *Twist,* יְעַקֵּשׁוּ, is not actually a participle but an imperfect verb in v. 9. Participial sequences are sometimes continued in imperfect verbs (e.g., Isa 5:23; 40:26; 46:6; Prov 7:8; Job 12:17, 19; 24:21). In this case the participle form עֹקְשִׁים might have been changed to the imperfect יְעַקֵּשׁוּ to offer a play on יַעֲקֹב, *Jacob.*

24. With many commentators, I am reading the plural participle בֹּנֵי instead of the MT's singular בֹּנֶה.

25. Hillers, *Micah,* 43.

who	abhor	justice	
	and twist	everything straight;	
who	build	Zion	with bloodshed
		and Jerusalem	with wickedness. (vv. 9–10)

The first participial phrase, *who abhor justice*, recalls the exposition, *Is it not for you to know justice?* and contrasts with the speaker, who is filled with justice. Whatever the prophetic poet means by *build[ing] Zion with bloodshed*—land seizures, forced labor, heavy taxation,[26] booty and captives of war, excessive animal sacrifices, profiteering of religious functionaries—the vivid image of cannibalism from the exposition colors the depiction of Jerusalem's blood-stained leaders. One also hears echoes from the development section, which represented the prophets as *ones who lead astray* (הַמַּתְעִים, *hammatʿim*), in this characterization of the leaders *who abhor* (הַמֲתַעֲבִים, *hamᵃtaʿᵃbîm*) *justice*.

As in the exposition, the recapitulation section continues with four parallel verb clauses. While the earlier passage employed those clauses to develop the characterization of the leaders as cannibals who eat the flesh of Israelites, flay their skin, and crack and scatter their bones; the corresponding passage describes the abuses of the leaders in Jerusalem, specifically the judges, priests, and prophets (v. 11):

Her heads	judge	for a bribe.	
Her priests	teach	for a price.	
Her prophets	divine	for silver,	
		and upon YHWH	
they	lean,		saying,

"Is not YHWH in our midst?

Disaster will not overcome us!"

No longer is Theme 1, the injustice of Israel's leaders, underdeveloped or vague. The voice of Micah exposes the specific identity of the leaders, matched with their corruptions: judges at the city gates take bribes; priests of Jerusalem teach Torah for profit; the prophets sell messages from YHWH and preach the dangerous, complacent dogma of YHWH's unconditional support of Zion, the holy city and its temple. No one but Micah is left *to*

---

26. Simundson, "Book of Micah," 560.

declare to Jacob his transgression / and to Israel his sin. Theme 1, injustice, is now well balanced with Theme 2, cannibalism, as the prophet specifies the injustices to match the vividness of the portrait of cannibalism and suggests that the viciousness and horror of cannibalism apply to the everyday abuses of the sacral offices. The depiction of rapacious judges, priests, and prophets extorting the goods and services of the Judean people, depriving them of justice, teaching them lies, and "building Zion with bloodshed" matches the image of cannibals sucking out marrow from bones.

The composition ends in a thundering "coda" which repudiates the corrupt prophets' confident assurances and reveals what the "codetta" sections of the exposition and development only implied. This is what it means for YHWH to turn his face:

Therefore on account of you

	Zion	shall be plowed	(as) a field,
	Jerusalem	shall become	a heap of ruins,
	and the temple mount		a wooded height.

Commentator Daniel Simundson aptly notes the irony of the judgment: "Since Jerusalem was built with bloodshed and wrongdoing, it is only fitting that the city should be reduced to a pile of rubble and a wooded hill. . . . What was built out of violence will be destroyed by violence."[27]

If one attributes the original version of this prophecy to Micah, whom the superscription to the book locates in the late eighth century BCE, this would be the first explicit announcement of the fall of Jerusalem and the temple included in the canonical prophetic books. In light of the theology of the inviolability of Zion expressed in the prophets' confidence in Micah 3:11 and in some of the Psalms (e.g., *For YHWH has chosen Zion; / he has desired it for his dwelling: / "This is my resting-place forever; / here I will dwell, for I have desired it"*—Ps 132:13–14), this pronouncement is utterly iconoclastic and equally as shocking as the image of cannibalism in the exposition. Like a Beethoven coda, this climax actually builds tension in its dramatic resolution.

Jerusalem did not fall in the late eighth century, but the power of the prophetic message lived on for the scribe who told the story of Jeremiah, set over a century later. Jeremiah 26 narrates the account of Jeremiah's temple sermon, in which the prophet, standing in the temple court, announced

---

27. Simundson, "Book of Micah," 559.

that the sacred city of Jerusalem would become desolate and the house of YHWH would be destroyed. When the Jerusalemite priests and prophets proclaimed that Jeremiah deserved to die for his iconoclastic message, the people and some of the officials quoted the warning of Zion's doom from Micah of Moresheth, giving him credit for moving the Judeans to repentance in his own day. But, they said, Micah's words are still alive, and *we are about to bring great disaster on ourselves!* (Jer 26:19) for the some of the same reasons that Micah had identified in his message: injustice, violence, and the corruption of Jerusalem's prophets. This illustration suggests that the powerful words of Micah 3, like a sonata-form movement, can be replayed over and over again as a message of warning to other communities which gloss over injustice and the corruption of officials. In this dynamic composition, the prophetic poet sets injustice alongside cannibalism to expose the former as rapacious and brutal and to warn that communities which tolerate such viciousness do not survive.

Of course Micah 3 is not a musical movement in sonata form but an ancient prophetic poem; Hosea 6:1–6 is not a diptych but a poem; and Isaiah 40:21–31 is not a building but a text. The metaphors I have employed to describe the shape of the poems are not the thing itself but ways of describing one reader's perception of the verbal and structural patterns in the poems. Although these descriptions are subjective, I am proposing them as examples of attentiveness by which the modern reader might communicate with the ancient writer and participate in the "soul-making activity" of prophetic poetry.

The next chapter offers a more detailed example of another shape, the chiasm (a pattern of repetition of elements in reverse order, named from the Greek letter *chi*, X), which interpreters frequently have recognized in biblical texts. In fact, the perception of chiasm is so common that some critics have complained that biblical interpreters have become "cross-eyed" as they view texts. I will continue to argue, however, that the value of a proposal about the design of a text is dependent on its power to show how form and content work together to convey the meaning of a poem; and I will suggest how a chiastic interpretation of the design of Isaiah 24 supports a proposal for the meaning of the poem which is relevant to both ancient and modern readers.

7

Divine Mayhem and Prophetic Rebuke

The "Fearful Symmetry" of Isaiah 24

Of Tygers and Prophetic Poems

Tyger Tyger, burning bright,

In the forests of the night;

What immortal hand or eye,

Could frame thy fearful symmetry?[1]

SO BEGINS ROMANTIC POET William Blake's "The Tyger" from his *Songs of Experience* (1794), expressing awe in a creature both terrifying and beautiful in design and wonder at its inscrutable Designer. I am particularly intrigued by that phrase "fearful symmetry," applicable not only to "Tygers" but also to much prophetic poetry, which is simultaneously beautiful and terrifying. In this case it is not so much the designer, the prophetic poet, but rather the divine subject and inspiration of the texts as well as the poems themselves which are the objects of wonder. The description "fearful symmetry" is particularly fitting for Isaiah 24. The poem's mesmerizing language is full of alliteration, assonance, sound plays, and evocative allusions and imagery; and its structure is characterized by clear and meaningful parallelism of lines, complex unfolding of an argument, and symmetry in the overall design. At the same time, the poem is fearful in the incantatory power of its language, in the severity of its judgment, and in its vision of YHWH on the rampage. In this chapter I will examine

---

1. Blake, "The Tyger," lines 1–4, in Erdman, *Poetry and Prose of William Blake*, 24.

the "fearful symmetry" of Isaiah 24, once again reading vertically through diagrams of parallels but now focusing more particularly on the logical development and overall design of the poem.

Seeing Cross-Eyed: The Chiastic Design of the Poem

Discovering logical development and overall design in Isaiah 24 is admittedly challenging, since there is no obvious connection from one section of verses to another, and the entire poem seems utterly shapeless. Verb tenses and unlabeled speakers shift suddenly, and hymnic acclamation sits side-by-side with announcement of judgment. In one verse a lone crier laments that all joy has vanished from the earth; then a few lines beyond the cry, a praise choir sings for joy, only to be cut off by a singular voice lamenting, *Woe is me!* (v. 16). Scholars attempting to make sense of the apparently disjointed poem propose multiple layers of editing to explain the rough seams;[2] identify discrete sections on the basis of patterns recognized by the biblical methodology of form criticism;[3] reconstruct a basic plot necessitating a rearrangement of verses;[4] or suggest that the text is an anthology of short units with "no prosodic structure on a higher level than these units . . . ."[5] Another option would be to start with the observation that Isaiah 24, like many of the poems in Jeremiah, is polyphonic; and the interplay among the voices is significant.

Further, I will argue that recognizing a chiastic pattern in Isaiah 24 helps readers perceive the dynamics of the poem. Although I grant the legitimacy of the critique that biblical commentators see chiastic patterns (abccba, abcddcba, etc.) in almost any text, and though I cannot say whether or not the writer intended a chiasm here, I nevertheless think that the interpreter who reads this particular poem as a chiastic composition discovers the richness of argumentation and a meaningful design in the whole poem.[6] The reader can perceive this chiastic pattern on the basis of shifts in focalization in Isaiah 24. Each section also includes a transition to the next

---

2. Wildberger, *Isaiah 13–27*, 447–60.
3. Sweeney, *Isaiah 1–39*, 325–32; and Johnson, *From Chaos to Restoration*, 14–17.
4. Polaski, *Authorizing an End*, 94.
5. Grol, "Analysis of the Verse Structure of Isaiah 24–27," 56. Van Grol divides all of Isaiah 24–27 into eighteen poems.
6. For some particularly useful examples of the way chiasm functions to illuminate the meaning of particular poems, see Fokkelman, *Reading Biblical Poetry*.

stanza, unifying the poem as the shifts occur. One can diagram the structure in this way:

A Cosmic Focus (vv. 1–3)

    YHWH as subject at beginning and end

    Link to B: earth as object → earth as subject

  B Whole-Earth Focus (vv. 4–6)

      ארץ (*earth*) appears multiple (5) times

      Link to C: opening אבל (*mourn*) and אמלל (*languish*)

    C Focus on City of Chaos—Description of Fall of the City (vv. 7–13)

        Emphasis on sound: silence, an outcry

        Link to C': reference to rejoicing

    C' Focus on City of Chaos—Response to Fall of the City (vv. 14–16c)

        Emphasis on sound: rejoicing

        Link to B': third person → first person narration (16bc)

  B' Whole-Earth Focus (vv. 16d–20)

      ארץ (*earth*) appears multiple (6) times

      Link to A': windows of sky opened

A' Cosmic Focus (vv. 21–23)

    YHWH as subject at beginning and end

Briefly surveying this design, we notice that the poetic lens is first focused from the transcendent realm, from whence the narrator previews a scene of divine mayhem as the cause of earthly chaos. Only when the focus is on this cosmic level (Sections A and A') is YHWH the subject of active verbs. In Section B the narrator's lens moves downward, panning the whole earth and horizon to survey the effects of the divine rampage from the perspective of an earthly viewer. Then the lens zooms in to focus on a particular city, the City of Chaos (קִרְיַת־תֹּהוּ *qiryat-tōhû*) and the vineyards surrounding it, where a joyful vintage festival has turned to mourning because the vines have withered and the city lies in ruins. With the lens still on the City of Chaos (Section C'), the prophetic narrator records the songs of a chorus of Yahwists rejoicing over the fall of the city. But the rejoicing is abruptly cut off by a new first-person voice, who insists on widening the lens to a panorama of the whole earth and horizon, as in Section B. Finally the imaginative lens returns to the realm of YHWH, once again the subject of active verbs. The poem, therefore, moves down the cosmic slide from the transcendent to the earthly realm and then slides back up from a concrete city scene to the realm of YHWH.

One consequence of viewing the design of Isaiah 24 in this way is the recognition of a specific event as the heart of the poem—the fall of a real city and reactions to its demise. This assertion does not mean that I think we can specify the date (usually considered to be vaguely post-exilic) or the writer (usually not identified as Isaiah of Jerusalem) or even the fallen city with any confidence. While I will offer a suggestion about the latter in the discussion below, my general point here is that this anonymous prophetic poet is presenting a transcendent view of a specific event of his own day, rather than an eschatological or apocalyptic vision of the distant future. To address the concrete event which is at the heart of the poem, the prophetic poet employs language that moves up the cosmic slide. That vantage point is transcendent and far-reaching but not really futuristic, and certainly not apocalyptic, despite the traditional label of Isaiah 24–27 as "The Isaiah Apocalypse."[7] Ironically, I will argue, the interpreter who views the poem as focused on a concrete event in the writer's own context will be in the best position to appreciate the continuing relevance of the poem for our own day.

Section A: Cosmic Focus—A Scene of Divine Mayhem (vv. 1–3)

Viewing the design of the poem as outlined in the chart above, we can follow the logical development from section to section and perceive the central theme of the prophetic message. In the opening stanza the narrator sees from a transcendent viewpoint as he previews a dramatic scene of divine mayhem, which we can diagram in this way:

¹Behold YHWH

	is emptying	the earth
	and wasting	it

---

7. Most modern scholars have abandoned the designation, "Isaiah Apocalypse," except as a traditional identification of Isaiah 24–27. An exception would be Childs, *Isaiah*, 173–4. However, most exegetes apply the term *eschatological* to these chapters. Many regard this section of Isaiah as a transition between prophetic and apocalyptic writing. See, for example, Millar, *Isaiah 24-27 and the Origin of Apocalyptic*; Plöger, *Theocracy and Eschatology*, 53–78; Hanson, *Dawn of Apocalyptic*, 313–4; and Cook, *Prophecy & Apocalypticism*, 108.

		and twisting	its surface
		and scattering	its inhabitants.

²It shall be	as people	so priest,
	as servant	so his master,
	as maid	so her mistress;
	as buyer	so seller,
	as lender	so borrower,
	as creditor	so debtor.

³The earth	shall be utterly emptied
	and utterly plundered.

For YHWH has spoken this word.

Several formal features of verses 1–3 identify this section as a unified stanza:

- YHWH as the subject of the first and last lines
- framing with בקק, *empty* (vv. 1, 3)
- closing reminder of YHWH's word (*For YHWH has spoken this word.*)
- shift in imagery from earthquake (vv. 1–3) to famine (vv. 4–6).

Behold YHWH dramatically announces that the narrative lens is at this point located in the height of the cosmos, focused on YHWH's ferocious activity and then its effects from that perspective. The abrupt announcement of YHWH's presence and the participle form of the initial verbs, *emptying* and *wasting*, draw readers into the middle of a scene of dynamic action, as if it were erupting before our eyes. Hebrew readers can also appreciate the appropriate, harsh plosive sounds and alliteration in the opening verbs בּוֹקֵק *bôqēq* and בּוֹלְקָה *bôleqāh*. YHWH is on the rampage—*emptying, wasting, twisting,* and *scattering*.

Still viewing from that transcendent perspective, the narrator previews the effects YHWH's devastating action will have on the earth, its surface, and its inhabitants as he focuses on various pairs of people to emphasize that the destruction will touch everyone regardless of social position (people/priest, servant/ master, maid/mistress) or economic status (buyer/seller, lender/borrower, creditor/debtor). Commentator Harm van Grol appropriately draws attention to the movement of the prophetic lens already in the objects of those first dynamic verbs and continuing through verse 2: "The attention is shifted from the earth to its (sur)face and to its inhabitants. The semantic buildup has a filmic quality. The strophe zooms in: the earth → its face → its inhabitants."[8] The summarizing line, *The earth shall be utterly emptied*, the passive form of the opening line announcing that YHWH *is emptying the earth*, implies that the effect of YHWH's rampage will be in perfect accord with divine intentions. The lens has turned to preview the earth from a distance, but the vantage point remains at the highest level of the cosmos, as the final line of the stanza suggests: *For YHWH has spoken this word*. Although the prophetic poet has not actually recorded any words from YHWH, we might imagine that this line recognizes YHWH as the "author" of this divine drama in which YHWH also assumes the opening role. From this point YHWH disappears as an active subject in the poem, surfacing again only in the final stanza, where YHWH's name reappears twice as the subject of dynamic verbs, *will punish* in verse 21 and *reigns* in verse 23.

Section B: Whole-Earth Focus—Languishing under a Broken Covenant (vv. 4–6)

Having previewed those effects only vaguely from a distance, the poetic lens now leaves YHWH behind and moves to earth in verses 4–6, lines with clear and forceful parallels:

⁴The earth	mourns	
	and withers;	
the world	languishes	
	and withers;	
the sky	languishes	with the earth.
⁵The earth	is polluted	under its inhabitants;
for	they have bypassed	instructions;
	they have transgressed	law;
	they have broken	an eternal covenant.

---

8. Van Grol, "Verse Structure of Isaiah 24–27," 55.

⁶Therefore	a curse	devours	the earth,
	and its inhabitants	bear guilt.	
Therefore	the inhabitants of earth	are emaciated,	
	and what remains of humanity		is a trifle.

The five-fold repetition of *earth*, underlined above, and the parallel term *world* in the initial subject column, implying that Hebrew אֶרֶץ (*'ereṣ*) here refers to the whole earth, rather than the land of Israel,⁹ keep the stanza firmly and broadly earth-bound. Dense repetition of words, sounds, and clear parallels bind the lines tightly together as the poetic lens surveys the wasted earth in images of famine and pollution. Earth's ruin has already been realized, as suggested by the succession of perfect verbs in Hebrew, often denoting completed action.

While the wide angle of the poetic lens surveys the entire earth, it records little movement but rather examines the languishing, polluted condition of personified earth and the cloudless horizon¹⁰ in the six parallel verbs: *mourns / withers / languishes / withers / languishes / is polluted*. The close repetition of *withers* and *languishes* conveys the impression of an exhaustion of effort, as if the prophetic poet himself wishes to demonstrate weariness linguistically; his semantic range languishes with the natural world he envisions.

---

9. The translation of *'ereṣ* remains a matter of dispute, with some scholars arguing that the text here focuses specifically on *the land* of Israel rather than the whole earth (see, for example, Johnson, *From Chaos to Restoration*, 26.) For additional technical support for reading a reference to the whole earth here, see Loete, "Premature Hymn of Praise, 228n; and Chisholm, "'Everlasting Covenant' and the 'City of Chaos,'" 240–1n.

10. The line I have translated *the sky languishes with the earth* is problematic. The MT reads אֻמְלְלוּ מְרוֹם עַם־הָאָרֶץ, with the semantically difficult subject and the problematic plural verb. 1QIsaᵃ, one Hebrew manuscript, Syriac, and the Vulgate read singular אֻמְלַל, which I am adopting here. 1QIsaᵃ reads עַם suspended above the line (Trever, *Scrolls from Qumran Cave I*, 26). Some see this as evidence of a scribal addition to the original text, but it could as well be a copyist's correction. Wildberger suggests a re-pointing of עַם as עִם and translating, "[I]t is disintegrated, that which is above, together with the earth" (*Isaiah 13–27*, 468, 470–1). I will accept that repointing and suggest that one can read מְרוֹם as definite without the article, since the definite article sometimes disappears in poetry. The poet might have wished to omit the article for better rhythm and *mem*-consonance: אֻמְלְלוּ מְרוֹם עִם. Understanding מְרוֹם as a reference to the sky, the location of the windows of heaven in 24:18, I read the line, *the sky languishes with the earth*, as a reference to lack of rain, appropriate to the imagery of famine in the verses. The reading also exposes a fine contrast between two destructive modes in the corresponding stanzas of the chiasm: famine in B and flood in B'.

In the following parallel clauses identifying the reason for earth's withering, one can recognize intensification in the sequence of the verbs *have bypassed / have transgressed / have broken* and in the objects referring to individual instructions, to law in general, and to an eternal covenant, the *berît ʿôlām*.[11] The text does not specify the content of the *berît ʿôlām*, a phrase which appears in that precise form sixteen times in the Hebrew Bible with various referents: the covenant with Noah and his descendants, that is, all humanity (Gen 9:16); the covenant with the Israelite patriarchs (Gen 17:7, 13, 19; 1 Chr 16:17; Ps 105:10); the Davidic covenant (2 Sam 23:5; Isa 55:3); observance of the Sabbath (Exod 31:16); offering of the Bread of the Presence (Lev 24:8); and YHWH's promises to restored Jerusalem or Israel (Isa 61:8; Jer 32:40, 50:5; Ezek 16:60, 37:26). In the context of this stanza with a whole-earth focus and the echoes of the flood story throughout Isaiah 24, one might best understand the *berît ʿôlām* as a reference to the Noahic covenant between Elohim and *every living creature among all flesh upon the earth* (Gen 9:17).[12] In the tradition represented in the flood story, that covenant, despite the adjective *eternal*, comes with conditions—a prohibition against eating animal blood and the strongest sanctions against human bloodshed, which pollutes the earth (Gen 9:3–6).[13] That the whole earth *has broken the eternal covenant* and consequently languishes polluted under its guilt probably reflects the prophetic poet's view that all humankind is responsible for violence and indiscriminate bloodshed.

If we survey the parallels in the two sets of lines beginning with *therefore* and relaying the consequences of breaking the covenant, we can recognize the

11. Wildberger, *Isaiah 13–27*, 471.

12. Scholars argue whether the *berît ʿôlām* refers to a covenant with Israel or the Noahic covenant, with Johnson being a strong supporter of the former (*From Chaos to Restoration*, 27–29) and Blenkinsopp a representative of the latter (*Isaiah 1–39*, 351–52; "Cityscape to Landscape," 43). For a good survey of arguments on both sides and a conclusion on the purposeful ambiguity of the phrase, see Chisholm, "'Everlasting Covenant' and the 'City of Chaos,'" 238–41, 245–9. The fullest discussion of the phrase appears in Polaski, *Authorizing an End*, 94–123. Taking an intertextual approach, Polaski surveys the use of the phrase in its reference not only to the Noahic covenant, but also to Israelite covenants regarding Sabbath, circumcision, priestly prerogatives, and the Davidic monarchy. As a new contribution to the discussion, he pays particular attention to parallels between the curses of the covenant in Deuteronomy 28 and the devastation in Isaiah 24 and to the oracles against foreign nations in Isaiah 13–23 and elsewhere. He concludes, "What emerges from this [intertextual] collision is a Deuteronomic covenant made cosmic and perpetually valid" (116–17).

13. Against earlier scholars, who read the unconditional promise in Genesis 9:8–17 as a distinct pericope from the prohibitions and obligations of 9:1–7, Mason makes a strong case that 9:1–17 is a unified covenant text, connected by the technical terminology *as for you* (v. 7) and *as for me* (v. 9). The covenant with Noah, then, was not unconditional, but included human responsibilities ("Another Flood?" 177–98.)

force of the contrast between the personified subjects—the active, voracious curse and the passive, defeated earth and its inhabitants. Alliteration and rhyme in the Hebrew text give the line *a curse devours the earth* incantatory power (אָלָה אָכְלָה אֶרֶץ *'ālāh 'āk^elāh 'ereṣ*). In a context in which the whole earth and its inhabitants are starving, withering, languishing, and emaciated,[14] there is ironically one eater—a voracious curse devouring the land.

Section C: Focus on the City of Chaos— The Sound of Silence (vv. 7–13)

Having surveyed the whole earth, the lens zooms in on a particular city and the vineyards round about, where there should be a celebration of the grape harvest:

⁷The new wine	mourns,
the vine	languishes.
All merry-makers	groan.
⁸The exaltation of hand-drums	has ceased;
the din of the jubilant	has stopped;
the exaltation of the lyre	has ceased.

⁹They no longer drink wine with song;
strong drink has become bitter to those who drink it.

¹⁰Crushed is	the City of Chaos.	
Shut up is	every house	from entering.

---

14. The meaning of חָרוּ here is uncertain in the line which I have translated *Therefore the inhabitants of the earth <u>are emaciated</u>*. Taking the root as חרר, one would understand the meaning to be *scorched*, or perhaps *parched* (see Ps 69:4; 102:4), not inappropriate to metaphors of famine. Millar emends to חרבו *are desolate*, with the Syriac (*Isaiah 24–27*, 27). 1QIsaᵃ has חורו, *they are pale*, and LXX reads the Hebrew verb as meaning *will become poor/destitute/humble*. Wildberger and Blenkinsopp cite G. R. Driver's suggestion (BZAW 77 [1958]: 44) relating the term to Arabic *hara(w)*, *be weak/be emaciated* (Wildberger, *Isaiah 13–27*, 471; Blenkinsopp, *Isaiah 1–39*, 350). With reservation I am adopting that suggestion in this translation.

¹¹An outcry over the [lack of] wine in the streets:

"All joy   has vanished;

the exaltation of the earth   has departed."

¹²There is left in the city [only] desolation.

A ruin—the gate has been beaten.

¹³For thus it shall be   in the midst of the earth,

                         among the peoples:

                                       like the striking
                                           of the olive,

                                       like the gleaning
                                            when the harvest is finished.

Apparently not appreciating the masterful shift in focus, many scholars regard this section of the poem as unimportant or trivial in comparison to the grand vision of the previous sections. For example, in his commentary on Isaiah 13–27, Hans Wildberger considers 24:7–9 an inadequate supplement to the original oracle in verses 1–6:

> Of course, it is an inadequate portrayal, one that actually minimizes the problem. If the entire earth has been devastated and its surface has been disfigured and even the heights of the heavens have been wilted and have disintegrated, what is so bad about the prospect that the vine branches would wither? And if there is to be only a pitiful few people who will survive the catastrophe, what is the point of the announcement that no one will sing any longer when they have their wine?[15]

Likewise Ronald Clements regards the verses as "rather trivialising in view of the awesomeness of the subject matter."[16] In my view of the poem, however, these two stanzas on the demise of the city and reactions to it (Sections C and C′) are the heart of the poem, revealing the concrete experience for which it was composed. The surrounding stanzas focusing on the whole

---

15. Wildberger, *Isaiah 13–27*, 484.
16. Clements, *Isaiah 1–39*, 202.

earth (BB') and the cosmos (CC') seek to orient that concrete experience from a transcendent viewpoint.

Several connections with the previous whole-earth stanza convey the message that the emaciated earth is the general context for this particular city and these particular vineyards. In addition to the appearance of the verbs *mourns* and *languishes* in both stanzas are the sections with six parallel clauses and repetition within the opening subject and verbal columns (*exaltation* and *has ceased* here; *the earth* and *mourns* and *languishes* in Section B), suggesting an exhaustion of possibilities. But new to this section is the prominence of auditory imagery. We do not so much *see* the scene as *hear* it. Through the stilled instruments[17] and voices, we "hear" the silence and muffled groan of the people who would normally be rejoicing at a vintage festival. The clear parallelism of the section on the stilled voices and instruments breaks down in the lines *They shall no longer drink wine with song; / strong drink has become bitter to those who drink it*. But here rhyme (*yēmar šēkār*), alliteration (*yištû, yāyin, yēmar*) and prominent sh/š-sound connect the words of the two non-parallel lines (בַּשִּׁיר לֹא יִשְׁתּוּ־יָיִן / יֵמַר שֵׁכָר לְשֹׁתָיו *baššîr lōʾ yištû-yāyin / yēmar šēkār lᵉšōtâw*); and, together with repeated sibilants throughout the section, the sh/š-sounds here perhaps suggest a hushing of the survivors. The only reported sound besides vague groaning is the voice of a desolate crier in the streets, from whose perspective the demise of the city seems like the end of all joy on earth: "*All joy has vanished; / the exultation of the earth has departed.*"

What is this mysterious, ruined City of Chaos (*qiryat-tōhû*, קִרְיַת־תֹּהוּ), which the prophetic poet describes in appropriately passive verbs, *crushed* and *shut up*?[18] Since I am arguing that the prophet is concerned about a concrete issue of his own day, it is important for my interpretation that the City of Chaos is a *particular* city recognizable to the original audience, even if its identity eludes a twenty-first-century reader. We are left to speculate, perhaps responding to clues from the context of Isaiah 24–27[19] and to inter-

---

17. For the identification of the instruments, תֻּפִּים as hand-drums and כִּנּוֹר as a type of lyre, see Wright, "Music and Dance in 2 Samuel 6," 203. Wright credits Braun, *Music in Ancient Israel/Palestine*.

18. For some good discussions of the mysterious city, see Chisholm, "'Everlasting Covenant' and the 'City of Chaos,'" 241–4, 249–53; Blenkinsopp, *Isaiah 1–39*, 347, 352; Wildberger, *Isaiah 13–27*, 472, 485–6; Tucker, "Book of Isaiah 1–39," 207–8, 211–2; Plöger, *Theocracy and Eschatology*, 56; Millar, *Isaiah 24–27*, 15–21; Johnson, *From Chaos to Restoration*, 29–35; Clements, *Isaiah 1–39*, 202–3; Redditt, "Once Again, The City in Isaiah 24–27," 317–35; Biddle, "City of Chaos and the New Jerusalem," 5–12; Carroll, "City of Chaos, City of Stone, City of Flesh," 45–61.

19. There are three other references to an unnamed city in this section of the Isaiah scroll: 25:1–5, a reference to a fortified city which has been oppressive but now lies in

textual allusions. Scholars debate among four main choices for the identity of the city in this chapter:

1. Babylon, the capital of the empire which conquered Judah in 586 BCE;
2. Jerusalem, criticized for its sinfulness in many sections of the Isaiah scroll (e.g., Isa 1);
3. a Moabite city, center of Israel's eastern neighbor singled out for a particularly wretched fate in Isaiah 25:10b–12;
4. a symbolic representation of oppressive cities in general, of all Israel's enemies, or even more generally of "the city of humankind, . . . the mother and father of us all."[20]

For my interpretation of Isaiah 24, it is most important to identify the *qiryat-tōhû* as a concrete, historical city (1–3) rather than a symbol (4). My view of the shape of the poem is that it begins in the abstract, transcendent realm; moves to the generalized earthly scene; and then zooms in on a specific issue arising from the fate of a particular city before reversing direction. That specific issue, which I will discuss below, is the heart of the poem; and the writer's effort to grant a cosmic perspective to that experience gives the poem its tension and dynamism. If, on the other hand, the City of Chaos is symbolic, then the whole poem stays on one level—the universal—and its theme is probably eschatological judgment. Therefore some discussion of the function, if not the precise identity, of the City of Chaos is important for my interpretation of the design and theme of the poem. After I have considered the case against a symbolic interpretation, I will offer my arguments for recognizing the appellation as a reference to a Moabite city, which I regard as the most likely choice among the historical cities.

Those who support a symbolic interpretation point to the fact that the poet has chosen to identify the city only by the appellative City of Chaos. This suggests, in their view, that the *qiryat-tōhû* is not intended to be one particular city but represents the aggregate of the foreign capitals mentioned in the oracles against the nations in the previous chapters of Isaiah (13–23) and the oppressive fortified cities in 25:1–5, 26:1–5, and 27:7–11; more generally, "all proud cities which oppose God's authority and become objects of his judgment";[21] or perhaps even the shadow side of any city

---

ruins; Isaiah 26:1–5, a contrast between a strong city inhabited by the righteous and a lofty city laid low by YHWH; and 27:7–11, a poem about a fortified city which has become a pasture. These cities might or might not be the same as the City of Chaos in Isaiah 24.

20. Carroll, "City of Chaos, City of Stone, City of Flesh," 60–61.
21. Chisholm, "'Everlasting Covenant' and the 'City of Chaos,'" 241.

where human corruption and oppression reside in any age. Those inclined to see proto-apocalyptic dualism, a stark contrast between good and evil, in this section of Isaiah particularly emphasize the symbolic implications of the distinctive term *tōhû*, recalling the primordial chaos of the beginning of Genesis. Hence, in this reading, the *qiryat-tōhû* is symbolic of all cities which oppose the good order of the Creator.

Arguing against this symbolic interpretation, one can point to comparable examples in which biblical texts portray prophets using appellations for *specific* cities to highlight their view of the essential character of the cities. Sometimes these appellatives play on the city's real name. For example, Hosea calls Bethel (=House of God) *Beth-aven* (=House of Wickedness—Hos 4:15; 5:8; 10:5). Similarly the Moabite city called *qîr ḥªreseth/qîr-ḥereś*, City of Potsherds or City of Silence, in 2 Kings 3:25; Isaiah 16:7, 11; and Jeremiah 48:31, 36, might be an appellation for a site with *qîr* (a form related to *qiryat*; also spelled *kîr*) as the initial element of its name, perhaps, as scholar Brian Jones suggests, Kiriathaim or Kiriath Huzoth.[22] The prophetic book Nahum designates Nineveh *ʿîr dāmîm*, City of Bloodshed (3:1). As a positive example, one can cite Isaiah's names for cleansed Jerusalem: *ʿîr haṣṣedeq*, City of Righteousness, and *qiryāh neʾemānāh*, Faithful City (1:26). In none of these cases does the appellative imply that the city is an archetype for all cities sharing the qualities of the title; rather, it simply highlights the essential nature of the one, concrete city in the writer's view. Similarly, in my interpretation *qiryat-tōhû* is a particular city, which the prophetic poet regards as chaotic because of its perceived opposition to the Creator, because of its present wasted condition, because of its status as a traditional enemy to the writer's audience, or for all these reasons.

Scholars supporting a symbolic interpretation of the City of Chaos also appeal to the immediate context, observing that the previous verses in Isaiah 24 depict YHWH's destruction of the whole earth. Those who identify an eschatological, universal perspective in verses 1–6 regard this portrayal of a ruined city and withered vineyards to be trivializing unless the city represents all cities or even all civilization. Furthermore, references to the whole earth within the description of the city itself (*The joy of the earth has vanished*—v.11; *For thus it shall be in the midst of the earth / among the peoples*—v. 13) suggest to some interpreters that "the world's inhabitants seem to be the city's residents."[23]

However, these interpreters do not recognize the signals within the poem which indicate shifts in focus away from the universal scenes of the

---

22. Jones, "In Search of Kir Hareseth," 3–24.
23. Chisholm, "'Everlasting Covenant' and the 'City of Chaos,'" 241.

opening stanzas toward a concrete, earthly site in verses 7–12. Most notably the change in Hebrew verb forms from verses 1–3b[24] (participles and imperfect verbs) to verses 4–12 (perfect verbs) signals the movement from a focus on YHWH's ongoing cosmic activity to a scene already realized on earth. The shift between the whole-earth perspective in verses 4–6 and the focus on the city in 7–12 is equally marked as the scene changes from vague mourning and pollution throughout the world to wasted vineyards and silenced music within a particular ruined city. Even Wildberger, who regards the city as symbolic in the final editing of the text, notes that the passage in verses 7–12 originally had a concrete city in view: "There is every indication that these verses reflect on something that had just happened [in the city] (יכת, 'smashed,' in v. 12, describes an event that took place at the same time; it is not an anticipated future event)."[25] In my interpretation the prophetic poet's effort to set the demise of a concrete, historical city and reactions to it into a broader perspective is the burden of the poem. If one understands the city to be a universal symbol from the outset, the poem has little tension or movement. The text is then an abstract pronouncement about YHWH's eschatological, cosmic activity rather than the attempt of a prophetic voice to persuade an audience to see its own present experience in a particular way. I regard this latter view as more attentive to the structure of the poem and to the role of prophetic poetry.

Those proposing a symbolic interpretation of the City of Chaos also argue that the motifs and language describing the city in Isaiah 24:7–13 are generalized and stereotyped, appearing in many passages about ruined cities: vines are withered, population is decimated, songs are silenced, and gates are smashed.[26] However, employment of stereotypical language does not imply a symbolic or archetypal subject. For example, the book of Lamentations borrows traditional motifs from Ancient Near Eastern laments and treaty curses, but its subject Jerusalem is nevertheless a concrete city undergoing a very real experience of defeat by Babylon in 586.

While it is most important for my interpretation of Isaiah 24 that the City of Chaos is a particular city known to the writer and his original audience rather than a universal symbol, I would also venture to suggest that the most likely referent in this poem is a Moabite city. The depiction of Israel's relations with Moab in biblical stories and poems, though not necessarily historical, reflects a range of attitudes from acknowledgement of Moabite kinship with the Davidic household (e.g., Ruth; 1 Sam 22:3–5) to extreme

---

24. Verse 3c uses a perfect verb, דִּבֶּר in a reminder of YHWH's previous word.
25. Wildberger, *Isaiah 13–27*, 486.
26. Biddle, "City of Chaos and the New Jerusalem," 7–8.

hostility (e.g. Gen 19; Num 21–25; Deut 2, 23; Judg 3; 2 Sam 8; 2 Kgs 3, 13; 2 Chr 20; Neh 13; Amos 2; Zeph 2; Ezek 25; see also the mid-ninth-century BCE Moabite Mesha' Inscription, in which the Moabite king describes his victory over Israel and the dedication of Israelite victims to his god Chemosh[27]). Israel's hostility toward its eastern neighbor is nowhere expressed more virulently than in Isaiah 25:10b–11, which depicts Moab as a swimmer drowning in a manure pile:

> Moab shall be tread down in his place
> as straw is trampled down in a dung-pit.
> Though he spreads out his hands in the midst of it,
> as a swimmer spreads out to swim,
> his pride shall be laid low
> despite the skill of his hands.

Though this bitterness does not express the ultimate viewpoint of the writer of Isaiah 24—as we shall see in 24:16d–20—or even the perspective of the poem about a banquet for all peoples immediately preceding the passage above, it does suggest that particular animosity between Israel and Moab is part of the context of the collection of poems in Isaiah 24–27.[28] Also several Moabite cities have names which begin with *qîr* (=*kîr*; meaning *city* or *town*) or the longer form *qiryat* (=*kiriath*): Kir, Kiriathiam, Kir-ḥareseth, Kerioth. Perhaps *qiryat-tōhû*, City of Chaos, is a play on the name of one of these Moabite cities. Furthermore, Isaiah 24 shares distinctive vocabulary and scenery of ruined vineyards and festival silence with Isaiah 16:8–10 and Jeremiah 48:32–33, both oracles against Moab. The saying about terror, pit, and snare in Isaiah 24:17–18 (*Terror and pit and snare / are upon you, O inhabitant of the earth! / It shall happen that whoever flees the sound of terror / shall fall into the pit; / And whoever rises from the midst of the pit / will be captured in the snare*) appears in almost identical wording but with an explicit application to Moab in Jeremiah 48:43–44 (*Terror and pit and snare / are upon you, O inhabitant of Moab!*). Perhaps one could also

---

27. Pritchard, *Ancient Near Eastern Texts*, 320–1.

28. Many scholars seek to "erase" this distasteful passage as a later intrusion into Isaiah 24–27. See, for example, Johnson, *From Chaos to Restoration*, 12; Wildberger, *Isaiah 13–27*, 455; Blenkinsopp, *Isaiah 1–39*, 364. Their reasons for this judgment include the jarring difference between the universalism and idealism of the depiction of a banquet for all people in 25:6–10a and this hateful text which abruptly cuts it off. Their comments, however, also express personal distaste and a strong wish to erase the lines. On the other hand, van Grol offers a strong defense for the integration of this passage on Moab into the context of the banquet scene ("Verse Structure of Isaiah 24–27," 69–70).

recognize word-plays on Moabite city names, geography, and history in some of the terminology of Isaiah 24. For example, *blq*, the root of the verb meaning "to waste" from 24:1, is also the consonantal base for the name of Balaq, the Moabite king from the stories in Numbers 22–24; מִבּוֹא (*mibbôʾ*) meaning *from entering* in the phrase, *Closed is every house from entering* (24:10), could be a play on the name Moab (מוֹאָב *môʾāb*); *ʿārebāh*, meaning *to grow dark* or *to vanish* in Isaiah 24:11, has the same consonants as the name of a wadi in Moab mentioned in Isaiah 15:7; the word for vintage in Isaiah 24:13, *bāṣîr*, has the same consonants as Boṣrah and Beṣer, cities in Moabite territory. While all this speculative word play seems far-fetched, we might point to several other examples related to Moabite place names in Isaiah 25 and 26[29] and to the strategy of play on place names in other biblical passages, most notably Micah 1:10–15. What is most important to my interpretation is the conclusion that the writer of Isaiah 24 refers to a *particular* city known to the audience as a City of Chaos, regarded as an opponent of the rule of YHWH. The denigration of Moab in the broader context of Isaiah 24–27; the common occurrence of *qîr* or *qiryat* in the beginning of names of Moabite cities; the focus on ruin of vineyards and stilling of music of vintage festivals, as in the oracles against Moab in Isaiah 16 and Jeremiah 48; common distinctive vocabulary with those other oracles against Moab; and word plays on Moabite names point to a Moabite city as the most likely City of Chaos in this poem.

The section concludes with a connection to the broader context of the destroyed earth, as in the previous stanza. The depiction of the ruined (probably Moabite) city *in the midst of the earth* becomes a vignette for the devastation of the whole world. As in Section B, the conclusion of this stanza laments the decimated population, but here the expression is more colorful with two similes: the number of people left will be as few as the number of olives left on a tree or the number of stalks of wheat left in the field after the harvests.

---

29. Some other possibilities for plays on Moabite names, history, and geography include the following (most names from Jer 48, an oracle against Moab):

גַּל *gal*, "heap" (Isa 25:2)—גִּלְעָד Gilʿād

מַדְמֵנָה *madmēnah*, "dung-heap" (Isa 25:10)—מַדְמֵן Madmēn (Jer 48:2)

מִשְׂגָּב *misgab*, "stronghold" (Isa 25:12)—The Misgab [of Moab] (Jer 48:1)

עָרִיצִים *ʿārîṣîm*, "terrifying" (Isa 25:3)—צֹעַר Ṣōʿar (צער) (Jer 48:34)

מֵישָׁרִים *mêšārîm*, "level" (Isa 26:7)—מִישֹׁר The Plain of Moab (Jer 48:8)

מַעְגַּל *maʿgal*, "track" (Isa 26:7)—עֶגְלַת ʿEglath (Jer 48:34).

Section C': Focus on the City of Chaos—A Yahwist Praise Choir Rejoices over Its Fall (vv. 14–16c)

The ears of the audience have been opened to hear the eerie silence, the indistinct groan, and the lone crier in the ruined city. Immediately to the west of that city, other voices, identified as *they*—a chorus of Yahwists—sing for joy, celebrating the fall of the (Moabite) city. Despite the clear shift to a new stanza, I have labeled this section the counterpart to verses 7–13 in my outline of chiastic structure, suggesting that the reader benefits from recognizing the connections between the two stanzas. Most obvious is the cause-and-effect relationship which the juxtaposition implies: verses 7–13 focus on the demise of the city, while verses 14–16c narrate the reaction from groups scattered over the earth. Furthermore, auditory imagery dominates both stanzas. While the previous verses portrayed the demise of the city through the silence of instruments and voices, here worshippers of YHWH lift their voices in praise.

> ¹⁴They lift their voice;
>
> they sing over the majesty of YHWH;
>
> they shout from the West:
>
> ¹⁵"Therefore in the East,
>
> glorify YHWH;
>
> in the coastlands of the sea
>
> the name of YHWH, God of Israel."
>
> ¹⁶From the extremity of the earth
>
> we hear songs:
>
> "Honor to The Righteous One!"

Certainly the identity of this new group, abruptly introduced only as *they*, is ambiguous.[30] However, if one interprets the City of Chaos as Moabite and understands the poetic lens to remain in the city in this stanza, the West could be a literal reference to Moab's western neighbor

---

30. For the most thorough analysis of the identity of *they* and *we*, see Loete, "Premature Hymn," 231–5, and Beuken, "Prophet Leads the Readers into Praise," 123–38.

Israel (more precisely, the Southern Kingdom of Judah). The one certain identifying feature of the singers is that they are worshippers of YHWH, singing *over the majesty of YHWH*.

The set of lines from verse 15 perhaps reads most smoothly as a quotation of the shouts from the Westerners, as they command peoples from the extremities of the earth to join them in glorifying *the name of YHWH, God of Israel*. The first word of their shout, *Therefore*, meaning *for this reason*, identifies the singers' words as a response to the previous scene depicting the fall of the city. While we could not realistically expect that peoples from the extremity of the earth would be interested in the fall of a city from the relatively insignificant little nation of Moab, the imagined voice here is conveying the perspective of the Judeans in the hyperbole of poetry. If one reads 24:11c from the previous stanza ("*All joy has vanished; / the exultation of the earth has departed*") as the voice of a city-dweller mourning the ruins and the failed vintage of his city, the contrast with the direct speech of the singers here is stark: a lone voice contrasted with multitudes; *in the streets* of the ruined city vs. *from the West, in the coastlands of the sea*, and *from the extremity of the earth*; and *an outcry* vs. *songs, they lift their voice, they sing, they shout*. In light of these contrasts, the words of the singers seem almost mocking. While the crier from the city hyperbolically mourns that all joy has vanished from the earth, singers from the corners of the earth praise YHWH, God of Israel.

Whereas YHWH's actions and even name have disappeared from the previous two stanzas, here the singers are insistent about reciting that name as an object of their praise, claiming their allegiance to this God. In this short stanza the name of the deity appears four times: twice as YHWH (vv. 14, 15), once as YHWH, God of Israel (v. 15), and once in the unique appellative *The Righteous One* (v. 16). Especially in light of the absence of YHWH's name in the previous stanzas, its four-fold appearance here underlines the singers' insistence that they are "on the side" of the one who is responsible for the demise of the City of Chaos. Such songs of praise over the fall of Israel's enemies and claim of divine favor are common in the prophetic literature, especially in Nahum, which celebrates the fall of the Assyrian capital Nineveh; in Obadiah, which confidently anticipates YHWH's judgment against Israel's neighbor Edom; and in the sections of oracles against the nations in almost all prophetic books.

The conclusion of this stanza abruptly introduces a first person plural perspective: *From the extremity of earth / we hear songs: / "Honor to the Righteous One!"* In my view of the movement of the poem, this change serves to connect the stanza to the previous and following ones. First, it reminds the reader where the poetic lens is situated: it is still on the city and its environs.

This new first-person narrator imaginatively stands among the few survivors in the City of Chaos listening to the singers from the West and from all over the earth praising the majesty of YHWH, evident in the fall of the city. Also, the first-person plural functions as a transition to the next stanza with its first person singular speaker.

Section B': Whole-Earth Focus—
A Lone Voice Reorients the Choir (vv. 16d–20)

Having heard the songs of praise, a first-person prophetic voice now stops the singing mid-note, first with truncated, wailing exclamations:[31]

¹⁶But I say:	"I waste away!	
	I waste away!	
	Woe is me!"	

Then with harsh, tumbling words full of repetition and word plays, this lone voice overrides the celebrations and attempts to broaden the singers' vision from the ruined city to the whole earth, a term repeated six times in this stanza. The language conveys dizzying madness as it conjures up a vision of the earth on the verge of collapse:

The treacherous	deal	treacherously.
Yes, the treacherous	deal treachery	treacherously.

---

31. The word רָזִי translated here as *waste away*, is problematic. Commentators are divided between those who understand the term to be related to Aramaic רז *secret*, supported by the Targum (for discussion see Blenkinsopp, *Isaiah 1–39*, 352-4) and those who interpret it from the root רזה *grow lean*. The latter view, in which the reading would literally be something like *Gauntness to me*, has the advantage of requiring no emendation; relating easily to *Woe is me*, also an expression of prophetic distress (Isa 6:5; Jer 4:31; 10:19; 15:10; 45:3); and contrasting with צְבִי לַצַּדִּיק in the singers' acclamation of *Honor to the Righteous One*. Perhaps the best discussion of the term is from Williamson, "Sound, Sense and Language in Isaiah 24–27," 1–9. Williamson understands רזי as an unusual noun form from רזה, created especially for the sake of contrast with צְבִי לַצַּדִּיק (3–5). Redditt appreciates "the contrast between צבי, which connotes that which is luxuriant and decorative, and רזי which connotes that which is shriveling or uncomely" ("Isaiah 24–27: A Form-Critical Analysis," 331).

¹⁷Terror

and pit

and snare

        are upon you, O inhabitant of the <u>earth</u>!

¹⁸It shall happen that whoever flees
        from the sound of terror

            shall fall   into the pit;

and whoever rises
    from the midst of the pit

        will be captured   in the snare.

For the windows of the sky   are opened,

and the foundations of the <u>earth</u>   shake.

¹⁹The <u>earth</u>   cracks,   cracking;

<u>Earth</u>   shakes,   shaking;

<u>Earth</u>   staggers,   staggering.

²⁰<u>Earth</u>   totters,   tottering   like a drunkard,

    and sways   like a hut.

Its transgression weighs heavy upon it;

it falls and will rise no more.

Dense side-by-side repetition and sound plays create the impression of stuttered words, beginning with the five-fold repetition of *treacherous/treachery/treacherously* with the harsh *b-g-d* sounds in Hebrew (בְּגָדִים בֹּגְדִים / וּבֶגֶד בּוֹגְדִים בָּגָדוּ *bōgᵉdîm bāgādû / ûbeged bôgᵉdîm bāgādû*). The alliterative Hebrew terms for *terror* (פַּחַד *paḥad*), *pit* (פַּחַת *paḥat*), and *snare* (פָּח *pāḥ*) also include guttural and plosive sounds appropriate to the harshness of the message. Side-by-side repetition of verbs in two different forms effectively conveys the cracking, shaking, staggering, and tottering of personified earth as the poetic lens returns to survey the wide world, as in Stanza B.

Here the prophetic voice disputes the singers' inadequate perspective[32] because their viewpoint has been too narrow and simplistic in its praise of YHWH. Although the demise of the City of Chaos might indeed testify to the majesty of YHWH—the prophetic voice never disputes this—there is no comfort in its ruin. The fall of the city is by no means the end of treachery on earth. From the larger perspective the whole earth awaits similar judgment for its transgression. Although the sin is not specified here, the correspondence with the previous whole-earth stanza implies that the transgression is breaking an eternal covenant, likely the Noahic covenant associated with sanctions against bloodshed. Reference to the opening of the windows of the sky reinforces the connection to the flood story. The word *weighs heavy* (*kābad*) in the line *Its transgression weighs heavy upon it* significantly echoes the previous stanza, in which one group of singers urges another to glorify (another meaning of *kābad*) YHWH. While the singers glorify YHWH for the ruin of the city, they do not perceive the larger truth which the prophetic voice now announces: the transgression of the whole earth, including that of the singers, weighs heavy upon it.

Besides the references to transgression, other connections between the two whole-earth stanzas (BB') strengthen their correspondence. In both cases earth is personified, first in the image of a mourner (v. 4) and then as a reeling drunkard (v. 20). The portrayals of a curse devouring earth (v. 6) and the inhabitants caught in a trap (vv. 17–18) both point to inescapable judgment. As was the case in the first whole-earth stanza, there is no mention the name of YHWH here. From an earthly perspective the prophetic speaker can see only disaster, described in terms of famine, with the sky (מרום) languishing, i.e., offering no rain in v. 4; and the contrasting image of a flood, with the windows of the sky (מרום) opened in v. 18. The depiction of ruin continues here with images of an earthquake: shaking foundations of earth and the cracking, staggering, tottering, swaying earth. This language reminds the audience of the opening stanza and prepares for a return to the transcendent realm. Having rebuked and warned those with an insufficient vision of YHWH, the prophetic voice can make no assertions about YHWH until the lens shifts to the cosmic realm in the next stanza.

---

32. Several scholars recognize the form of a *disputation* in 24:14–20 or 24:14–23 (Sweeney, *Isaiah 1–39*, 328–31; Johnson, *From Chaos to Restoration*, 37–42; Loete, "Premature Hymn," 231–7). The form begins with a *thesis*, here praise of YHWH for the fall of the city (vv. 14–16c). Then follows the *counterthesis*: "YHWH's actions, praised by the inhabitants of the earth in vv. 14–16aα, will in fact lead to their demise" (Sweeney, *Isaiah 1–39*, 329). The form ends with a *dispute*, in which the prophet develops his argument by supplying a contrary perspective (vv. 18f–20 in Loete and vv. 21–23 in Sweeney).

Section A': Cosmic Focus—YHWH Reigns (vv. 21–23)

Opening with a traditional announcement of the impending Day of YHWH, *It will happen on that day*, the final stanza returns to the vantage point of the realm of YHWH from which the poem began. As in Section A, YHWH is named twice as the subject of dynamic activity:

²¹It will happen on that day
that YHWH will punish

        the host of the sky   in the sky
        and the kings of the earth   on the earth.

²²They   will be confined   [as] a group,
                                [as] a prisoner   in a pit,
        and shut up   in a dungeon,
        punished   after many days.

²³Then the moon   will be abashed,
and the hot sun   will be ashamed.

For YHWH Seba'oth reigns
        on Mount Zion
        and in Jerusalem
        and among his elders: Gloria!

As in my discussion of Joel 2, I do not view *that day*, the Day of YHWH, as a reference to eschatological judgment, but rather as the signal to a cosmic perspective on a specific earthly scene, here the fall of the City of Chaos and the Yahwists' response to that fall. Moving up the cosmic slide, the language in this final stanza conveys YHWH's wrath over the breaking of the eternal covenant, as well as over the narrow-minded celebrations in a world collapsing under the weight of treachery and bloodshed. The language sounds futuristic because the lens is on YHWH, whose vision extends throughout time and space; it is language which expresses the prophetic poet's interpretation of YHWH's vantage point.

As in the opening stanza, the prophetic poet uses merism to express the conviction that YHWH's judgment affects everyone: priests and others, masters and slaves, buyers and sellers, debtors and creditors in verse 2; and here the oppressive earthly kings and the divine beings, *the host of the sky*. Perhaps the inclusion of the divine beings in the judgment is another echo of the flood story, related in tradition with a narrative of heavenly beings' illicit transgression of the boundary between heaven and earth to mate with women and teach humans secrets of the heavenly realm (Gen 6:1–4; 1 Enoch 6–16). In any case, this is a loftier version of the initial announcement that the whole earth, now also including the divine realm, is the object of YHWH's "visitation."

Paradoxically, just as the lens focuses on the cosmic realm, with even the sun and moon intimidated and ashamed before King YHWH, the poet identifies a direct connection between YHWH and the earth—a very specific, concrete location, the only place explicitly named in the whole poem. In the previous stanzas of the poem, YHWH had disappeared as a subject when the lens shifted away from the cosmic level; but here is a straight shot between heaven and earth: *YHWH Seba'oth reigns / on Mount Zion and in Jerusalem / and among his elders: Gloria!* That final line skillfully weaves together the Sinai tradition, concerned with stories of exodus and wilderness wandering, and the Zion tradition, centered in the temple. As most commentators recognize, the reference to YHWH's presence among the elders probably alludes to the story of the grand theophany with Moses, Aaron, Nadab, Abihu, and the seventy elders of Israel at Sinai, where *they beheld Elohim, and they ate and drank* (Exod 24:11).[33] *For YHWH [Seba'oth] reigns* is the formulaic shout celebrating YHWH's kingship in the temple liturgies of the Psalms (Pss 47, 93, 96–99); and the usual perfect verb form in the Hebrew here suggests that YHWH's reign is not primarily a futuristic, eschatological event, but is already realized in the worship of the community on Mount Zion. With that final acclamation, "Gloria!" (*kābôd*)—now appropriately oriented, contrary to the singers' earlier use of the term—the prophetic voice aligns his conclusion with the ancient liturgical tradition:

> The voice of YHWH whirls oaks
> and strips forests bare.
> And in his temple all declare: "Gloria (*kābôd*)!"
> YHWH sits over the flood;
> YHWH sits as king forever. (Ps 29:9–10)

33. Polaski explores the political implications of this reference to leadership of elders in place of the imprisoned kings (*Authorizing an End*, 138–42). The suggestion is certainly worth exploring but is beyond the scope of my study.

The only proper response of the community to that straight shot between heaven and earth is the awed, open-mouthed acclamation *"Kābôd!"* All disparate voices have now been merged in that singular affirmation of YHWH's reign.

What Has Ancient Moab to Do with Modern Baghdad?

I remember the moment the apparent jumble of lines in Isaiah 24 took on a symmetrical, chiastic design for me. It was Lent, April 9, 2003. Studying Isaiah 24–27 on a sabbatical leave from teaching that spring, I had worked on translations, read numerous commentaries and articles, reread the texts countless times, and had even memorized the words of Isaiah 24 so they could rattle around in my brain while I was occupied with daily tasks. But the poem remained stubbornly shapeless to me. Taking a break from studying, I traveled to Leipzig with my husband to visit my daughter and attend performances of Bach's *St. Matthew, St. John, and St. Mark Passion* oratorios. When we switched on the television for a news program on April 9, the screen lit with the image of a US Marine Corps armored vehicle toppling the twenty-foot statue of Saddam Hussein in Firdos Square, Baghdad. As the crowd which was gathered in the square dismantled the statue, there was dancing and jubilation celebrating the imminent fall of Saddam Hussein and the city of Baghdad. Although we have since learned that the iconic image of the toppled statue and jubilation of the crowds was in some sense staged and that responses to the event and its meaning were much more nuanced than the image implied, those disturbing scenes of rejoicing over the fall of an enemy have been repeated on numerous other occasions of military missions, terrorist attacks, and retaliatory strikes.

Swirling around in my unsettled mind on that April evening in 2003 were fragmented words and images:

> smoke over the ruins of Baghdad
> news reports of hundreds of wounded civilians and casualties
> *Seht! Wohin? Auf unsre Schuld (Behold! Where? Behold our guilt.)*[34]
> *Crushed is the City of Chaos*
> the toppled statue of Saddam Hussein
> dancing and rejoicing in Firdos Square
> excited news reporters

---

34. Bach, *Matthäus-Passion*, BWV 244, "Text and Translation of Bach's St. Matthew Passion," Part One, Chorus and Chorale.

> *They lift their voices; / they sing over the majesty of YHWH*
> American armored vehicles
> *The treacherous deal treachery treacherously*
> the US flag over the face of the statue
> *Woe is me!*
> *The earth is polluted under its inhabitants*
> *For they have broken an eternal covenant*
> *Erbarm dich unser, O Jesu (Have mercy upon us, O Jesus.)*[35]

Suddenly Isaiah 24 assumed a shape for me. The stanzas about the ruined City of Chaos and Yahwist singers rejoicing over its fall emerged as the concrete experience at the center of the poem. The portrayal of a wasted earth and the prophetic voice silencing the singers to expose the treachery of all earth's inhabitants pulled at the center, insisting on a broader vision. Finally even that broad whole-earth vision calling all humanity to account widened to a cosmic perspective of an outraged Deity, whose reign can only be greeted with a stunned acclamation of awe.

Did the prophetic poet design Isaiah 24 with that chiastic shape as a protest against those who rejoiced over the fall of their (Moabite) enemies and ignored their own accountability for an earth tottering under the weight of human violence and bloodshed? Or did I simply see that shape because my own experience of news reports and Passion oratorios connected with the words of the poem? Perhaps we can think of reading prophetic poetry as receiving a gift from the distant past. Honoring the gift and respecting its integrity, we carefully prepare to receive it in various ways, some through historical and language study and translation, some through prayer and meditation, through reading and rereading, perhaps through disturbance and sleeplessness, through sharing ideas with others in discussions or commentaries and articles, maybe through memorization so that the words can rattle around in our minds. The ancient writer does not share with us a historical context nor supply a metanarrative about authorial intention but offers a poem, which assumes shape and yields meaning as we prepare to receive it and its "fearful symmetry" finally resonates with our own experience and works forcefully on our hearts.

---

35. Bach, *Matthäus-Passion*, BWV 244, "Text and Translation of Bach's St. Matthew Passion," Part One, Chorale..

Bibliography

Aaron, David H. "Idolatry: The Most Challenging Metaphor." In *Biblical Ambiguities: Metaphor, Semantics, and Divine Imagery*, 125–56. Boston: Brill Academic, 2002.
Ahlström, Gösta W. *Joel and the Temple Cult of Jerusalem*. Supplements to Vetus Testamentum 21. Leiden: Brill, 1971.
Alonso Schökel, Luis. *A Manuel of Hebrew Poetics*. 1988. Reprint, Subsidia Biblica 11. Rome: Pontificio Istituto Biblico, 2000.
Alter, Robert. *The Art of Biblical Poetry*. Rev. ed. New York: Basic Books, 2011.
———. *The Hebrew Bible: A Translation with Commentary*. Vol. 2, *Prophets*. New York: Norton, 2019.
Andersen, Francis I., and David Noel Freedman. *Hosea: A New Translation with Introduction and Commentary*. Anchor Bible 24. New York: Doubleday, 1980.
Anderson, Gary. *A Time to Mourn, A Time to Dance: The Expression of Grief and Joy in Israelite Religion*. University Park: Pennsylvania State University Press, 1991.
Andiñach, Pablo. "The Locusts in the Message of Joel." *Vetus Testamentum* 42 (1992) 433–41.
Attridge, Harold W., ed. *The HarperCollins Study Bible, New Revised Standard Version, Including the Apocryphal/Deuterocanonical Books*. Rev. ed. San Francisco: HarperSanFrancisco, 2006.
Bach, Johann Sebastian. "Matthäus-Passion," BWV 244. "Text and Translation of Bach's St. Matthew Passion." https://gbt.org/music/St_Matthew_text.pdf.
Bakhtin, Mikhail. *The Dialogic Imagination: Four Essays*. Edited by Michael Holmquist. Translated by Michael Holmquist and Caryl Emerson. Austin: University of Texas Press, 1981.
———. *Problems of Dostoyevsky's Poetics*. Edited and translated by Caryl Emerson. Minneapolis: University of Minnesota Press, 1984.
Ball, Ivan. *A Rhetorical Study of Zephaniah*. Berkeley: BIBAL, 1988.
Barker, Joel. "One Good 'Turn' Deserves Another? Rhetorical Strategy in Joel 2:12–17." In *Why? . . . How Long? Studies on Voice(s) of Lamentation Rooted in Biblical Hebrew Poetry*, edited by LeAnn Snow Flesher et al., 115–31. Library of Hebrew Bible/Old Testament Studies 552. London: Bloomsbury T. & T. Clark, 2015.
Barton, John. *Joel and Obadiah*. Old Testament Library. Louisville: Westminster John Knox, 2001.

Berges, Ulrich. "Isaiah: Structure, Themes, and Contested Issues." In *The Oxford Handbook of the Prophets*, edited by Carolyn Sharp, 153–70. New York: Oxford University Press, 2016.

———. "Personifications and Prophetic Voices of Zion in Isaiah and Beyond." In *The Elusive Prophet: The Prophet as a Historical Person, Literary Character and Anonymous Artist*, edited by Johannes C. De Moor, 54–82. Oudtestamentische Studiën 45. Leiden: Brill, 2001.

Berlin, Adele. *The Dynamics of Biblical Parallelism*. Rev. ed. Biblical Resource Series. Grand Rapids: Eerdmans, 2008.

———. *Zephaniah: A New Translation with Introduction and Commentary*. Anchor Bible 25A. New York: Doubleday, 1994.

Berridge, John M. *Prophet, People, and the Word of Yahweh: An Examination of Form and Content in the Proclamation of the Prophet Jeremiah*. Zurich: EVZ, 1970.

Beuken, Willem. "The Prophet Leads the Readers into Praise: Isaiah 25:1–10 in Connection with Isaiah 24:14–23 Seen against the Background of Isaiah 12." In *Studies in Isaiah 24–27: The Isaiah Workshop—De Jesaja Werkplaats*, edited by Hendrik Jan Bosman et al., 123–38. Oudtestamentische Studien 43. Leiden: Brill, 2000.

Biddle, Mark. "The City of Chaos and the New Jerusalem: Isaiah 24–27 in Context." *Perspectives in Religious Studies* 22 (1995) 5–12.

———. "The Figure of Lady Jerusalem: Identification, Deification and Personification of Cities in the Ancient Near East." In *The Biblical Canon in Comparative Perspective: Scripture in Context IV*, edited by K. Lawson Younger et al., 173–94. Ancient Near Eastern Texts and Studies 11. Lewiston, NY: Mellen, 1991.

———. *Polyphony and Symphony in Prophetic Literature: Rereading Jeremiah 7–20*. Studies in Old Testament Interpretation 2. Macon, GA: Mercer University Press, 1996.

Blenkinsopp, Joseph. "Cityscape to Landscape: The 'Back to Nature' Theme in Isaiah 1–35." In *'Every City Shall Be Forsaken': Urbanism and Prophecy in Ancient Israel and the Near East*, edited by Lester L. Grabbe and Robert D. Haak, 35–44. Journal for the Study of the Old Testament Supplement 330. Sheffield: Sheffield Academic, 2001.

———. *Isaiah 1–39: A New Translation with Introduction and Commentary*. Anchor Bible 19. New York: Doubleday, 2000.

Braun, Joachim. *Music in Ancient Israel/Palestine: Archaeological, Written, and Comparative Sources*. Translated by Douglas W. Stott. Grand Rapids: Eerdmans, 2002.

Bright, John. *Jeremiah: Introduction, Translation, and Notes*. Anchor Bible 21. Garden City, NY: Doubleday, 1965.

Brueggemann, Walter. *A Commentary on Jeremiah: Exile and Homecoming*. Grand Rapids: Eerdmans, 1998.

Carroll, Robert P. "City of Chaos, City of Stone, City of Flesh: Urbanscapes in Prophetic Discourses." In *'Every City Shall Be Forsaken': Urbanism and Prophecy in Ancient Israel and the Near East*, edited by Lester L. Grabbe and Robert D. Haak, 45–61. Journal for the Study of the Old Testament Supplement 330. Sheffield: Sheffield Academic, 2001.

———. *Jeremiah: A Commentary*. Old Testament Library. Philadelphia: Westminster, 1986.

———. "The Polyphonic Jeremiah: A Reading of the Book of Jeremiah." In *Reading the Book of Jeremiah: A Search for Coherence*, edited by Martin Kessler, 77–85. Winona Lake, IN: Eisenbrauns, 2004.

Childs, Brevard S. *Isaiah*. Old Testament Library. Louisville: Westminster John Knox, 2001.

Chisholm, Robert B. "The 'Everlasting Covenant' and the 'City of Chaos': Intentional Ambiguity and Irony in Isaiah 24." *Criswell Theological Review* 6 (1993) 237–53.

Claassens, L. Juliana. "God and Violence in the Prophets." In *The Oxford Handbook of the Prophets*, edited by Carolyn J. Sharp, 334–49. New York: Oxford University Press, 2016.

Clements, Ronald. *Isaiah 1–39*. New Century Bible Commentary. Grand Rapids: Eerdmans, 1980.

Clines, David J. A. "The Parallelism of Greater Precision." In *Directions in Biblical Hebrew Poetry*, edited by Elaine R. Follis, 77–100. Journal for the Study of Old Testament Supplement 40. Sheffield: JSOT Press, 1987.

Coggins, Richard James. *Joel and Amos*. New Century Bible Commentary. Sheffield: Sheffield Academic, 2000.

Collins, Terence. *Line-Forms in Hebrew Poetry: A Grammatical Approach to the Stylistic Study of the Hebrew Prophets*. Studia Pohl 7. Rome: Biblical Institute Press, 1978.

Coogan, Michael D., et al., eds. *The New Oxford Annotated Bible: New Revised Standard Version with the Apocrypha*. 5th ed. New York: Oxford University Press, 2018.

Cook, Stephen L. *Prophecy & Apocalypticism: The Postexilic Social Setting*. Minneapolis: Fortress, 1995.

Couey, J. Blake. *Reading the Poetry of First Isaiah: The Most Perfect Model of the Prophetic Poetry*. Oxford: Oxford University Press, 2015.

Crenshaw, James L. *Joel: A New Translation with Introduction and Commentary*. Anchor Bible 24C. New York: Doubleday, 1995.

———. "Who Knows What YHWH Will Do? The Character of God in the Book of Joel." In *Prophets, Sages, & Poets*, 147–52. St. Louis: Chalice, 2006.

Dearman, J. Andrew. "Daughter Zion and Her Place in God's Household." *Horizons in Biblical Theology* 31 (2009) 144–59.

Dobbs-Allsopp, F. W. *On Biblical Poetry*. New York: Oxford University Press, 2015.

———. *Weep, O Daughter of Zion: A Study of the City-Lament Genre in the Hebrew Bible*. Biblica et orientalia 44. Rome: Pontificio Istituto Biblico, 1993.

Elliger, Karl, and Wilhelm Rudolph, eds. *Biblia Hebraica Stuttgartensia*. 2nd ed. Stuttgart: Deutsche Bibelgesellschaft, 1984.

Erdman, David V., ed. *The Poetry and Prose of William Blake*. Commentary by Harold Bloom. Garden City, NY: Doubleday, 1970.

Everson, A. Joseph. "The Days of Yahweh." *Journal of Biblical Literature* 93 (1974) 329–37.

Faust, Avraham. *Judah in the Neo-Babylonian Period: The Archaeology of Desolation*. Archaeology and Biblical Studies 18. Atlanta: Society of Biblical Literature, 2012.

Fisch, Harold. "Hosea: A Poetics of Violence." In *Poetry with a Purpose: Biblical Poetics and Interpretation*, 136–57. Indiana Studies in Biblical Literature. Bloomington: Indiana University Press, 1990.

Fitzgerald, Aloysius. "*Btwlt* and *Bt* as Titles for Capital Cities." *Catholic Biblical Quarterly* 37 (1975) 167–83.

———. "The Mythological Background for the Presentation of Jerusalem as a Queen and False Worship as Idolatry in the OT." *Catholic Biblical Quarterly* 34 (1972) 403–16.

Floyd, Michael H. "The Daughter of Zion Goes Fishing in Heaven." In *Daughter Zion: Her Portrait, Her Response*, edited by Mark Boda et al., 177–200. Ancient Israel and Its Literature 13. Atlanta: Society of Biblical Literature, 2012.

———. "Welcome Back, Daughter of Zion!" *Catholic Biblical Quarterly* 70 (2008) 484–504.

Fokkelman, J. P. *Reading Biblical Poetry: An Introductory Guide*. Translated by Ineke Smit. Louisville: Westminster John Knox, 2001.

Freedman, David Noel. "Pottery, Poetry, and Prophecy: An Essay on Biblical Poetry." *Journal of Biblical Literature* 96 (1977) 5–26.

Gafney, Wilda. *Women Prophets in Ancient Israel*. Minneapolis: Fortress, 2008.

Geller, Stephen. *Parallelism in Early Biblical Poetry*. Harvard Semitic Monographs 20. Missoula, MT: Scholars, 1979.

Gelston, Anthony, ed. *Biblia Hebraica Quinta*. Vol.13, *Minor Prophets*. Stuttgart: Deutsche Bibelgesellschaft, 2010.

Goh, Samuel T. S. *The Basics of Hebrew Poetry: Theory and Practice*. Eugene, OR: Cascade Books, 2017.

Greenstein, Edward. "How Does Parallelism Mean?" In *A Sense of Text: The Art of Language in the Study of Biblical Literature—Papers from a Symposium at The Dropsie College for Hebrew and Cognitive Learning, May 11, 1982*, 41–70. Jewish Quarterly Review Supplements. Winona Lake, IN: Eisenbrauns, 1983.

Grol, Harm van. "An Analysis of the Verse Structure of Isaiah 24–27." In *Studies in Isaiah 24–27: The Isaiah Workshop—De Jesaja Werkplaats*, edited by Hendrik Jan Bosman et al., 51–80. Oudtestamentische Studiën 43. Leiden: Brill, 2000.

Haak, Robert D. *Habakkuk*. Vetus Testamentum Supplements 44. Leiden: Brill, 1992.

Habel, Norman. "The Form and Significance of the Call Narratives." *Zeitschrift für die alttestamentliche Wissenschaft* 77 (1965) 297–323.

Hamori, Esther J. *Women's Divination in Biblical Literature: Prophecy, Necromancy, and Other Arts of Knowledge*. Anchor Yale Bible Reference Library. New Haven: Yale University Press, 2015.

Hanson, Paul D. *The Dawn of Apocalyptic*. Philadelphia: Fortress, 1975.

Henderson, Joseph M. "Who Weeps in Jeremiah VIII 23 (IX 1)? Identifying Dramatic Speakers in the Poetry of Jeremiah." *Vetus Testamentum* 52 (2002) 191–206.

Heschel, Abraham J. "A Prayer for Peace." In *Moral Grandeur and Spiritual Audacity: Essays*, edited by Susannah Heschel, 230–4. New York: Farrar, Straus & Giroux, 1996.

———. *The Prophets*. 1962. Reprint, Perennial Classics. New York: Harper & Row, 2001.

Hillers, Delbert R. *Micah: A Commentary on the Book of the Prophet Micah*. Hermeneia. Philadelphia: Fortress, 1984.

Hirsch, Edward. *How to Read a Poem and Fall in Love with Poetry*. New York: Harcourt, Brace, and Company, 1999.

Hoffmann, Yair. "The Day of the Lord as a Concept and a Term in the Prophetic Literature." *Zeitschrift für die alttestamentliche Wissenschaft* 93 (1981) 37–50.

Holladay, William L. *Jeremiah 1: A Commentary on the Book of the Prophet Jeremiah, Chapters 1–25*. Hermeneia. Philadelphia: Fortress, 1986.

Jakobson, Roman. "Grammatical Parallelism and Its Russian Facet." *Language* 42 (1966) 399–429.
Jeremias, Jörg. *The Book of Amos*. Translated by Douglas W. Stott. Old Testament Library. Louisville: Westminster John Knox, 1998.
Jindo, Job. *Biblical Metaphor Reconsidered: A Cognitive Approach to Poetic Prophecy in Jeremiah 1–24*. Harvard Semetic Monographs 64. Winona Lake, IN: Eisenbrauns, 2010.
Johnson, Dan G. *From Chaos to Restoration: An Integrative Reading of Isaiah 24–27*. Journal for the Study of the Old Testament Supplement 61. Sheffield: Sheffield Academic, 1988.
Johnson, Marshall. "The Paralysis of Torah in Habakkuk I 4." *Vetus Testamentum* 35 (1985) 257–66.
Jones, Brian C. "In Search of Kir Hareseth: A Case Study in Site Identification." *Journal for the Study of the Old Testament* 52 (1991) 3–24.
Kaiser, Barbara Bakke. "Poet as 'Female Impersonator': The Image of Daughter Zion as Speaker in Biblical Poems of Suffering." *Journal of Religion* 67 (1987) 164–82.
King, Martin Luther Jr. *I Have a Dream: Writings and Speeches that Changed the World*. Edited by James Melvin Washington. San Francisco: HarperSanFrancisco, 1992.
Korpel, Marjo C. A. "Who Is Speaking in Jeremiah 4:19–22? The Contribution of Unit Delimitation to an Old Problem." *Vetus Testamentum* 59 (2009) 88–98.
Kugel, James. *The Idea of Biblical Poetry: Parallelism and Its History*. New Haven: Yale University Press, 1981.
———. "Poets and Prophets: An Overview." In *Poetry and Prophecy: The Beginnings of a Literary Tradition*, edited by James Kugel, 1–25. Ithaca: Cornell University Press, 1990.
Kumaki, F. K. "A New Look at Jer 4, 19–22 and 10, 19–21." *Annual of the Japanese Biblical Institute* 7 (1982) 113–22.
Landy, Francis. "Poetics and Parallelism: Some Comments on James Kugel's *The Idea of Biblical Poetry*." *Journal for the Study of the Old Testament* 9 (1984) 61–87.
———. "Spectrality in the Prologue to Deutero-Isaiah." In *The Desert Will Bloom: Poetic Visions in Isaiah*, edited by A. Joseph Everson and Hyun Chul Paul Kim, 131–58. Ancient Israel and Its Literature 4. Atlanta: Society of Biblical Literature, 2009.
Lee, Nancy. "Prophet and Singer in the Fray: The Book of Jeremiah." In *Uprooting and Planting: Essays on Jeremiah for Leslie Allen*, edited by John Goldingay, 190–209. Library of Hebrew Bible/Old Testament Studies 9. New York: T. & T. Clark, 2007.
Linville, James R. "The Day of Yahweh and the Mourning of the Priests in Joel." In *The Priests in the Prophets: The Portrayal of Priests, Prophets and Other Religious Specialists in the Latter Prophets*, edited by Lester L. Grabbe and Alice Ogden Bellis, 98–114. Journal for the Study of the Old Testament. Supplements 408 London: T. & T. Clark, 2004.
Loete, Joseph. "A Premature Hymn of Praise: The Meaning and Function of Isaiah 24:14–16c in its Present Context." In *Studies in Isaiah 24–27: The Isaiah Workshop—De Jesaja Werkplaats*, edited by Hendrik Jan Bosman et al., 226–38. Oudtestamentische Studien 43. Leiden: Brill, 2000.
Lowth, Robert. *Isaiah: A New Translation with a Preliminary Dissertation and Notes, Critical, Philological, and Explanatory*. 3rd ed. Perth: Morison, 1793.

———. *Lectures on the Sacred Poetry of the Hebrews*. Translated by G. Gregory. London: J. Johnson, St. Paul's Church Yard, 1787.
Maier, Christl M. "Daughter Zion as Queen and the Iconography of the Female City." In *Images and Prophecy in the Ancient Eastern Mediterranean*, edited by Martii Nissinen and Charles E. Carter, 147–62. Forschungen zur Religion und Literatur des Alten und Neuen Testaments 233. Göttingen: Vandenhoeck & Ruprecht, 2009.
———. *Daughter Zion, Mother Zion: Gender, Space, and the Sacred in Ancient Israel*. Minneapolis: Fortress, 2008.
Mandolfo, Carleen R. *Daughter Zion Talks Back to the Prophets: A Dialogic Theology of the Book of Lamentations*. Semeia Studies 58. Atlanta: Society of Biblical Literature, 2007.
Martin, Dale B. *Sex and the Single Savior: Gender and Sexuality in Biblical Interpretation*. Louisville: Westminster John Knox, 2006.
Mason, Steven D. "Another Flood? Genesis 9 and Isaiah's Broken Eternal Covenant." *Journal for the Study of the Old Testament* 32 (2007) 177–98.
Mathews, Jeanette. *Performing Habakkuk: Faithful Re-enactment in the Midst of Crisis*. Eugene, OR: Pickwick Publications, 2012.
Mays, James Luther. *Hosea: A Commentary*. Old Testament Library. Philadelphia: Westminster, 1969.
Millar, William R. *Isaiah 24–27 and the Origin of Apocalyptic*. Harvard Semitic Monograph 11. Missoula, MT: Scholars Press, 1976.
Miller, Patrick D. "The Book of Jeremiah: Introduction, Commentary, and Reflections." In *The New Interpreter's Bible 6*, edited by Leander E. Keck et al., 553–926. Nashville: Abingdon, 2001.
Moyers, Bill. *Bill Moyers Journal: The Reverend Jeremiah Wright Speaks Out*. Produced by Gail Ablow et al. 58 min. Princeton: Films for the Humanities and Science, 2008. Videorecording.
Newsom, Carol. "Bakhtin, the Bible, and Dialogic Truth." *Journal of Religion* 76 (1996) 290–306.
Nissinen, Martii. "What Is Prophecy? An Ancient Near Eastern Perspective." In *Inspired Speech: Prophecy in the Ancient Near East—Essays in Honor of Herbert B. Huffmon*, edited by John Kaltner and Louis Stulman, 17–31. Journal for the Study of the Old Testament Supplements 378. London: T. & T. Clark, 2004.
Nogalski, James. *Interpreting Prophetic Literature: Historical and Exegetical Tools for Reading the Prophets*. Louisville: Westminster John Knox, 2015.
O'Brien, Julia, and Chris Franke, eds. *The Aesthetics of Violence in the Prophets*. Library of Hebrew Bible/Old Testament Studies 517. New York: T. & T. Clark, 2010.
O'Brien, Julia. "Edom as (Selfish) Brother." In *Challenging Prophetic Metaphor: Theology and Ideology in the Prophets*, 153–74. Louisville: Westminster John Knox, 2008.
O'Connor, Kathleen. *Jeremiah: Pain and Promise*. Minneapolis: Fortress, 2012.
———. "Reclaiming Jeremiah's Violence." In *Aesthetics of Violence in the Prophets*, edited by Julia M. O'Brien and Chris Franke, 37–49. Library of Hebrew Bible/ Old Testament Studies 517. New York: T. & T. Clark, 2010.
O'Connor, Michael. *Hebrew Verse Structure*. Winona Lake, IN: Eisenbrauns, 1980.
Perry, Peter S. *Insights from Performance Criticism*. Reading the Bible in the 21st Century. Minneapolis: Fortress, 2016.
Petersen, David L. *Late Israelite Prophecy: Studies in Deutero-Prophetic Literature and in Chronicles*. SBL Monograph Series 23. Missoula, MT: Scholars, 1977.
———. *The Prophetic Literature: An Introduction* Louisville: Westminster John Knox, 2002.

Pilarski, Ahida Calderon. "A Study of the References to בת־עמי in Jeremiah 8:18—9:2(3): A Gendered Lamentation." In *Why?. . . How Long? Studies on Voice(s) of Lamentation Rooted in Biblical Hebrew Poetry*, edited by LeAnn Snow Flesher et al., 20–35. London: Bloomsbury T. & T. Clark, 2015.

Plöger, Otto. *Theocracy and Eschatology*. Translated by S. Rudman. Oxford: Blackwell, 1968.

Polaski, Donald C. *Authorizing an End: The Isaiah Apocalypse and Intertextuality*. Biblical Interpretation 50. Leiden: Brill, 2001.

Polk, Timothy. *The Prophetic Persona: Jeremiah and the Language of Self*. Journal for the Study of the Old Testament Supplements 32. Sheffield: JSOT Press, 1984.

Pritchard, James B., ed. *Ancient Near Eastern Texts Related to the Old Testament*. 3rd ed. Princeton: Princeton University Press, 1969.

Rahlfs, Alfred, ed. *Septuaginta*. Vol 2, *Libri Poetici et prophetici*. Stuttgart: Württembergische Bibelanstalt, 1935.

Redditt, Paul. "Isaiah 24–27: A Form-Critical Analysis." PhD diss., Vanderbilt University, 1972.

———. "Once Again, The City in Isaiah 24-27." *Hebrew Annual Review* 10 (1986) 317–35.

Rendsburg, Gary. *How the Bible Is Written*. Peabody, MA: Hendrickson, 2019.

Roberts, J. J. M. *Nahum, Habakkuk, and Zephaniah: A Commentary*. Old Testament Library. Louisville: Westminster/John Knox, 1991.

Seitz, Christopher R. "The Book of Isaiah 40-66: Introduction, Commentary, and Reflections." In *The New Interpreter's Bible* 6, edited by Leander E. Keck et al., 307–552. Nashville: Abingdon, 2001.

Sharp, Carolyn. "Hewn by the Prophet: An Analysis of Violence and Sexual Transgression in Hosea with Reference to the Homiletical Aesthetic of Jeremiah Wright." In *The Aesthetics of Violence in the Prophets*, edited by Julia M. O'Brien and Chris Franke, 50–71. Library of Hebrew Bible/Old Testament Studies 517. New York: T. & T. Clark, 2010.

Sherwood, Yvonne. "'Darke Texts Needs Notes': On Prophetic Prophecy, John Donne and the Baroque." *Journal for the Study of the Old Testament* 27 (2002) 47–74.

——— and Jonneke Bekkenkamp, "Introduction: The Thin Blade of Difference between Real Swords and Words about 'Sharp-Edged Iron Things'—Reflections on How People Use the Word." In *Sanctified Aggression: Legacies of Biblical and Post-Biblical Vocabularies of Violence*, edited by Yvonne Sherwood and Jonneke Bekkenkamp, 1–9. Journal for the Study of the Old Testament Supplement 400. London: T. & T. Clark, 2003.

Simkins, Ronald. *Yahweh's Activity in History and Nature in the Book of Joel*. Ancient Near Eastern Texts and Studies 10. Lewiston, NY: Mellen, 1991.

Simundson, Daniel J. "The Book of Micah: Introduction, Commentary, and Reflections." In *The New Interpreter's Bible* 7, edited by Leander E. Keck et al., 531–89. Nashville: Abingdon, 1996.

Stökl, Jonathan, and Corinne Carvalho, eds. *Prophets Male and Female: Gender and Prophecy in the Hebrew Bible, the Eastern Mediterranean, and the Ancient Near East*. Ancient Israel and Its Literature 15. Atlanta: Society of Biblical Literature, 2013.

Stulman, Louis. "Jeremiah as a Polyphonic Response to Suffering." In *Inspired Speech: Prophecy in the Ancient Near East—Essays in Honor of Herbert B. Huffmon*, edited by John Kaltner and Louis Stulman, 302–18. New York: T. & T. Clark International, 2004.

---. "Reading the Prophets as Meaning-making Literature for Communities under Siege." *Horizons in Biblical Theology* 29 (2007) 153–75.

Sweeney, Marvin A. *Isaiah 1–39: With an Introduction to Prophetic Literature.* Forms of the Old Testament Literature 16. Grand Rapids: Eerdmans, 1996.

---. "Structure, Genre, and Intent in the Book of Habakkuk." *Vetus Testamentum* 41 (1991) 63–83.

---. *The Twelve Prophets.* Vol. 1, *Hosea, Joel, Amos, Obadiah, Jonah.* Berit Olam. Collegeville, MN: Liturgical, 2000.

---. *The Twelve Prophets.* Vol. 2, *Micah, Nahum, Habakkuk, Zephaniah, Haggai, Zechariah, Malachi.* Berit Olam. Collegeville, MN: Liturgical, 2000.

---. *Zephaniah: A Commentary.* Hermeneia. Minneapolis: Fortress, 2003.

Toorn, Karel van der. "From the Mouth of the Prophet: The Literary Fixation of Jeremiah's Prophecies in the Context of the Ancient Near East." In *Inspired Speech: Prophecy in the Ancient Near East—Essays in Honor of Herbert B. Huffmon,* edited by John Kaltner and Louis Stulman, 191–202. Journal for the Study of the Old Testament Supplements 378. London: T. & T. Clark, 2004.

Trever, John C., ed. *Scrolls from Qumran Cave I: The Great Isaiah Scroll, The Order of the Community, The Pesher to Habakkuk.* Jerusalem: Albright Institute of Archaeological Research, 1974.

Tucker, Gene M. "The Book of Isaiah 1–39: Introduction, Commentary, and Reflections." In *The New Interpreter's Bible* 6, edited by Leander E. Keck et al., 25–305. Nashville: Abingdon, 2001.

Vayntrub, Jacqueline. *Beyond Orality: Biblical Poetry on its Own Terms.* New York: Routledge, 2019.

Volz, Paul. *Der Prophet Jeremia: Übersetzt und Erklärt.* Kommentar zum Alten Testament 10. Leipzig: Deichert, 1922.

Walker, Clarence E., and Gregory D. Smithers. *The Preacher and the Politician.* Charlottesville: University of Virginia Press, 2009.

Webster, James. "Sonata Form." https://doi.org/10.1093/gmo/9781561592630.article.26197.

West, Nathanael. *Miss Lonelyhearts & The Day of the Locust.* 1933. Reprint, New York: New Directions, 1962.

Westermann, Claus. *Isaiah 40–66: A Commentary.* Translated by David M. G. Stalker. Old Testament Library. Philadelphia: Westminster, 1975.

Whiting, J. D. "Jerusalem's Locust Plague." *National Geographic* 28 (1915) 511–50.

Wildberger, Hans. *Isaiah 13–27.* Translated by Thomas A. Trapp. Continental Commentaries. Minneapolis: Fortress, 1997.

Williamson, H. G. M. "Sound, Sense and Language in Isaiah 24–27." *Journal of Jewish Studies* 46 (1995) 1–9.

Wolff, Hans Walter. *Joel and Amos.* Translated by Waldemar Janzen et al. Hermeneia. Philadelphia: Fortress, 1997.

Woude, Annemarieke van der. "'Hearing Voices while Reading': Isaiah 40–55 as a Drama." In *One Text, a Thousand Methods: Studies in Memory of Sjef van Tilborg,* edited by Patrick Chatelion Counet and Ulrich Berges, 149–73. Biblical Interpretation Series 71. Boston: Brill, 2005.

Wright, David P. "Music and Dance in 2 Samuel 6." *Journal of Biblical Literature* 121 (2002) 201–25.

Yee, Gail A. "The Book of Hosea: Introduction, Commentary, and Reflections." In *The New Interpreter's Bible* 7, edited by Leander E. Keck et al., 195–297. Nashville: Abingdon, 1996.

www.ingramcontent.com/pod-product-compliance
Lightning Source LLC
Chambersburg PA
CBHW050347230426
43663CB00010B/2018